SURPRISED AT BEING ALIVE

# SURPRISED AT BEING ALIVE

## AN ACCIDENTAL HELICOPTER PILOT IN VIETNAM AND BEYOND

ROBERT F. CURTIS

CASEMATE
*Philadelphia & Oxford*

Published in the United States of America and Great Britain in 2014 by
CASEMATE PUBLISHERS
908 Darby Road, Havertown, PA 19083
and
10 Hythe Bridge Street, Oxford, OX1 2EW

ISBN 978-1-61200-275-0
Digital Edition: ISBN 978-1-61200-276-7

Cataloging-in-publication data is available from the Library of Congress and
the British Library.

Printed and bound in the United States of America.


For a complete list of Casemate titles please contact:

CASEMATE PUBLISHERS (US)
Telephone (610) 853-9131, Fax (610) 853-9146
E-mail: casemate@casematepublishing.com

CASEMATE PUBLISHERS (UK)
Telephone (01865) 241249, Fax (01865) 794449
E-mail: casemate-uk@casematepublishing.co.uk

# CONTENTS

*"Now this is no shit,*
*There I was, 10,000 feet,*
*I had a pocket full of nickels and*
*There wasn't a soft drink machine for miles,*
*So I turned to my copilot and said, 'Alice,'*
*When all of a sudden, there was Plexiglass flying everywhere.*
*The men, they were scared, but not me.*
*Down below us we saw a man on a bicycle.*
*We knew he was going to church,*
*Because it was Sunday.*
*So, we rolled in on him.*
*It was ten to one!*
*But we finally got that little SOB"*

—Typical flying war story, circa 1971

*This book is dedicated to the maintenance men who kept all the aircraft I flew whole through their non-stop labors. I trusted you with my life every day and your skill validated that trust. It is dedicated to the crewmen who flew with me and trusted me to bring them back as I trusted them to keep the helicopters ready, because after all, the aircraft was theirs, not mine. It is dedicated to the pilots who sat in the other seat while I flew and vice versa, each of us trusting the other's skill and judgment. It is dedicated to the wives and families that watched us all go out in our fragile machines full of potential single-point failures. Watched us go and hoped for our return. Finally, it is dedicated to those who ran out of luck and superstition. We miss you.*

# PROLOGUE

A perfect flight is usually one you don't remember. When you are old, and if you are a military pilot, should you live to be old, you discover that you tried your entire flying career for perfect flights. Sometimes, very rarely but sometimes, you have a perfect flight in that everything you did was spot on—you could do no wrong that day. But somehow, some of them, when you were not that good, some of the less than perfect ones, stick in your mind even when you are well past flying and should have forgotten them . . .

The thing is, for helicopter pilots at least, war stories don't even require a war. War is only marginally more dangerous for transport helicopter pilots than peace is, since there is very little difference in wartime missions and peacetime missions. The nights are just as dark, the weather just as bad, the loads just as heavy. Today you can't even say that you only get shot at in wartime—get close enough to someone's marijuana patch stateside and you will take incoming; maybe not a missile, but an assault rifle shot is still incoming fire. And it's not just gunfire—flying a premature baby on a medevac from Camp Lejeune, North Carolina, to Norfolk, Virginia, at night, in bad weather, is just as terrifying as doing a night combat resupply to a mountain top in Vietnam.

Someone once told me that the primary, and perhaps only, difference between a fairy tale and a war story is that a fairy tale starts off with, "Once upon a time, a long time ago . . ." while a war story starts off with, "Now this is no shit, there I was . . ." At some point in my military life I figured out that both fairy tales and war stories are equally true.

Now, this is no shit, for serious aviators, especially military aviators, flying is far closer to being a religion than being a job. All the things necessary to a religion are present, except perhaps a deity. But as with many people's personal religion, a deity is not really necessary; all you need are rituals to provide purpose and comfort and therefore a reason to believe. The comfort comes through prayer, singing, and the promise of better things to come. The purpose is to do something most people cannot, be it getting to heaven or being respected by your brother pilots.

9

If flying is a religion, then the instructor pilots are the priests. Instructors show you the way to come through the trials and tribulations of the present into a better future, or any future at all, period. They teach you which sins are venial and which are mortal. They introduce you to the secrets of the order, test your virtue during your check flights to determine if you are worthy, and instill the rituals of aviation into you until no pilot can fly without performing the proper ceremonies. If you cannot meet the instructor priest's stern tests or if you show unorthodox tendencies, they will excommunicate you as a heretic. Learn well, show the proper attitude and you may become one of them. And, if you make a mistake that kills you, they will come to your memorial service and sing about God guarding and guiding the men who fly through his great spaces of the sky.

The Holy Books of Flying are the operator manual for your aircraft, The Federal Aviation Regulations (FAR), the Aeronautical Information Manual (AIM), International Civil Aviation Organization (ICAO) Regulations—the international version of the FAR if you are going to be flying outside the US, the military directives which each service issues by the pound, and texts on weather and aerodynamics. The novice studies them to learn the right path and the masters return to them often to maintain their orthodoxy.

Most religions teach that if one follows the path laid out in the Holy Books and the guidance of the Holy Men, the future will be some form of paradise. Flying also preaches that the path to heaven or the future or, as noted, any future at all, lies in complete orthodoxy: the following of the rules, a course of actions that spells out precisely how to behave in all situations and thereby know exactly what will happen in the immediate future. The entire process of flight training, therefore, becomes teaching the student pilots how to plan and predict the future.

Any pilot who has been flying for a number of years can tell the future, a fact self-evident in that the pilot is still alive. But in learning to predict the future, pilots, like the very religious, become the most predictable of people. After all, a pilot must know in advance when he will start the engine, which route to taxi the aircraft, where to takeoff, to what altitude to climb, at what speed to climb, the route to follow, how much fuel will be burned en route, where the landing will be, how the landing will be done, and finally which route to taxi the aircraft to the gate or ramp spot. All events are timed to the second and each has a fallback, in case the first plan does not work. There is another third fallback in case the second fallback doesn't work either, and finally, the pilot knows how to crash the aircraft in the way most likely to let the crew survive if nothing at all works.

In other words, the pilot has been trained in what to do and how to react to all possible situations. The Holy Books give him THE WORD and the instructor/priests have drilled the pilot and tested the pilot and passed judgment on the pilot until, at last, the pilot is prepared and blessed. But unlike most modern religions, the price of failure to follow the Holy Writ of Aviation is not paid in the future on some judgment day, it is often paid right then and there if the pilot does the wrong thing during a failure or flies into unsuitable weather for his machine and/or level of skill and training, or he just loses concentration for a moment. More likely though, he will pay when he strays from the path of righteousness and tries something on his own, something not taught him by the instructors/priests. The pilot becomes a heretic; that is, he gets "creative," which brings us back to war stories.

The Holy Books cannot contain everything: there are just too many possibilities. So, like many people living in primitive, pre-literate societies, pilots tell each other stories, war stories or flying stories. The purpose of these stories is to pass on knowledge that is not written. Often with great embellishment and even exaggeration, the storyteller in effect says, "This happened. I did this about it. It worked or it didn't work." The listener takes it all in and files it away for later. He may or may not use it, but at least he knows that as Ecclesiastes 1:9 says, "The thing that has been, it *is that* which shall be: and that which is done *is* that which shall be done: and *there is* no new *thing* under the sun." Whatever happens to your aircraft, someone has seen it before.

One of the primary lessons of war stories, one of the things the Holy Books never say, is that you must always be calm. This does not mean that you do not have to react very, very quickly at times—failure to reduce the power when the engine quits, in some helicopters within two seconds, means the rotor blades slow to the point where they cannot provide enough lift and you will fall from the sky and die—but it does mean that even when you do have a situation that requires immediate action, you must remain cool and calm.

---

*Once, right after I reached my first assignment as a brand new Army warrant officer, a WO-1, I flew as copilot/map holder on a U-8, a small twin-engine 1960's fixed-wing. Being strictly a rotary-wing pilot, I knew nothing about fixed-wing aircraft, but the aircraft commander on this flight was my boss, a major, and was a god in my eyes. He had flown C-46s (large twin-engine cargo planes) during WWII and had been flying helicopters ever since the Army had them. Now we were flying the U-8 down to Atlanta and he wanted some company, so I was along in the copilot seat, tuning radios and holding the charts as we flew southeast. We were in the clouds over the Smoky Mountains and some ice was building up on the wings, not a good thing in my eyes, but the aircraft had rubber de-icing boots on the leading edges of the wings to knock the ice off when it got too thick.*

*Then, an hour into the flight, the major turned to me and smiled, calm and collected. From his position in the left seat, he reached over with his right hand and pointed at one of the myriad gauges on the plane's dash, the one marked "number 2 engine oil pressure." It had fallen well into the red zone on the low side, signaling the engine would fail soon from lack of oil. Looking over at the right wing, I could see oil streaming back from the leaking engine across the wing. He reached for the lever to feather the engine, to bring the prop's pitch back to zero so that it would not windmill and keep turning the engine after he shut it down. If it did windmill without oil, the engine might explode and take us out of the sky. The lever would not move. Ice had gotten into the control cables and locked it up. He looked at me and smiled; cool, calm, and collected.*

*"Center, Army U-8, declaring an emergency: We are losing one of our engines and cannot maintain altitude. Request you vector us down one of the long valleys around here in our descent," he called over the VHF radio. The entire time his voice was a calm and smooth as if he were ordering lunch at the Officer's Club, not dropping an airplane out of the sky, quite possibly into a mountain ridge.*

*"Roger, Army. Turn heading 120. There's an airport straight ahead ten miles away." The tone of the controller's voice matched the major's—calm, routine.*

*The major reduced power and we started down, still unable to see any-*
*thing through the gray of the clouds. A few minutes later the controller said,*
*"Losing you on radar in ground clutter. Call when you are clear of the clouds."*

*After an eternity, an eternity being perhaps five minutes when you are*
*headed down through the clouds not knowing what is below you, we came*
*out the bottom of the cloud and could see we had descended into nearly the*
*center of a broad valley, mountain ridges rising above us on both sides. Good*
*job, FAA radar. As we got below the icing level the ice in the cables went away*
*and the major feathered the number 2 engine without difficulty, and the now-*
*feathered prop stopped turning. The airport was directly in front of us as the*
*controller said it would be, and our landing was utterly routine. After we*
*were parked on the ramp and the other engine was shut down, the major*
*looked over at me and smiled again.*

---

Cool and calm, always be cool and calm even when you have to move
fast to keep something bad from happening. Be cool and calm, something
the books can't say, but something the religion of flying requires of you if
you are to face the fire successfully and come through. Always, because the
mission must be done.

The purpose of the following stories is not to provide any startling new
truths or show a slice of flying that has not been written about in great and
bloody detail by nearly everyone that ever controlled an aircraft or thought
about controlling an aircraft. Rather, I have written this to show places and
moments out of a flying career that have stayed with me when all the others
have faded into a blur with the years. These stories in it are as true as all
war stories are.

Jean Renoir is quoted as saying, "The only things that are important
in life are the things you remember." Yet a perfect flight is one you don't
remember. You look at your log book later in wonder, as if some magic
happened to you and you never knew it. Did someone make a false entry?
A perfect flight went completely as planned. It was planned and briefed
on time. The preflight inspection found no new faults, takeoff and climb-
out were unremarkable, and flight en route to your destination was normal.
You descended to the runway, ship deck, or landing zone; landed; dropped
your load or your passengers; and returned home. The aircraft worked like

it was supposed to. Neither you nor the copilot, nor any of the crew, did anything that they weren't supposed to do. You didn't scare yourself even once. And an hour after the flight was debriefed, it was well on its way to being forgotten. By the next week, the flight was forgotten altogether. Even looking at it in your log book does not bring it back. It's gone.

Perfect flights are always what a pilot wants, or at least pilots who live to be old want. These imperfect flights I remember . . .

## INTRODUCTION *Helicopters*

To understand helicopter-flying war stories we, the storyteller and the listener, must have a common ground. The storyteller must remember that things, such as acronyms and common aviation terms, are a foreign language to non-aviation folk. He must also remember to explain why some things are more important than others. The reader must understand the basic principles of helicopter flight to have a better understanding of the nature of the machines that figure in all these war stories and why the storyteller considers some events more important than others.

First, "helicopter," "aircraft," "helo," "bird," even in rare cases "copter" are all names for a helicopter used by the aircrews that fly them, the controllers that handle them, and the maintainers who keep them in the air. Notice that "chopper" is not listed among the names of these machines. Few, if any, of the pilots and crewmen I know or have known ever use that term and cringe when they hear others use it, perhaps because they do not like the image of rotor blades doing anything except lifting the aircraft.

According to an old saying, helicopters really don't want to fly. Unlike most fixed-wing aircraft, the best helicopter design in the world is inherently unstable. A trimmed up airplane in flight will hold its flight path indefinitely. Most of the older helicopters will hold their trimmed-up flight path for a very short while, after which they veer off in a random direction. Without the computer-controlled stability systems installed into modern helos, the pilot must manually fly them all the time or they fall from the sky in the aforementioned random directions.

Stability system or no, a helicopter pilot must learn first thing to anticipate what is going to happen next and correct it *before it happens*, a point that becomes all too clear the first time you try to hover a helicopter that does not have the stability systems. You chase the aircraft movements all around the sky, always a step behind until you learn to anticipate.

Even a pilot trained to anticipate what is going to happen is subject to mechanical failures, the worst of which is a "single-point" failure. A single-point failure is quite simply something that, if it happens, the entire machine comes crashing down. A single-point failure in a helicopter is the equivalent of a wing falling off an airplane. A common, and very true, saying is that helicopters are "a collection of thousands of parts flying in close formation." Among this vast collection of parts there are many, many single-point failures waiting to happen, meaning that if one thing fails, the aircraft will stop flying or at least stop controlled flight: things like failure of the control system that lets the pilot move the rotor heads, things like a rotor blade coming off, tail rotors stopping turning, drive shafts breaking, transmissions failing, and on and on.

Fire is another good one that can lead to myriad single failure points and is one of the reasons helicopters rarely fly very high. If the aircraft is burning, how long will it take the pilot to get it on the ground? Will he make it before a control rod burns through and the aircraft goes out of control, and with no parachute to save them, the crew falls screaming with the aircraft until they lose consciousness or the aircraft hits the ground?

That's the hardest thing, I think, the possibility of falling out of the sky with no control and having time to think about it—falling and screaming and wondering what comes next, instead of a quick explosion, a flash and then nothing. Even a few seconds can be a very, very long time when you are beyond hope and falling with the world spinning around you. A fellow pilot told me about it when it happened to him yet instead of dying, somehow he lived.

---

It *happened this way: his CH-46 came apart in flight with no warning, a single-point failure of the worse kind. One second he is flying—everything is normal, blue sky above and earth below. Then he is in a violent spin—out of control, the world flashing by too quickly to take it in. He is conscious and so has time to think about what is happening and in that second decides he does not want to die in the aircraft. He jettisons his emergency door, releases his seat belt and tries to jump. But he can't—centrifugal force holds him in the seat. He does not know that a single-point failure in the aft rotor system has allowed the aft rotor blades to chop the aircraft in half. He is falling in the cockpit with stumps of the forward blades spinning free, the aft cabin section gone and disintegrating as it falls. Somehow, randomly really, the cockpit hits the ground, relatively softly and upright. By now he is unconscious, probably from the impact, but he does not die.*

*Several years later the exact same single-point failure in the aft rotor system happened to another CH-46 flown by another two friends with a third friend acting as crew chief. We had been a flight of six CH-46s hauling Marines in simulated combat assaults at Marine Corps Base 29 Palms, California. I had just released them and a second aircraft to return to the base at Yuma, Arizona, 60 miles away, while I led the other four helicopters to the refueling pits prior to completing the last mission of the day. We had only four loads of Marines remaining to be brought back to base, so the other two helicopters were not needed. As my CH-46 was taking on fuel, I heard, "Mayday, Mayday, Mayday" over the UHF radio Guard channel. Looking off to the south, toward the direction the two aircraft had gone, I could see a column of smoking rising up from the desert.*

*The second aircraft was in a loose trial formation, maybe six or eight rotor diameters behind the lead when right before the crew's eyes, the first aircraft just came apart. As the lead 46 broke up in flight immediately after the single-point failure, the wingman made the Mayday call and started an approach down to where the wreckage now lay, the pieces burning. The wingman told me later that he thinks they all three died instantly because the aircraft just disintegrated in front of him, cockpit included, instead of coming down with the cockpit more or less whole as my other friend's did. I hope they did die immediately. I hope they didn't have time to think about it.*

---

Beyond the mere possibility of death from any number of failures in the spinning parts, helicopters are different from airplanes just by their nature. Airplanes are aerodynamic and sleek, sealed against the force of the wind as they hurtle through the air. Their wheels move and their wings do not. Most helicopters are aerodynamic drag monsters that are fat and slow, at least by fixed-wing standards. Helicopter's wings move and on most of them, their wheels don't.

Helicopters, at least cargo helicopters, have windows that open so that you can stick your hand out in flight, like you did in Dad's car when you were a kid, although this is not recommended when flying at over 100 MPH. Once, when bored after yet another eight hours of flying sling loads in Vietnam, I was looking out the side window at the fields and forest below us while my copilot flew the aircraft. Without thinking, I stuck my arm out the window of the Chinook to move my hand like an airfoil, like I had done as a child in the back seat of my Dad's Chevy. The 140-knot wind nearly jerked me out of the seat, trying to pull my left arm and the rest of me out through the narrow window opening. My copilot never said a word as I extracted my arm, but it was clear from his look that he considered me insane.

Helicopters are not sealed like airplanes. Helicopters have windshields that leak water in the rain and leak air in the cold. Some military helicopters have armored seats to protect you from small arms fire from below, but the seats also sometimes fill up with water when the aircraft has been sitting outside in the rain, leaving your backside wet and cold until your body heat dries them. If your crew chief likes you, he might remove them the night before so they will be dry, or he might not.

Sometimes the seats collapse from the optimum upright position to their lowest setting at just the wrong time, leaving the pilot just barely able to see over the glare shield above the dash as he tries to put the aircraft down in a tight landing zone or hover over a ship's deck.

It is not all bad, though. Sometimes you will get a helo that has just the right frequency vibration. I've never asked a female helicopter pilot, but for males, a bird with the right vibration can give you a strong sexual reaction, that is, a very strong erection, at least when you are a young male pilot. Don't know about old pilots because I quit flying before I got that old. Gives a whole new meaning to the phrase, "getting a buzz out of flying." That's something you rarely ever mention to the other pilot at the time, though. Except you might say, "Good one" and get just get a smile in return.

All helicopters are slow by airplane standards. A very fast helicopter would be a very slow military airplane. In fact, most helicopters are slower than the speed at which a fighter stalls and falls from the sky. This means that the enemy has a long time, relatively speaking, to get you in his sights and shoot at the cockpit to take out the crew, if their weapon is a gun— or at the hot parts of the helicopter, like the engine exhausts, if their weapon is a missile. And sometimes, sometimes, you can even see the man who is trying to kill you. It gets very personal, down low and slow where the helos fly.

Even so, all in all, for me, helicopters are better to fly than airplanes of any type, even jets, simply because they can land anywhere there is a relatively flat, open spot slightly larger than the aircraft. You fly low and slow enough to see what the world looks like, what mountain peaks and valleys look like up close. Though helicopter pilots cannot land the entire aircraft if the zone is on a mountaintop or a building roof that is too small, they can land one skid or two wheels and hover the rest of the aircraft while cargo or people off-load. Or they can do a "one wheeler," hovering with just one wheel or skid touching, just so the crew can enjoy the view from the top of a mountain. Helicopters can land on a beach between missions and let the crew cool off with a swim.

Poor limited airplanes, even Vertical/Short Takeoff and Landing (V/STOL) aircraft like AV-8 Harriers and very short takeoff landing aircraft like the Helio Courier, they are mostly restricted to airport runways or ship decks; no beaches or mountain peaks for them. Then too, airplanes mostly fly high above the clouds and the top of one cloud looks pretty much the same as another. Helicopters fly below the clouds and the crews get to see the ever-changing face of the earth. And occasionally, somewhere where you know that there is no one else flying but you, you can do magic things with your helicopter.

In the middle of the ocean, when you know there are no other aircraft or mountains below you, and there is lots of room between the bottom of the clouds and the surface of the sea, on a day with puffy cumulus clouds, you can pretend that the clouds are solid and "land" your helicopter on top of them. You slow your aircraft as you descend toward the cloud's top, coming to a stop and putting your power all the way down, down as you would if you were landing on a solid surface. Then, with the power completely off, you hold the aircraft level and fall straight down through the cloud toward the sea below. The cloud's surface churns as your rotor wash hits it and the white mist disappears in a swirl around you as you fall. The world goes white until you come out the bottom and the blue sea is below you again and the illusion must end, so you lower the nose to regain airspeed and start flying again. Or, is "normal" flight the illusion, and the act of falling straight down through clouds to the sea the reality?

# FLYING LIFE ONE

---

## THE ARMY
## 1968–1972

# 1

# THE ACCIDENTAL AVIATOR
## COVINGTON, KENTUCKY ■ FEBRUARY 1968

---

*The posters showed a young man of the classical All-American type, clean cut, moderate length dark hair, brown V-neck sweater, sitting on the steps of what appeared to be a high school. His hand was resting on his chin and he looked upward, off upward toward a clear blue sky. Below him, printed in large letters were the words, "90 days between you and the sky." In smaller type below that, the poster announced the US Army would take a young man with a high school diploma or a general educational development (GED) certificate, 20–20 vision (or correctable to 20–20), and who would be at least 19 years old upon completing the program and make him into a helicopter pilot. If you could meet these minimal requirements, pass a flight physical, and complete the training, you could become an Army Aviator and find the freedom of the sky. And, although the ad did not say it, in 1968 you would also find the Vietnam War.*

---

I received the notice from my local draft board to take the draft physical in early March, 1968. I would turn 19 in May and had been relatively certain that this letter would be forthcoming. In March, 1968 there were no draft numbers, only the near certainty of being drafted if you did not have a ready deferment, like college. The physical itself was a long boring day of lines and forms and being herded from one room to another for tests of one sort or another in the big downtown Cincinnati Federal Building. As I walked into the building that morning, an anti-war protester about my age standing just outside the door handed me a flyer. I glanced at the words just long enough to see what it was, and then I wadded it up and bounced it off his forehead as I continued inside. At the end of the day, I was certified mentally and physically qualified for military service. After passing the physical, I knew the "Greetings" letter would soon come to the two-room apartment I shared with my wife of six months. We rented it from one of her cousins and, both of us being 18, kept their kids entertained through the walls, or must have since they always giggled for some reason whenever they saw us.

In '68, being a high school dropout with a GED certificate, 18, married with no children, not a student or an objector or a sole-surviving son, completely settled the issue. A week after I got the letter confirming I had passed the physical, I called the draft board. "Yes, you will be drafted, probably in July; unless, of course, you want to volunteer to be drafted, in which case you could leave next month."

There were other choices: objector, Canada, immediate entry into school (if I could find one that would take me and that I could afford, both doubtful) but I really did not see any other choices except one. Instead of waiting for the draft I could enlist and gain some small measure of control over my fate. The other alternatives, if I thought of them at all, which I didn't, were unacceptable, not because I was a burning anti-Communist, or believed "my country, right or wrong," or because I pretended to understand the war one way or another. My people were from the mountains of Kentucky and there were some things the men always did. Going into the military was one of them.

All my life I played among the dusty uniforms hanging in the closets and looked at the fading photographs of my dad and my uncles from their military times, war and peace. I played in their old "Ike" jackets from the 40's and 50's and treasured the spent cartridge cases and old unit patches they had given me. I had my "science cabinet" (an old china cabinet) full of these things and others, patches from various Army units, a Nazi party pin one of my uncles brought back from the war, a WWI Victory Medal given to me by an old veteran neighbor, an empty ammo clip from an M-1 rifle, all displayed next to the buffalo skull I brought back from a visit to relatives in Oklahoma, plus the dead tarantula sent me in a match box by my Uncle Bill, a veteran of the war in the Pacific who lived in Texas.

All my life, too, I saw the well-oiled and cleaned rifles and shotguns hanging on the walls of the houses in the Kentucky hollers (mountain valleys) of my childhood. No matter how poor the family, the weapons were always there along with pictures of the men in uniform. Few men were drafted out of the hollers because most enlisted when their war came. In fact, in Breathitt County during one of our wars, no one was drafted because all the men enlisted. Again, not from burning patriotism, although patriotic they were and still are—it was just what the men in their families had always done. The hardships of military service were often a rest from the reality of the true hardships of mountain life, coal mines and small farms. After all, in the military you always had clothes and food and a paycheck, small perhaps, but more than welfare.

My then wife's people were of the same mountain stock as mine; in fact, we were distant cousins. But for her, it was not so simple. At 18 her life as a woman had just begun. She was only now becoming adjusted to our life together and she saw clearly that it could end all too soon. One of our high school teachers even told us, as we sat in the cafeteria before I quit high school for the second and final time, that we would get married; I would then get drafted and would be killed in Vietnam. But running away never occurred to her either.

The next day I drove our first new car, a blue '68 Mustang that my factory laborer's job allowed us to buy, across the bridge from Newport over the Licking River to Covington, to the nearest recruiter's office. The street the recruiting office was on had been the center of town—you could still see the streetcar tracks in between the cobbles laid down by the German immigrants—but in '68, Covington was fading fast. Empty storefronts displayed "for lease or sale" signs in the windows and the streets were not swept as often as they once had been. The litter of city trash sat in the curb and on the sidewalks and made everything feel even more rundown than it was.

The recruiting office had once been a restaurant, but as the businesses that provided the customers for the lunch trade folded, the restaurant joined them. Where the tables and chairs of the diner had been, were the desks of the three service's recruiters, Navy, Marines, and Army, all in a row. The tiles on the floor still spelled out the restaurant's name. During the race riots of the year before, I had worked at a very similar restaurant, just down the street from the recruiter's office. The restaurant's owner hid guns throughout the place—a rifle and a shotgun in the kitchen and a pistol under the counter, and told me, "If they start breaking in, just grab the first gun you are close to and open up." My plan was simpler—"they" break in the front, I am out the back and gone. It's all "theirs."

When I walked in, the Army recruiter was talking to two other young men, which was fine—I didn't want to talk to him anyway. One of my uncles was a Marine gunnery sergeant, a "Gunny." Because of him, I had wanted to be a Marine since I was a little boy. The Marine recruiter was sitting alone reading a western novel when I walked to the front of his desk and stood there, waiting for him to look up. When he did, the Marine smiled.

Motioning me into a chair by the desk, the Marine introduced himself as the Gunny, non-commissioned officer in charge, NCOIC, of the Marine Corps portion of the recruiting station. What could he tell me that was not already common knowledge? "The greatest fighting outfit the world had ever seen and after boot camp, you become one of us, you become a Marine. A two-year enlistment in the infantry would be the perfect start on life and an experience that you could tell your grandchildren about." Still with a smile the Gunny said, "Boy, we'll put you in the rice paddies and you can kill all the Cong you can find."

As the Marine talked about his own infantry experiences in "the Nam" I looked at the three rows of ribbons on his chest and the hardness of his smile. My Marine uncle's experiences from boot camp, Korea, and Vietnam came back to me, and the Gunny lost his recruit. Rifles and rice paddies would be only a last resort. I would not voluntarily sign on for what the draft promised anyway. After listening politely for a decent interval, I thanked the Marine and told him I would think about what he said. As I turned to go I saw the Army recruiter was now free.

As I walked toward the Army recruiter he turned his head slightly and gave the Marine a little grin. After a few questions about my background the recruiter asked, "How would you like to be a helicopter pilot?" Leafing through the pamphlets on his desk, he selected one, and laid it in front of me. The leaflet began, "90 Days Between You And The Sky." As I read, the thought came to me that if I were to die, it would be better to fly to the spot rather than walk to it. Six months later I reported to Fort Polk, Louisiana. Nearly all warrant officer candidates (WOCs) went through Fort Polk and it was exactly what you would think it would be with the

Vietnam War in full swing. Everyone smart enough to get out of military service had, leaving mostly National Guard and reserve enlistees, draftees and those of us who enlisted to "beat the draft."

Twelve weeks later, a couple hundred candidates-to-be boarded Greyhound buses immediately after graduation from basic training and traveled to Fort Wolters, Texas, for a month of pre-flight training and then primary flight training. The demand for pilots was so strong that the Army had ten companies of WOCs under training at once for many years. I joined 9th WOC, the Tan Hats.

# 2

# CHASING BUZZARDS

## FORT WOLTERS, TEXAS ■ FEBRUARY 1969

---

*The OH-23 Raven was a three-man bubble helicopter designed by one of the pioneers of vertical flight, Stanley Hiller. The first ones came out in the early 1950's and the final versions lasted long enough to see service as scouts in Vietnam. Even in 2013, a few OH-23's soldier on as crop dusters or toys for people with the money to keep an old helicopter operational. The 23 was a typical bubble helicopter, i.e., slow, with a manual throttle that works opposite of a motorcycle (the grip was black rubber and read "Harley-Davidson"), and was a very rugged machine, as I discovered when I bounced one about 20 feet into the air after screwing up a simulated engine failure, with no damage to the machine.*

---

Seventeen flight hours into my aviation career, I couldn't say I really had much of an understanding of the process of flying in general, and the process of flying helicopters in particular. All us warrant officer candidates (WOCs) struggling to get through Primary Flight Training at Fort Wolters were in about the same position; that is, scared and confused, but never admitting anything, even to each other. To admit any fear meant running the risk of having the staff wash you out of flight school, or maybe having one of your classmates write you up in a peer review that would accomplish the same thing, whereupon the Army would hand you a rifle and send you wading into the Vietnamese rice paddies. This, of course, is exactly what they did do in 1968 when you washed out of flight school. You still owed Uncle Sam a year and a half—plenty of time for a Vietnam tour.

I had soloed in the OH-23D helicopter the week before. After six-and-a-half hours of dual flight, my instructor looked over at me, smiled, and said, "Take it around the pattern three times, then come back and pick me up." As he opened the door to climb out of the little helicopter, he started laughing, laughing so loud that I could hear him over the engine noise. I watched him walk to the ready shack where we waited between flights without even looking back, still laughing.

My first solo flight was uneventful, despite the pounding of my heart. After the three wobbly landings and takeoffs, with shaky hovering in between, my instructor came back to the aircraft, no longer laughing but smiling broadly.

"Congratulations! Looks like you won't get washed out after all, well, not yet anyway. Let's take it home now, while we're on a roll," he said.

He let me hover back out to the runway and make the takeoff. I remembered where our home field was, more or less, and after more or less leveling off (plus or minus 100 feet or so, i.e., the height of a ten-story building) I turned the aircraft toward it. Feeling very pleased with myself, I actually felt like I was in control of the aircraft, for once. Five miles from the outlying field we had just left, the instructor said, "I've got it" and as we had been taught, I immediately let go of the controls.

Looking over at the instructor, I wondered what I had done wrong, since they did not normally take the flight controls without a reason. He was still smiling as he took the controls. With his left hand he pointed out to the front of the bubble.

"See that buzzard at one o'clock, just a little high," he asked?

"Yes, sir. I saw it and was going to avoid it," I replied, thinking he thought I was going to get too close to the bird and have it hit the bubble of our aircraft.

"Watch this," he said and turned directly for the bird.

The vulture saw us, or had been watching us already, and turned to escape from the larger "bird" attacking him. As the vulture turned, we turned with him. As he dove, we dove, always staying far enough away to ensure we did not hit him. For what seemed to be three or four minutes, we followed him through the sky, turning, twisting, climbing, diving, and then, laughing, my instructor turned the H-23 back toward the base, resumed level flight, and gave me back the controls.

It was the first time I had ever been in a maneuvering helicopter. We were not just taking off, climbing out and flying level around the traffic pattern—we were actually twisting and turning through the sky! With the assurance of a god-like flight instructor sitting next to me, I knew there was no danger to us and it was fun! After the grind of basic training, the terror of preflight training and the pressure to solo, it was the first time that "90 days between you and the sky" seemed real, the first feeling of freedom, of real flying, like the old war movies.

Now, another week and another five hours of flight time later, I was being entrusted with flying an aircraft the fifteen miles from the stage field back to Fort Wolters, all by myself. I was sure it would be no problem. I felt good, having had a good flight earlier in the day. So I pulled up on the collective, and not wobbling too much, took off to head for home. I leveled off at 500 feet, plus or minus only 50, instead of the 100 feet of last week; this time it was a five-story building instead of a ten-story. At about the same place as the week before, a vulture was circling.

"That was fun, chasing the buzzard last week," I thought as I turned toward the bird. The only problem was that this buzzard was either the same one or one that had been chased once too often. Instead of turning way, the buzzard, or maybe it was a hawk, turned toward the helicopter, intending to fight.

For a moment I panicked. A good-sized bird, or even a small one for that matter, will do a lot of damage to an aircraft, if it hits the right parts, like the bubble and/or the pilot. To avoid the buzzard, I turned hard right, pulled a lot of power while rolling on as much throttle as I could. The bird passed beneath the H-23, clear and gone. My heart pounding, I rolled the aircraft level and started to lower the collective to descend to the mandated 500 feet. I was already passing through 800 feet, climbing rapidly, and knew I would get in trouble (thoughts of rice paddies passed through my mind) if I went higher. But as I tried to lower the collective pitch lever, I found it would not go down. The collective was stuck up and I was climbing faster than I ever had.

Climbing into the Texas sky, I was passing through 1,200 feet when the thought occurred to me that I had no idea how high this aircraft could go or what happened if you tried to go higher than that. Unable to think of anything else except getting the helicopter started on its way back down, I loosened my seat belt and half stood in the cockpit, all the while keeping my feet on the rudders. Holding the cyclic stick with my right hand, I put all my weight on the collective stick with my left and it came down. All the way down, leaving me almost floating in the air as the aircraft entered mild negative "G," like when you almost leave the ground in your car taking a rise in the road too fast. I was now mostly a passenger, instead of the pilot. The aircraft wobbled around the sky, upright as it fell but not really under control.

As the slight negative G faded, I managed to regain control, more or less, and after stopping the descent, did the first thing all men do when they have done something stupid or clumsy or something they know they shouldn't have done. I looked around to see if anyone had seen me. There were no other helicopters in sight, so no one had.

It took a few minutes for me to get my heart under control, get to more or less the right altitude, and to figure out exactly where I was, and to head back toward the base. The bird was nowhere to be seen. In the following 24 years I spent as an aviator, I never chased a bird again, although I did hit a duck at about 160 MPH once, but that's another story.

# 3

# ENGINE FAILURE
## FORT CAMPBELL, KENTUCKY ■ NOVEMBER 1970

---

*The OH-13E Sioux was a Korean War aircraft, the same one used for the opening sequence of the TV show M.A.S.H. The E models I flew were all built in 1951. They had wooden rotor blades that warped a little when the aircraft sat out in the damp, causing it to have a slight vibration until they straightened out after turning for a while. The OH-13E also came with a hand crank, just like a Ford Model-T, in case the battery was dead. It had only two seats, but with only 190 horsepower it couldn't lift much more than two people anyway. As old, slow, and weak as the OH-13E was, I loved flying it, mainly because it was the first aircraft I could truly take out on my own.*

---

The student pilot was a captain, a recent returnee from Vietnam, and a good stick (jargon for a smooth pilot). He was doing very well flying the old OH-13E even though he was used to modern turbine powered helicopters and not old reciprocating engine-powered ones. The aircraft's altitude had remained right where it was supposed to be, 1000 feet, since we had started down the flight corridor from the airfield out to the rear area of Fort Campbell. The captain's control of the manual throttle was good too; RPM steady at 3100 in cruise flight, just as required.

As normal, the heater in the OH-13E was barely putting out any heat at all. Not surprising, since the heater, like that on Volkswagens of similar vintage, was just a shroud around the exhaust pipe of the engine. In the just-above freezing November air, both of us were bundled into winter-weight flight suits that resembled gray nylon children's playsuits. Even though we both had on two pair of socks, our feet were still cold inside our black leather combat boots.

I was the instructor pilot and was more than slightly intimidated, as I always was then, by Vietnam vets, like the older man in the right seat. Even though I was the instructor, I was also a nearly brand new warrant officer 1 (also known as a "Wobbly One") and not yet a Vietnam vet.

---

*Instead of the usual direct ticket to in-country, my flight school class, for reasons unknown to us, was assigned to various forts around the states when we graduated from flight school at Fort Rucker, Alabama—the first time that had happened in ten years. Assigned to the 3rd Army at Fort Campbell, Kentucky, I was so excited at the prospect of being a real aviator that I did not even take the full 30-day leave I had coming, but instead, bundled up my wife into our green '68 Impala Custom Coupe and proceeded to the base less than two weeks after flight school graduation. I was the first of the wave of new WO's headed for Campbell. I walked in the door to the Standardization Office and the boss said, "Looks like we will need some more instructors. Kid, take that H-13 and get 100 hours, then we'll make you an instructor pilot (IP)." Thus, I was selected to become an instructor. I, the brand new WO1, straight from flight school at Fort Rucker, Alabama, was now to be an instructor pilot.*

*"Take that H-13, get 100 hours in it and we'll give you a local instructor's course," the major in charge of the standardization section told me on my first day of real duty in the Army and the words rang in my ears. A new pilot's dream, but I wondered when I would get the God-like confidence most instructors had.*

*The other two pilots assigned to standards were older Chief Warrant Officer 2's (CW2), both of them between Vietnam tours and in no big hurry to fly an excessive number of hours in an 18-year-old, wooden-bladed, Korean War-vintage, two-man bubble helicopter, and as such, were only too glad to let the new kid fly. And fly I did, as soon as my ten-hour transition course was finished, any mission, any day, every day, to build the 100 hours. I flew the MPs on tours of the back areas of the fort looking for poachers. I flew basic training company commanders on tours of their bivouac areas. I flew "flour bombing" missions, where my passenger would throw paper bags of flour out at marching trainees to simulate real bombs. My wife understood the inconvenient Sunday missions and short cross-countries to Bowling Green, Kentucky, and Nashville, Tennessee. In a month and a half I had over 100 hours of flight time in the Sioux and began the ten-flight-hour instructor course. I learned a lot in that course, for example, to be very, very careful what you say when you are flying.*

*In the OH-13E a maximum performance takeoff is not very maximum. The helicopter had a very small engine, so a vertical takeoff over a 50' obstacle was difficult to impossible unless it was very cold, you had a very strong head wind, and/or had a very light load. The procedure consisted of picking up to a 3' hover and hovering backwards in the landing zone as far as you could go without hitting anything. When you were ready to begin the takeoff, you rolled the throttle on as far as it would go for maximum power, while lifting the collective to keep your engine RPM at the takeoff speed of 3,200 RPM. You kept the nose of the helicopter level with the horizon. This nose attitude would give you around 20 knots forward airspeed, just enough to bring you into translational lift, that point in flight where smooth, undisturbed air comes down through the rotor system and reduces the amount of engine power required to fly. When you cleared the obstacle you reduced throttle slightly to prevent engine over speed as you lowered the collective to reduce power from maximum while lowering the helicopter's nose to transition to forward flight.*

*If it appeared that you would not clear the 50' obstacle, the procedure was to move the cyclic stick backwards and fly, slide really, back into the landing zone tail first. This was not something any of us ever wanted to do, even though we had done it back at Fort Wolters in primary training. If the tail slide was successfully accomplished, you would then lighten the aircraft by burning off fuel or sending your passenger on a hike to a bigger landing zone where you could pick him up and try again. Finally, if the landing zone was big enough, you could fly in tight circles close to the ground until you got enough speed to get through translational lift and climb out using a cyclic climb that traded airspeed for altitude, again something that few of us wanted to do.*

*On this syllabus flight, I was the "instructor" and was talking my "student" (a very experienced instructor pilot) through the maximum performance takeoff procedure as we sat in our turning helicopter on the north side of Fort Campbell's airfield. When I had talked him through what we were going to do, he lifted the helicopter into the prescribed three-foot hover.*

*"OK, instruments are good. We are clear to go. Now, holding the nose level, smoothly roll on full throttle while increasing collective to keep the RPM under control."*

*My student followed my words exactly and our takeoff was going perfectly. In seconds we were smoothly clear of our imaginary 50-foot obstacle and ready to transition to forward flight.*

*"Now, we are clearing our obstacle, so roll off the throttle . . . "*

*That's as far as I got because my "student" completely closed the throttle, leaving us at 50 feet and 20 knots with no engine power, firmly in the middle of the "dead man's curve," i.e. that point in the height-velocity diagram where your airspeed, plotted against your altitude, puts you completely out of the area of flight where a safe landing can be made without engine power. Lose power while you are in the dead man's curve, and you will crash. Period. As he closed the throttle, I looked at him in complete amazement, my mouth wide open. He was looking back at me, cool, calm, and smiling.*

*The OH-13E's wooden rotor blades did not have weighted tips, meaning that there was minimal inertia to keep them turning without power from the engine. No turning blades, no lift and you just fall. As the blades rapidly slowed, I grabbed the flight controls, trying to keep the fuselage level and stop the sideward drift we picked up instantaneously, while desperately rolling the throttle back on as we wobbled toward the ground. I didn't quite get the aircraft back to full RPM before we hit the ground, shaky but level and with only one bounce. Mouth still open I looked at my "student," completely speechless.*

*Still smiling and cool after our near crash, the real instructor said, "Never, ever, say anything like that unless you really mean it. When you say "roll off the throttle," a student will do just that, like I just did. And, when a student does something stupid, like I just did, you, Mr. Instructor Pilot, must be ready to recover, like you just did."*

*Lesson learned in a way I would not forget, and I never had that particular problem again. No, there were many others waiting for me.*

---

Now, a month after completing the instructor training course, I was out with my fourth student, the captain. My first had also been a more experienced pilot just back from Vietnam, who could obviously fly the helicopter with more skill than the brand new instructor pilot in the right seat. My confidence grew with the next two students, both new WO's like me, straight from flight school and not yet into and back from the war. But now I had another old hand, a captain, and again felt more than slightly inadequate to train him. The thought went through my mind that he should have been training me instead of the other way around as we flew toward our training area.

The outbound route from the airfield at Fort Campbell to our gravel and dirt training airfield ran down a road through the middle of the base, over WWII wooden training barracks that now housed the basic trainees who were the only remaining soldiers at the normally crowded base while the 101st Airborne Division (Airmobile) was off in Southeast Asia. When the road left the main base proper and started through the woods that make up the Fort Campbell rear area and the majority of the reservation, it went down into a small valley. On both sides of the road at that point were large grassy fields, nicely open, smooth and flat.

I made it a habit to give my student the first simulated engine failure of each familiarization flight over the highway bridge between the fields. Simple, the student had only to turn right or left and he was set up perfectly for the autorotation from the standard 1000 feet out-bound altitude.

Simulated engine failures were a very important part of helicopter training in the old, reciprocating-engine aircraft; the reciprocating engines in 1950's helicopters quit fairly often, at least compared with modern turbines. When the helicopter loses full engine power, the pilot has only seconds, as in maybe two or three seconds, to lower the collective pitch lever, the power control on helicopters, and enter autorotation. If he does not lower the collective in time, the rotors will slow to the point where a recovery cannot be made, the blades bend upwards, stall, and the aircraft literally falls from the sky.

The simplest way to think of the process is to understand that in normal, powered flight, the engine drives the rotors. When the pilot pulls up on the collective pitch lever, air is pulled down through the rotors and produces lift. When the engine stops, the power to turn the rotors, and to thereby produce lift, is gone. By entering autorotation the pilot trades altitude for lift, with the power coming from gravity. The pilot rapidly lowers the collective all the way down, and as the helicopter starts to descend, the air flow reverses, providing lift to keep the aircraft flying and under control. With the airflow now coming up through the rotors, the pilot is trading altitude for lift. The helicopter has entered autorotation.

All the pilot must do once autorotation is established is to get his airspeed right in order to glide the proper distance and, of course, find a place to land. Properly done, an autorotation is a steep, fast, but relatively normal landing. Done wrong, the result is a sure crash; hence, all helicopter pilots were taught engine failure procedures from nearly the first day of flight school. Every time the student flew the helo over a spot where he could not make a safe autorotative landing, a large set of woods for example, the instructor would cut the throttle. After a few flights, all students flew over areas where autorotations were possible as much as they could, their helicopters flying zigzag through the sky, almost like they were dodging ground fire.

There was little conversation between us on the outbound trip. The captain had completed his work at the main airfield practice area—hovering, landing and lifting off, simple things—and was on his way to the first confined area landings (small fields, usually surrounded by trees, instead of wide open areas of airfields) of the ten flight hour transition syllabus. All his work had been well within standards and his control touch was smooth, so I felt no apprehension about his ability to handle a simple forced landing, the same kind all Army pilots had practiced a thousand times in flight school.

I lit a cigarette. Trying to match the practiced skill of the instructors at Fort Wolters and Fort Rucker, who could induce a simulated engine without the student suspecting what was coming, I started to put my cigarette lighter back into my pocket, but instead quickly grabbed the throttle and turned it to idle. Whether or not he was fooled, the captain responded perfectly. I felt slightly light in my seat as the collective came down rapidly to enter the auto. As the captain adjusted the rudders to keep the aircraft in trim and turned right, lining up neatly for the level green field below, he kept the airspeed at exactly 70 knots, just as the book called for.

I relaxed again. The captain had done everything correctly. Since practice engine failures like this one were not continued all the way to a landing, as we passed through 500 feet I called for the captain to recover. As he rolled the throttle back on to get engine power restored, there was a slight cough from behind us, and then silence. In flight school, the instructors described the sound of a dead engine as the same as "a mouse pissing on cotton." That was an inadequate description since the silence was closer to going completely deaf, at least to me it was.

After the slightest moment of hesitation, my flight school and instructor training took over. Throwing the freshly lit cigarette to the captain I yelled what instructors always yell when the situation is getting beyond the other pilot's control, "I've got it" and grabbed the flight controls.

Turns, the rotation speed of the rotor, are life in a helicopter. Without the correct speed of rotation the rotor blades do not produce lift and the aircraft, with no flight capability, just falls and your life ends. I immediately checked to see that the rotor speed was high enough, "in the green," and simultaneously made sure the airspeed stayed at the specified 70 knots and kept the H-13 lined up for the spot in the green field the captain had already picked out.

As I had practiced a thousand times, at an estimated 75 feet above the ground I pulled the nose back, flaring the helicopter to reduce the airspeed and break the high rate of descent. At about 20 feet above the ground I pushed the cyclic stick forward to level the aircraft. As I did the rate of descent immediately started to build again, so at 10 feet I jerked the collective pitch lever about halfway up to trade rotor speed for lift, to break the final rate of descent.

As the helicopter slowed its rate of descent, I smoothly used the remaining collective to touch down so gently that neither of us felt the actual touch. The remaining forward speed stopped as I lowered the collective after we touched, allowing the OH-13E to slide the two skid lengths the operator's manual, the "-10," called for. From the time the engine stopped, until the aircraft was motionless on the ground, was less than 20 seconds.

In the post landing silence I realized that the captain was still holding the lit cigarette as we watched the rotor blades slowly spin to a stop. The helicopter was very, very quiet.

"You stay with the bird, Sir, and I'll go find a phone." I said to the captain, who opened the Plexiglas door and threw out the un-smoked, but still burning, cigarette.

Before I left the helicopter to walk the 100 yards to the road, I got the rotor blade tie down out of its storage, slid the padded metal loop over the rear blade and tied the ribbon ends to the tail boom, securing the blades so that they did not flap around in the wind. Satisfied the bird was OK, or at least certain there was no damage beyond a dead engine, I began to walk across the grass over to the road. From the first day of flight school, the instructors had prepared us for this by making us do countless simulated engine failures, and now it had happened. And I had made it without further damage to the aircraft. But as I walked toward the road on the other side of the field, my knees went weak, a little wobbly.

Flagging down a car on the road between the fields, I asked the driver to take me to the Rod and Gun Club about a mile away, the closest place with a phone. The enlisted man that answered back at the airfield passed me to the maintenance officer, an old, very experienced chief warrant officer 4 (CW4).

"No, I didn't do any damage landing it," I said in answer to his first question. He didn't ask if I was OK, since if I was making the call, that much was obvious.

"No, I have no idea why it quit," I said in answer to his second question.

"See you in a few minutes," he said as he hung the phone up.

---

*I was in total awe of the maintenance officer. He had been in one of the very first helicopter training classes that the Army ever held in the early '50s, and was later one of the pilots in the Army's equivalent of the Blue Angels, the helicopter demonstration team. He could make a helicopter sing. Once he took me up on a maintenance check flight and instead of doing a normal takeoff, he took the OH-13E off backwards. We slowly flew around the traffic pattern, turned final, and then came to a hover, all facing 180 degrees from the normal heading. Another time, after an ice storm, he said, "Let's go flying," but instead of having the helicopter towed out onto the ice-covered ramp he had it moved to the edge of the hanger and then had the hanger doors opened wide. He started it up and ground taxied, moved it forward with the skids dragging on the concrete instead of coming to a hover, until we were clear enough to lift up without blowing things around inside the hanger. The entire airfield was covered in a coat of glaze ice, so we had it to ourselves. Flying out to the main runway he climbed to 1000 feet and then entered autorotation. He flared at 75 feet like we were supposed to, leveled, "popped" up the collective to break our rate of descent, but instead of stopping after touch-down, the helicopter slid down the runway without even slowing down. After a hundred yards he rolled the throttle back on and back up we went again. He did two more before he hovered back over to the ramp. When he rolled the throttle off to shut down, the torque caused the helicopter to spin slowly on the ice until all momentum was lost.*

---

Thirty minutes later the CW4 pulled up in his personal pickup truck accompanied by one of the sergeants who worked for him. He parked on the side of the road between the two green fields and looked out at the helicopter sitting in the middle of the spot the captain had picked. It was so near the center, it looked like it had been towed out there. Leaving the captain with the aircraft, I walked over to him. He didn't say anything until I was about 20 feet away from him.

"The least you could have done was land the Goddamn thing closer to the road, you dumb shit! I'm going to get my boots muddy just walking out there," he shouted, loud enough for the captain and the sergeant to hear.

I was surprised and slightly hurt by the comment. Somehow I expected praise, thank-God-you-are-OK, or some other expression of relief, but not that comment. The best I could manage in reply was a weak, embarrassed smile, until it dawned on me slowly that this was praise. Praise, because he implied that I had enough skill to put the helicopter anywhere, even with a dead engine.

The CW4 quizzed me on what happened. When I got to the simulated engine failure part, he held up his hand to stop me and walked to the cockpit of the helicopter. Looking inside, the CW4 pointed to the carburetor heat. The lever with the round black knob marked with an "H" was in the up position. It was off.

In cold weather, the fuel flowing through the carb needs heat to keep moisture in the air from forming ice and stopping the fuel flow when you reduce power. The heat from the engine exhaust is ducted to the carb to make this happen. If the outside air temperature is near or below freezing, carb heat must be used, particularly when making rapid power changes. I had forgotten to pull the heat on when I cut the throttle; ice formed, the engine quit, all as advertised in the most basic helicopter flying classes.

Quickly examining the aircraft, the CW4 found no damage. The ice in the carb went away as soon as the fuel flow stopped.

"Get in and fly it home," the CW4 snapped.

Again, I was surprised and even more, apprehensive. After all, I had just survived my first engine failure, but the CW4 was adamant. The captain and I got back onboard and started the H-13 up. When I looked, the maintenance officer was already gone. He did not even wait to see if we got off alright.

The flight home was without incident, but the ragging I got from the other instructors hurt, at first. Then I realized that they all had done similar, stupid things, things like cutting down a flag pole with the rotors or chopping down bushes from landing too close, and they all had survived them and learned from them. Now I had joined the club with my first real emergency, even if it was self-induced.

I never did that particular stupid evolution again. But, I managed a variation on a theme and caused another engine on another OH-13E to shut down in flight again a few months later. I survived that one, too, with no damage to helicopter, pilot, or passenger, but the maintenance officer was mad at me again. That too is another story.

# 4

# THE PLAYTEX CLUB

## PHU BAI, VIETNAM ■ SEPTEMBER 1970

The black lacquer plaques with the enameled squadron patch in the center and the flags of the Allies participating in the war across the top were hung around the walls of the bar in the Playtex Officer's Club. They were just about at eye level, and below each plaque was a Polaroid of the pilot who owned the plaque, the man who would have it presented to him when he left country. The plaques were hung in order of "shortness." That is, the newest man had his hung at the far end of the room, next to the door out onto the patio. Around the wall back toward the bar itself, they were ordered until, over the bar, there were only five left.

In the center of the bar, over the chrome and red vinyl barstools, stolen from who knows where, was the plaque of the next man to leave. When that man received his plaque from the commanding officer, the CO, and took the jeep ride over to the Phu Bai airfield to catch the C-130 south to Cam Rahn and back to the states, the next man in line would move all the plaques up until his was in the center.

If you were killed, the executive officer, the XO, would go to the Club that same day, usually as soon as he received the word, and remove your plaque. It would be placed in the boxes containing the personal effects of the man and mailed to his family with the date not filled in. The photo was never mailed. It was just discarded or put with the other small things that were the un-official company history. By the time the pilots came back from that day's missions, no sign would remain that the man or his plaque had ever been there.

Most units gave out plaques when you left, but not "C" Company, 159th Aviation Battalion, 101st Airborne Division (Airmobile) in 1970. The radio call sign of "C" Co was Playtex (unofficial motto, "We give living support") and the day you checked in, you were presented with your plaque and had your picture taken with the safety officer's Polaroid. As soon as the gook shop (casual, racist slang, common then, for the concession shop run by Vietnamese that sold hats and cowboy holsters for our .38s, made unit patches, did sewing, etc.) down the mud street from the officer's area got the steel plate engraved with your name and in-country date, the plaque was put up at the end of the line.

The officer's area in Playtex consisted of SEA (South East Asia) Huts. They were plywood, gray painted, single story buildings with tin roofs, built quickly by combat engineers. The Club was a rectangular room that occupied the southern half of the eastern-most shack. It had been built two years before when Playtex moved into the compound. The walls were varnished plywood, an attempt to make it seem more like some of the real world Officer's Clubs the older pilots had seen in their travels. The floor was covered with those one-foot squares of linoleum that everyone that ever served in the Army spent so many hours pushing a buffer over. The northern half of the Club building contained two rooms, the one next door was a single room occupied by the company XO and the one on the far end was home to two of the company warrant officers.

In front of the wall of the Club that adjoined the XO's room was the bar. The builders had done a good job on the woodwork, very professional looking carpentry amid the squatter's-camp look of the rest of the company area. The mirror behind the bar reflected bottles of liquors, mostly unfamiliar to the pilots since nearly all were too young to drink stateside. Displayed over the top of the mirror was a bra and various bits of female underwear, souvenirs of R&R exploits. Under the counter, were the cabinets where the hard liquor was supposed to be locked up, but these shelves stayed empty because the Club never closed and no one ever bothered to lock the booze up. To the right of the mirror was a door that led to the storeroom where the extra beer and soft drinks were kept.

To the right of the storeroom door were the two refrigerators that held the beer and soft drinks ready for consumption. The freezer compartments of both held long stainless steel trays from the mess hall that were used to make ice. An ice pick was usually handy on top of the refrigerator so that the pilot who wanted ice could break some off. The water used to make the ice was potable but only just. When frozen, the water had swirls of dirt, like marbling in praline ice cream. The pilots just broke the ice around the swirls and left most of the grit in the tray until someone got disgusted enough to throw it out and start over again.

Because the Club was an "unofficial" one, it received no support from the official system of alcohol distribution. To buy the hard liquor, the pilots pooled their ration cards and gave them to the Club Officer. This system ensured plentiful booze because each officer was authorized two quarts of hard liquor each month and the non-drinker's cards provided for the heavy drinkers. The Club Officer would check out a helicopter and take the ration cards to the Class 6 (liquor store in military language) store in Da Nang once a month or so and buy the booze. The beer and soft drinks mostly came from the small post exchange (PX) over by the runway at Phu Bai, a mile or so away. Both soft drinks and beer were in steel, not aluminum, cans and were often flat from the long shipment from the states and the months in storage.

On the wall near the ceiling, to the right of the two bar refrigerators, was an exhaust fan with bend blades and a motor that made a labored sound as it turned. The wall around the fan was scared and stained from being a target. Once a month or so, the company would order and receive a shipment of bar glasses and just as regularly break them all that night. The game was to see who could get a glass, or at least most of the glass, through the fan without stopping it. If there were no glasses, beer cans were tried, but since they were steel cans, the fan usually stopped when the first one made it into the blades.

Below and to the right of the fan, among the stained and drooping Playboy Playmates of the Month, hung two rocket propelled grenade (RPG) launchers, one a Russian RPG-7 and the other a Chinese RPG-2. Scrounged from the grunts, they were operational weapons, but only served as decorations since no one could get any of the grenades to fire from them. The Chinese one was more like a piece of pipe with a crude trigger hanging on the bottom than a weapon. The Russian version was more advanced and even had the telescopic sight still attached. The bell-shaped exhaust of the Russian RPG looked like one of the blunder-busses in the old drawings of the Pilgrims.

Around the walls, below the plaques were bookshelves, two and sometimes three high, full of paperbacks of all kinds. Textbooks, sex books, westerns, science fiction, novels, non-fiction, all types of books, mostly supplied by Special Services, these books generally represented more sophisticated taste than that held by the members of C Co. Westerns, pornography, and science fiction were the favorites, easy to spot by their worn covers and falling-out pages. Among the bookcases were stereo speakers in varying stages of disrepair from the hand-pumped fire extinguisher water fights that were a semi-regular feature of company life. The stereo itself had disappeared, probably thrown away after being soaked and shorted out by the water.

Below the plaques and books was a bench that went around half the Club. Like the varnished walls and well-built bar, someone had put a lot of time into building it. Even the upholstery of red vinyl from the paraloft was of a high enough quality to be mistaken for a professional, but cheap, upholstery job.

Opposite the bar, at the far end of the rectangular room, were two Plexiglas picture windows, made from sheets of the plastic intended to cover someone's desktop. Scratched and dirty, the windows looked out on the wooden deck and the yard of the officer's area; no grass, just all sand. The tin roofing that made up the privacy fence around the officers compound prevented anyone inside the Club from seeing the two-hole outhouse or the pipe stuck in the ground to serve as the piss-tube (urinal) just beyond the fence.

From inside the Club, the sand volleyball court, horseshoe pit, and the barbecue grill, made from real stone like those grills in the better national parks, were invisible. Even the few sickly banana trees planted to give the yard a green look could not be seen. The smoke from the diesel fuel used to burn the shit from the outhouse could be seen when the weekly cleaning was done by the hired Vietnamese cleaning crew. Even when you couldn't see it, you could smell the shit burning.

To the right of the windows were more bookshelves and the poker table. Boxes of chips and the dirty packs of cards used by the casual players were stacked haphazardly on the shelves among the special service books. The hard-core players used new decks for every game. Used decks of cards and $500 or $600 poker hands mixed no better here than anywhere else such games are played. Unlike the mythical old west of the movies, everyone here really did carry a gun.

The windows along the wall by the poker table were screened but contained no glass or even Plexiglas, only a sheet of plywood over each that could be lowered to keep the winter wind, such as it was, out. The covers were almost always down since no one was ever in the Club during the day to need the ventilation they were supposed to provide.

The door was a sheet of plywood cut to the size of a normal screen door. The spring that was to hold the door closed nearly always dangled loose, since the wood where the screw attached the spring to the wall had been pulled out so many times that no wood was left and the door stood open or closed, depending on which way the wind was blowing.

Between the door and the bar was another sheet of plywood, painted white and covered with Plexiglas. A grease pencil on a string hung on the left side of the board. The board listed the rules under which the Playtex Club operated:

Rule 1—There are no rules.
Admission free, Exit $50
Broken Cherries, $50
Drink Prices—Mixed drinks $.30, Beer $.25, soft drinks $.20
Operating Hours—24 Hours per day, 365 days a year.

Some Clubs operated with rules that mimicked the rules of the "real world" Officers Clubs: enter with your hat on and buy everyone at the bar a round; entered armed and buy the bar; throw six aces when playing one of the dice games and buy the bar; hat on the bar and buy the bar, step on the mascot painted in the tile floor and buy the bar. But Playtex held no such pretensions. Because you had to pass the bar to get to the showers, it was not uncommon to see a naked pilot with a towel over his shoulder having a beer with a pilot just back from flying, still wearing his hat embroidered with his wings and rank insignia and his .38 pistol in the customary cowboy holster from the gook shop. Leave your hat in the bar and someone would wet it thoroughly, ball it up, and put it in the freezer, leaving you a ball of ice with your hat in the center.

The "Admission free, Exit $50" reflected a local custom. On their first night in the company, new pilots drank free, were expected to drink a lot, and were expected to still be able to show up for work in the morning. They would be hung over badly at the least and more likely, still drunk when they reported to the XO for their job assignments. On their last night in the squadron, before they took the ride to Cam Rahn and on to home, they were expected to put $50 on the bar for those whose time was not up yet to drink on.

"Broken cherries, $50," meant that the first time a pilot had bullet holes in his aircraft, he had to put $50 on the bar. It was to celebrate a passage, from "Newbie," new boy, to real company member. After the first hits, no one owed anything. Unless of course they were promoted or made aircraft commander or had a birthday or a child born back in the world, or just felt like it.

Below the rules were the names of all the pilots and a line for grease pencil marks. The bar ran on the honor system, so each time a drink was taken a mark would be made under the appropriate column, soft drink, beer, or hard stuff. Once a month, the Club Officer would total up the marks and bill each pilot. Even with those prices, some would have a large bill. Some of the high bills reflected events, promotion, birthday, etc., but most just reflected an early tendency toward alcoholism produced by stress or whatever causes alcoholism anywhere.

Next to the rules was another Plexiglas-covered plywood board. This one had a two-column list of names. On the left was the aircraft commander, on the right the copilot for the next day's missions. Next to each name was a number which marked what priority you were for the next day's missions. The lower the number, the more missions you would have.

Playtex was a Chinook company, flying the CH-47C, the big, twin-rotor, twin-engine helicopters made by Boeing in their plant just south of Philadelphia. The number of aircraft Playtex operations had determined were required for the next days' missions could be seen by the number of crews listed, with those on standby at the bottom. Being number one through number four always meant you would be flying from between eight to ten hours the next day, but from there on down, you might or might not have a mission. Usually there were two standby crews. Standby crews were listed at the bottom and were required to at least preflight and start their aircraft so that when one of the primary birds broke, as they always did, the aircraft commander could jump in and make takeoff on time. Those crews drawing missions such as aircraft recovery standby, or flare drop standby, were noted on the very bottom of the board.

In the evening, the assistant operations officer (Ops O) would walk up from the Ops bunker down the street from the officer's area and grease pencil in the names. Sometimes he would tape a stenciled sheet of paper with names on it over the board but this didn't work too well, since it was likely to be covered in thrown drinks and be totally unreadable before the evening was over. In theory, the pilots looked at the board before they turned in, but since the crews were formed on the basis of flight time (the man with the least in the last 30 days would fly the longest missions and the man with the most would not fly) the pilots usually already knew whether or not they would be flying. In any case, the duty clerk would wake them in time to get ready for launch if they were flying.

The lights were always on in the Club. That is, they were always on unless the generator that provided power to the entire company ran out of fuel or broke down or was shut down for maintenance. And the light they provided reflected off the black lacquer plaques and the already fading Polaroid's of their owners, 24 hours a day, 365 days a year during 1971.

# 5

# FIRST TAKEOFF OF THE DAY
## PHU BAI, VIETNAM ■ DECEMBER 1970

---

*"Liftmaster Tower, Playtex One Two, three miles east for landing. I've got six turnin' and two burnin', my gear is down and bolted, my pistol is cold" (typical call for landing at Playtex's home airfield, circa 1971. Translation: I am Chinook with all six rotor blades going around, both engines running, my landing gear is not retractable, and I am not shooting my pistol.)*

---

You are the aircraft commander (AC) for your helicopter today. The duty clerk woke you up to give you the mission sheet at around 0430, an hour and a half before daylight and takeoff time. The mission sheet lists all the missions Playtex has for today. The mission sheet lists them in the order that they are to be flown and highlights the ones that you will fly. You get the complete listing of all missions because if someone else's aircraft goes down for maintenance or battle damage, you will have to pick up their missions. All the missions must be completed before the last aircraft is shut down for the day. No matter what, the missions must be done.

Because there are no windows in your Southeast Asia (SEA) hut hootch, you had to turn on the lamp on the homemade desk next to your bed to find your clothes, survival vest, pistol, and boots even though you had laid them out the night before. Your roommates and you sealed all the windows with plywood to better insulate the hootch, hoping the Sears air conditioner built into the wall would have a better chance against the heat. You put the mission sheet on your clipboard so that it stays unwrinkled through the coming long humid day. Your roommates do not wake up or move when your light comes on since we go through this every morning when at least one of the three of you is flying.

Walking through the plywood door to the back room that served as kitchen and bath, you run water in the sink. Shaving using water warmed by your room's personal electric hot water, the only hot water heater in the company at this time of day, quickly completed the wake up process. Back through the door and into the main room, you finished dressing quickly: white T-shirt, green issue wool and cotton socks, green trousers made of flame-proof nomex with lots of pockets, matching nomex shirt with your company patch sown over the left breast pocket and 101st patch on the left shoulder, tail tucked in, strap on the .38 pistol in a black leather cowboy holster from the gook shop, and lastly pull on the olive drab (OD) green baseball hat with your wings and a CW2 bar sown on the front. You made the bed by pulling the camouflage-patterned nylon poncho liner over the sheets. Last thing before you were out the door was to turn off the fan oscillating over the bed—it kept you cool and the mosquitoes off in the night—and turn off the lamp.

A fast piss into the tube stuck in the ground on the other side of the tin fence on the far side of the officer's area next to the plywood shitters and then to breakfast across the peniprime (black material like thick oil that almost, but not quite, turned the dirt into blacktop) street to the mess hall, greasy eggs, limp, coarsely baked bread, semi-raw bacon cooked in an oven and hot, bitter black coffee. No conversation with other pilots sitting around the table in the officer's dining room, the food is just fuel for your body and then it's back out the door into the dark. Back to the hootch and pick up your flight gear. Carrying your helmet bag, wearing your 15-pound ceramic and steel bullet bouncer—at least the front plate of the bullet bouncer since wearing the back was just too uncomfortable for 10 hours of flying—and your survival vest, you walked in the darkness down the company street to the operations bunker on the right, next to the company headquarters. Your copilot joins you and walks beside you, but you don't talk to each other—nothing to talk about. A hundred feet down the street, he turns left toward the wire surrounding the flight line to start the pre-flight, while you turn right into the operations bunker.

Company operations, the S-3 or just "Ops" is in a sandbag-protected SEA hut, but the sandbags are starting to leak from all the exposure to sunlight they get every day. Weeds have started growing up through the spaces between them. Every day, every time you walk past Ops you wonder if they would stop the shrapnel from a mortar round or are they just psychological protection, like the plastic windows on your helicopter.

In the Ops bunker, you sign for the KY28 encryption box for the fox mike (FM) radio. The KY28s are square, gray, armored, heavy things that scramble your radio signal so you can speak to other users of KY28s, each other, and controllers without the enemy understanding you. You sign for the Signal Operating Instructions (SOI, a classified small rectangular notebook with all the frequencies and call signs listed for all of I Corps) for the northern-most part of Vietnam where you are based. You pick up your blood chits, the pieces of paper printed in several languages telling of a gold reward for the return of the bearer should you get shot down and have to E&E (escape and evade) back to friendly lines.

Blood chits always remind you of the Flying Tigers from WWII, but you don't know why—old movies you saw when you were a kid, maybe. You also know that the enemy usually executes helicopter crews because they are captured in the thick of battle by regulars, not farmers with pitchforks. Trying to get the helicopter crews back to enemy rear areas puts their soldiers to unnecessary risk, so they don't usually do it.

There are several other pieces of survival gear too, all in an OD green steel 7.62MM machine gun ammo can, but you know if you crash you will not drag the ammo can out of the wreckage of the aircraft, so you don't even look inside.

After five minutes in the Ops bunker, you are outside again and walking to the helicopter across the steel PSP (pierced steel planking) mat to the two-sided steel revetment where today's bird is parked, carrying all the things you just signed for as well as your flight gear. The wire around the mat is supposed to keep infiltrators out, and the high steel walls of the revetments protect the aircraft from in-coming mortars. You walk through the gap in the barbed wire by the little two-story control tower and across the slick, damp PSP to your Chinook.

The crew is already there—the flight engineer, the crew chief, and the door gunner. They probably have been there for hours, sometimes they sleep in the aircraft. It's easier to go that way, just sleep out there most nights on stretchers stolen from who knows where and eat C-rations stolen out of the pallets for the grunts. Keep the machine ready, but even more, have a place to yourself, a place where you are king. No roommates or sergeants to give you hassle or to keep you awake with drugs or drink. Just the night sounds a quarter mile from the wire around the base. Sometimes mortar fire and a burst of machine-gun fire in the distance, but most nights just flares drifting down on their parachutes over the raw red dirt of Phu Bai.

The flight engineer, called "Chief" in this company, owns the aircraft. The pilots change every day but this Chinook is his. He supervises the other crewmen, the crew chief—a flight engineer in training and a gunner—often a grunt who got tired of walking and now owns the two door guns. The Chief owns everything aft of the cockpit when you fly. You know that he can kill you by his actions or inactions. He knows you can kill him and the rest of the crew in a second if you don't do your job right. But you trust each other because you must, because you will all die together if one of you fails. The missions must get done.

Your copilot climbs to the top of the aircraft to begin his preflight. It's slick up there from spilled oil and hydraulic fluid and dew in the morning dark; better he falls than you. Besides, you already did your climbing up there while you were a copilot, while you were a "newbie" like he is. Now you are the AC, and as is your right, you preflight the inside and the bottom of the Chinook. Nothing unusual to see, and in ten minutes you are telling the flight engineer about what's up for the day, or at least as much of it as you can tell by the mission sheet. Not much is required in the way of crew briefing when you fly together for eight or ten or twelve hours every day. The Chief wants to know seats up for internal cargo or seats down for PAX or sling loads starting off, but today, as most days, it's sling loads all day. The seats are fine in the down position for now.

No missions on the sheet call for Cobra escort, so Ops didn't know for sure you'd be shot at today. You wouldn't know either until it happens, maybe not even then. Lots of times in a Chinook, you don't hear small arms rounds hitting over the whine of the transmissions and the roar of the two turbine engines, so unless someone sees holes starting to appear or the bullets hit something that shows up on the gauges or the master caution panel, you just don't know.

Now both pilots are in their seats, AC on the left and pilot on the right. You like the left seat because it somehow seems as if you can see better over here on the left. You command from the left seat, the pilot flies from the right. Seats on the Chinook adjust not only up/down and forward/back, but also in tilt. It always seems you start the day out bolt upright and somehow finish it ten hours later in a slump, seat tilted all the way back. Your "chicken plate," aka "bullet bouncer"—a ceramic-over-steel plate that covers your chest—is not hurting you yet but you know it will before the day is over. It's heavy and rests on the top of your legs. Around your neck on a dog tag chain is the SOI with all the current radio frequencies and call signs listed. It fits neatly into a pocket on the front of the armor.

Before things get too far along in your start up, you pull your grease pencil out of the pocket on your left upper sleeve and get out the SOI. You write the frequencies and call signs you will need first thing on the lower left portion of the windshield. You copy them from the SOI because they change all the time and it is too hard to remember what your call sign is today—once it was "Rancid Killer," someone's idea of a joke no doubt. Looking at the clipboard all ACs carry, you scan the first of today's missions. The fox mike frequency of the pickup zone (PZ) and their call sign, the call sign of the firebase where you will take the first loads of the day, the artillery clearance frequency, all these things go on the windshield, making it classified at least "Secret," but you will erase it before you leave the cockpit at the end of the day. When you are finished you put the clipboard down to the right of your seat, next to the center console where you can get it easily. Underneath the mission sheets are pictures of your wife and son covered in acetate to remind you to live through the day. If you crash, you hope the clipboard is destroyed so that the enemy does not get to see your family.

You are in your seat and ready for the start checklist. Four-point seat belt and shoulder harness on over the chicken plate, .38 pistol in its cowboy holster moved from your right side to between your legs for a little extra protection, even if it is just psychological. The copilot calls the items on the checklist and you do them and the checklist goes quickly by. The small turbine engine, auxiliary power unit (APU), which drives the flight boosts and powers the electronics when the engines are not running, comes on line and then you are starting the engines. Since there is no rotor brake on a Chinook to hold the rotors still, as you start the engines the noise increases and the aircraft starts rocking unevenly as the big blades, three on the front and three on the back, start to turn slowly. It's a rhythmic rocking until the blades get into phase (90 degrees apart), and then it smoothes to a steady vibration. Then the blades turn faster and faster. Using the condition levers in the center of the console, you take the engines from the ground position to the fly position and with the increasing whine of the turbines, the individual blades become a solid disk to the eye. As the blades achieve sync, the rocking goes away and the motion becomes a smooth vibration, almost a hum.

Checklist complete, you are ready to taxi and your flight engineer sees you are the first ready out of all the aircraft flying this morning. He stands in front of the aircraft and motions you forward out onto the main taxiway. Before you move, you call Liftmaster tower for taxi clearance and you are cleared into position and hold. Because you were parked in the front row, you get first place in line on the short runway facing east, waiting for takeoff clearance.

There are eight aircraft turning now, though only six are required for missions today. If one of the six breaks on run-up, the AC will unstrap and go to one of the two backups while the original copilot completes the shutdown of the broken bird.

Ground taxiing a Chinook using all four sets of wheels is a two-man operation. The copilot works the thrust and cyclic, while holding the rudders neutral. The AC works the brakes and steers using the power steering knob on the center console. Only the right wheel is power driven, the left just trails along. When you are ready to move, the copilot adds a little thrust and moves the cyclic to two inches aft. The AC releases the brakes and uses the power steering to move the aircraft in the direction he wants to go. With familiar teamwork, the two of you smoothly move the Chinook into takeoff position on the runway.

The Chinook's familiar roar through your helmet ear pads and vibrations through the seat, floor, and flight controls feel good, feel strong. You are fully awake now and are ready to go, ready to go fly. You are 21 years old and your body is whole and none of your joints hurt and your eyes are clear with 20/10 vision and you command this machine and this crew. The sky is lighter in front of you now and as you wait for takeoff clearance, you get a sense of power that wasn't there when you were half asleep going through the routine motions of those things that you must do before you fly, satisfying the religious flying rituals. As the sun starts to move above the horizon, takeoff clearance comes from the control tower.

As AC, you always make the first takeoff of the day. An inexperienced copilot might not feel something wrong with the aircraft before it's too late. You pull the cyclic back two inches with your right hand and add power with your left as you smoothly pull the thrust lever up.

The big helicopter comes off the ground smoothly, front wheels first as the first rim of the sun becomes visible. At 20 feet you hold the aircraft steady in a hover while last minute checks of all the systems are made—"All set in the back"—"gauges look good"—and then you are free to go.

As you pull up on the thrust lever to add more power and lower the nose, and as you begin the first climb out of the day, you feel so strong, like your machine can lift the world and take it high into the sky. You are young and strong and nothing can ever change that for you—Ever. You can fly.

# 6

# LUCK AND SUPERSTITION
## DA NANG, VIETNAM ■ JANUARY 1971

---

*I have no idea if pilots are more or less superstitious than people
in other professions. Some have their "lucky" objects, some must
do an obsessive/compulsive certain thing every time before they
fly, while still others show no superstition at all. During Vietnam, mine became "petting" my aircraft, a soft pat on its nose
or a rub on the skin by the door, as I boarded. It was a promise
to the machine that I would take care of it and in return it
promised to bring me back. I don't think I had or needed any
superstitions until I flew with the oldest pilot I have known before or since, but I did afterwards on the grounds that if it
worked that long for him, it would work for me.*

---

Sometimes when flying missions in northern I Corps, we would see a
single gray and black Huey, usually high above us and always alone.
Sometimes it would be headed off toward the mountains that marked the
border of Laos. Other times, we would see it sitting on the ground, just
sitting by itself, in the middle of nowhere. Occasionally, we would see a
man in a white short-sleeve shirt leaning against the side of the aircraft as
it sat outside a small village. We always looked upon this as something of
a wonder in our world of green uniforms and green helicopters above the
green forest.

To those of us in the 101st Airborne, it always seemed an insane thing
to do, to fly a gray and black helicopter without door guns by yourself
and to wear a white shirt and tie, to put yourself outside the protective
wall of the military and fly alone into unknown places. Of course, the Air
America pilots that flew the gray and black Huey's probably felt the same
way about us, flying above the green for paltry military pay into hot landing zones and dusty mountaintops, day after day. And, of course before
they were Air America pilots, they were us, learning their trade in the same

helicopters we flew before leaving the green nomex for a shirt and tie.

Air America also flew many other types of aircraft, but we seldom saw them. Once, while waiting out some bad weather at the small, crumbling airstrip in the old imperial capitol, Hue City, I watched an Air America Helio Courier (a very short landing Swiss-built aircraft) drop from the clouds, roll to a stop in what seemed like its own length, off load a passenger, and after taking off in less than 100 feet, climb back into the sky in about two minutes flat. It disappeared into the clouds nearly as soon as it broke the ground. I had no idea how the pilot even found that airfield through the clouds, let alone land his fixed-wing in the same space a helicopter would have taken. Another time, it seemed I was flying through a cloud of what looked like snow, but then realized it was actually white paper, and looking up, I saw an old C-47 dropping Chu Hoi ("I surrender") leaflets on the I Corps forest below us.

Strange aircraft, operating alone, were just part of the background of the war. All in all, Vietnam was a strange war—at least compared to what I had read about WWII—but a war that offered unusual opportunities to the participants. Opportunities like the two-week leave to anywhere in the world you wanted to take it, introduced in late 1970.

The two-week leave program was designed to keep morale up, always a good thing. Anyone could take two weeks of leave, right in the middle of the war and go anywhere they liked, albeit at your own expense, unlike Rest and Recuperation leave (R&R) when Uncle Sam pays for your flight. Patriotic airlines immediately introduced cheap fares from Vietnam back to the United States. Wishing for a nice break from the war, I immediately looked for the best deal and found it in a North West Orient ad.

For $350 all-in-all-done, I could fly commercial air from Da Nang, South Vietnam, to Nashville, Tennessee and back, and have nine days with my wife and son in the middle. Plus, because of their flight scheduling, I would have one night on the airline in Hong Kong between flights, not a bad deal anytime but especially nice in war time. A few phone calls later, I found out that I would have to buy my ticket in person at the Air Vietnam Airlines counter in Da Nang, about 60 miles and one small mountain pass to the south of Phu Bai.

Normally, getting to Da Nang from Phu Bai was as easy as finding another pilot who had a day off and wanted to do some shopping at the big Post Exchange (PX) there. Then you went to Playtex Ops and signed out a Chinook for the day and went, taking a jeep with you in the back for transportation when you got there. The advantages of a big aircraft . . . but this time it was not so easy.

There were four different models of Chinook in Vietnam, the "A", "B", "Baby C," and "Super C." The A and B were older model aircraft with two fuel tanks and much less range than either of the two C models we flew with their six fuel tanks. Playtex had both Baby C's and Super C's, the difference being the Super C engines produced far more power than the ones in the Baby C. Everything has a price, and the price was that the engines on the Baby were good for 1,200 hours between changes, while because of the higher stress on them, the engines on the Super were only good for 300 hours.

The stress turned out much worse than the Army thought. The engines on the Super C weren't making it to 300 hours; instead they were blowing up before it was time to change them. So, all Super C's were grounded until the engines could be replaced with the weaker, but more reliable engines on Baby C's. Unfortunately, Playtex had ten Super C's out of a total of sixteen aircraft, leaving only six of the Baby C's for missions until the engines on the Supers could be changed, bringing them back to Baby C's. Optional flying was temporarily ended.

The second choice for getting to Da Nang was the Bus Run. As the name implied, Chinooks from one of the three companies in the 159th Assault Support Battalion flew a daily mission that was exactly like a city bus route. Ten hours long, the Bus Run went from Landing Zone (LZ) to LZ all over I Corps, including Da Nang, picking up and dropping passengers at set stops along the way. But the engine problem stopped the Bus Run, too.

Other than trying to hitch a ride on a truck, a very long and dangerous trip, the only option left was to go over to the base ops room at Phu Bai airfield and wait for someone to pass through on their way down to Da Nang. Having flown over 100 hours in last 30 days, company Ops gave me the day off and I bummed a ride in the company jeep for the mile over to the Phu Bai airfield.

The Base Ops Department was doing the usual paperwork when I came into their small office. When I finally got their attention, they told me to talk to the pilot of an Air America light twin-engine, fixed-wing parked on the ramp out in front of the building. I thanked them and walked through the front door, out onto the concrete ramp.

I could see a pilot in a white shirt studying a map in the cockpit. I walked to the right side and yelled into the open door, "You going to Da Nang."

As the pilot turned toward me, I was surprised to see the oldest man I had ever seen at the controls of an aircraft sitting there. He must have been 70—a 70-year-old active pilot.

With a smile on his very lined face he said, "Sure am. You want a ride?"

When I replied yes, he motioned for me to climb in. I strapped myself into the right seat as he watched, smiling all the time.

Looking at the Playtex patch on my flight suit pocket, he asked, "Enjoy flying Chinooks?"

"Yes, sir. Great aircraft. They're a lot of fun," I replied.

He smiled at that. "We'll get going in a minute," he said, turning back to his chart.

In 1971, at Playtex and all the other aviation companies, the average age of the pilots was around 21, maybe 23 tops. The old-timers, for example our major commanding officer (CO), were probably 35. In the states, I had seen colonels and some ancient, passed-over-for-promotion majors who were in their 40's, but this man looked at least 70. A 70-year-old pilot. In his black pants and short-sleeved white shirt he looked even stranger, since I was familiar with green flight suits and rolled down sleeves and pistols worn in cowboy holsters, just like the uniform I had on. No pistol, no flight suit, just a short-sleeved white shirt and black trousers on a 70-year-old pilot. . . .

Handing me a headset instead of a flight helmet, he put down the chart and began to start the airplane. Unlike the military procedures where one pilot calls out the steps from a checklist, he just started moving the switches at a rapid pace without referring to anything.

He talked as he started the aircraft, "I used to fly helicopters, but they're just too noisy for me now. I liked the CH-21 though. You ever fly a CH-

21? Nah, you're too young for CH-21's. Maybe a CH-34? Nah, you're too young for them, too. Probably flew OH-23's at Wolters, I'll bet, you being tall and all," he said, as the left, then right engines started. Obviously he had been an Army pilot in another life, another life a long time ago.

Reaching across in front of me he got the door to the airplane and pulled it closed. We put on our headsets as he pointed at a thumb switch on the control wheel that operated the intercom.

"We'll be on our way in a minute or two. Here, you can navigate," he said with a laugh, throwing me the rumpled chart he had been studying.

He laughed because no navigation was required between Phu Bai and Da Nang today. From the ramp where we were parked, we could see the mountains that ran down to the sea to the southeast. Mountains on your right and the water on your left and you would find Da Nang just on the other side of the first ridgeline you came to as you flew south. Just don't take the easy path through the gap in the hills. It's called the Hai Van Pass, and is littered with the wreckage of four or five aircraft that found out the North Vietnamese Army (NVA) likes to set up machine guns there every now and then to catch pilots sneaking through the pass under the clouds, instead of going out to sea between the shore and the island a mile out. Watch for them coming and then just hold the trigger down as they go by, easy . . .

He was already taxiing when he called tower for clearance and just glanced down the runway before pulling out. The throttles were already coming on as we left the taxiway, and in a short distance we were in the air and climbing out toward the mountains over a junkyard full of wrecked aircraft just off the end of the runway and the perimeter wire and bunkers. Never having had much to do with fixed-wing aircraft, I was somewhat surprised that he handled all the controls as easily as I did a helicopter. It would be logical that he did, but flying fixed-wing aircraft was not a natural act to me.

Reaching 5,000 feet, he turned the aircraft south. How different the ground looked from the cockpit of a fixed wing. No chin bubble to look through, wings in the way when you looked off to the side. No door gunners in the rear and no rotor vibrations, it felt unnatural. Instead of heading out to sea to fly between the islands and the mountains as we always did, he just climbed a little higher and went over the Hai Van well above machine-gun range.

On the 20-minute flight he never stopped talking. He talked of Beavers and Otters and Bird Dogs and other old fixed-wing aircraft that were disappearing day by day. Canadian built, Beavers and their bigger brothers, Otters, were single-engine tail-draggers meant for hard service in the bush of Canada and Alaska and other wild places. They carried two pilots and cargo/passengers. The Bird Dog was a Cessna, Kansas-built and tough in its own right. It was an observation aircraft with a pilot and observer flying seated in tandem for controlling artillery. He told of putting the aircraft into a tight turn over people on the ground and lowering down a bucket on a rope with a message in it. He talked of dirt strips and bad weather in Germany and all the other things pilots talk to other pilots about—hot landing zones, strips too short or too narrow and snow and ice on the runway and cheap copilots who wouldn't buy you a drink. He was still talking as we taxied up to base operations at the Air Force Base (AFB) in Da Nang.

As the engines went quiet, I reached up to take off my headset. One last transmission came through before I took it off—he looked over at me with a huge grin and said, "Well, son, looks like we cheated death again, didn't we? Luck and superstition, that's all it is."

As I walked away from the aircraft where he was still shutting things down, it struck me that he was right. When you break the ground and go flying in war zones, you really are risking death every time. And while you try to keep the odds on your side by following what you have been taught, by being orthodox and obeying the holy rules of flying, in the end, it is only luck and superstition that keep you alive.

I petted my aircraft as I boarded, and said those words after the rotors stopped on every flight for the rest of my career, "Cheated death again. Luck and superstition, that's all it is."

**7**

# SURVIVAL INSTRUMENTS
## I CORPS, VIETNAM ■ FEBRUARY 1971

---

*During the height of the war in Vietnam, the Army could not afford the extra time to train pilots to fly only on the flight instruments to the level that the Air Force and Navy and Marines did. The Army needed bodies to fill the seats of the thousands of helicopters throughout the country. In the other services, newly minted aviators had a "standard" instrument ticket, meaning that they could fly during instrument meteorological conditions (IMC) under instrument flight rules (IFR) anywhere in the world, a necessary thing for pilots flying off ships and airfields at night and under all weather conditions. Army helicopter pilots, on the other hand, had a "tactical" instrument ticket, meaning that they could not fly IFR anywhere except in a war zone. Most of the time, this worked well because nearly all missions were conducted in daylight and under visual meteorological conditions (VMC). But sometimes . . .*

---

The missions didn't stop when the monsoon clouds and rain brought the weather down to near zip, because the war did not stop. The missions had to be done, they just took longer since the aircraft had to hover along, at times just above the trees, to deliver their external loads of food, ammunition, and even water in the midst of low clouds, rain, and fog. Instead of flying high above the reach of small arms, we flew low, down among the trees where the NVA might hear us or even see us but where we were usually long gone before they could react.

No one ever told us that there was such a thing as "mission categories," i.e., routine, urgent, and mandatory, and that you could refuse missions. There were just missions and you had to try them, no matter the weather, enemy situation, or anything else. You had to try because the grunts and the gunners knew you would come and so you always did, hovering along in the rain and fog if you had to. Sometimes you might not make it, but you had to try.

This morning over the green coastal low lands, the clouds had lifted into a high overcast. It felt odd to be so high after weeks of monsoon rain, flying to the PZ instead of more or less hovering slowly forward over the trees. In the right seat of the CH-47C Chinook, the 21-year-old WO1 copilot that was me shivered slightly from the cool, damp air that came in around the sliding window on my side. It was supposed to be hot in Vietnam, but with November monsoon rain at 800 feet, it was probably in the 50's and I had not brought my flight jacket.

To the north, ahead of us, was the base at Quang Tri and PZ that held the loads for this mission. If the visibility had been better, you could have seen up into North from here: scary when you first see it, but like most things, once you got past the novelty of looking into your enemy's homeland, it was just normal, a fact that just was, not something you needed to talk about. The South China Sea out to the right was invisible in the mist.

The AC in the left seat, a CW2, called the PZ Control to let them know we were on our way in and got a "Line 1, mission 293" in response. The AC checked the mission sheet the duty clerk had given him before he left and said, "Shit."

"What is the load?" I asked, curious about his comment since copilots did not get to see the mission sheet.

"It's a generator. Goddamn thing weighs 6,500, maybe 7,000 pounds."

"So what's the problem?" I asked. "We can handle that no sweat." Generators are nice loads, heavy without too much surface area to make them swing.

The AC looked over at me and said, "It's not how much the damn thing weighs. It's where it is going—check the LZ" and handed me the clipboard.

"Shit," was all I could say after looking at the board.

The generator was going to a mountain top firebase right up on the demilitarized zone (DMZ.). The firebase was under easy observation from the jungle around the river that ran through the middle of the DMZ and therefore, it was easy to direct mortar fire onto the top of the hill. The North Vietnamese Army (NVA) gunners would wait to drop the mortar rounds down the tube until the aircraft was on short final (just about to touch down for landing), the most critical stage of flight for the helicopter. The pilots, concentrating on getting heavy loads to an exact spot, were always surprised when the booms that marked the explosions from the mortars came faintly through the aircraft noise, even though when you worked this base you halfway knew they were coming.

But today with the bad visibility, they would not see us before we were in and out. They might hear us, but timing the mortars was that much harder with only sound to work with.

That was the theory anyway . . .

"Kilo Alpha 1, Bravo Hotel 12, inbound on mission 1134, line 1," the AC called over the fox mike so that LZ control team would know which load to have ready for us.

The hookup man was ready as the Chinook began its final approach to the pick up pad at Dong Ha, just north of Quang Tri. When the load came in sight, we could see that the sling was fouled, caught under the load, so that he had to lay on his back on top the load, but he had the donut (the reinforced nylon ring that joins the legs of the sling together) up as high as he could get it and was ready as our Chinook moved forward over him. The steel hook and belly of the aircraft would be inches above him during the hookup. One twitch by the pilot or any malfunction of the aircraft during the hookup would crush him between the load and the belly of the aircraft instantly.

To make sure we understood the danger of externals, we had to stand on top of loads and hook them up back at Fort Rucker while we were learning to fly Chinooks. To doubly reinforce the danger, after hookup, the student pilot at the controls would bring the helicopter even lower so that the student pilot doing the hookup could climb up from the top of the load and then climb through the hellhole into the aircraft's cabin.

"Load coming under. Forward 30," meaning bring the helicopter forward 30 feet, the Chief said over the intercom from the back of the aircraft. Lying on his belly on a stretcher looking down through the hellhole, the chief could see the load as the aircraft moved forward. The hellhole is the square or rectangular hatch-covered hole in the center of the helicopter's cabin floor, that, when opened, allows the crew to see the cargo hook and the external load, as well as the ground below the aircraft.

"Forward 20, down 10." The numbers were approximations but were good enough to allow the pilot an idea of how high he was above the load.

"Forward 10, down 5."

"Hold down, forward 5. Steady"

"Load hooked. Up slow. Steady. Tension coming on the sling. Up slow, hookup man clear, tension."

As the weight of the load was taken by the aircraft, I could feel the aircraft stop in its climb. I slowly applied more power by moving the thrust lever upward.

"Load's off. Up 10," the Chief called.

"Lots of power, gauges look good, clear to go," called the AC from the left seat.

"Loads clear," called the Chief.

Increasing power a little more, I thought "light thoughts" to make the load easier to carry, and applied forward stick. The Chinook began to move forward. Passing around 20 knots forward speed, the big helicopter shuddered as translational lift was achieved and we climbed above the perimeter barbed wire. The aircraft accelerated and climbed slowly into the mist as we moved off north toward the firebase on the DMZ.

Normally we would climb to at least 1500 feet above the ground so that we would be above the range of small arms fire, but today, the best we could do was about 800 feet. Above that we began to go into the clouds. Since there was no instrument approach to the firebase and further, neither of us was exactly what you would call "well trained" in instrument flight, I leveled the aircraft off below the clouds and hoped that there was no one with a rifle or machine gun waiting along our flight path. The load was riding well; it was not swinging back and forth since it was heavy and dense. The 6,000-pound generator had a small surface area for its weight and stayed in place below us as we flew toward the firebase.

At three miles from where the firebase should be, the mountain it sat on came into view. That is, the rising terrain that marked the base of the mountain was visible. Starting about half way up, clouds ran into the jungle that covered the sides.

Without comment, I began a right hand turn to take the generator back to the PZ. If the clouds were covering the firebase, we obviously could not see to deliver it.

"Turn back toward the hill," the AC said over the intercom.

Rolling wings level, I looked over at the AC in the left seat. Then, seeing no reaction from him, after a moment I reversed course back toward the cloud-covered firebase.

"We can't get in there," I said, stating what I thought was readily apparent, given that the base was invisible in the clouds.

"Sure we can. All we have to do is shoot an approach to the hill just below the base of the clouds. Once we are stabilized in a hover, we will just hover up the side of the hill in the goo. You'll be able to see the trees through the chin bubble. Just don't look out the windshield," the AC replied.

I was still fairly new to Vietnam. My aviation experience was a little more than usual for a first tour pilot, due to a year stateside flying OH-13E's before coming to I Corps, but this little bit of experience did not prepare me for anything like this. Clouds look soft but sometimes they are very hard, like when they hold mountains inside their white mask. Like fog, clouds stop you from seeing forward and all pilots live by visibility when they are not taking off and landing on instrumented runways. If you can't see, you don't know where you are and there may be one of those "hard clouds" in front of you. And besides, clouds scared me after all the horror stories about vertigo and pilots coming out of clouds upside down, not healthy in a helicopter.

Being new to flying in Vietnam, I gave a mental shrug and continued on toward the firebase. The AC was like an instructor; you knew that he knew things you did not. The AC called the Pathfinder (the ground controller who directed helicopter traffic on every firebase) on the hill on the fox mike and asked him if they were ready for the load. When the Pathfinder replied they were, I noticed his voice sounded slightly surprised that we would even try to land a load on his hill in the fog. He told us that the visibility on the top was at or near zero. The AC "rogered" the Pathfinder, completed the landing check, and the crew reported ready. To my surprise, he left me at the controls instead of taking over himself. I began the approach to the green hillside halfway up the mountain.

I completed a more or less normal approach. Shuddering and shaking, the Chinook came to a hover over the trees at what I estimated to be about three quarters of the way up the mountain. Above us the trees all went white as they disappeared into the ragged clouds covering the upper portion of the hill.

I added more power and began to move the aircraft up the slope into the clouds. Just like the AC said, I could see the top of the trees well enough to hover the aircraft as we moved forward and up the hill. Sneaking a peek up through the windshield only showed a solid whiteness with no breaks. Quickly I returned my eyes down to the tops of the trees where there was some reference to right side up.

Coming onto the top of the hill, the trees were gone and I could see the rows of barbed wire passing under the nose of the aircraft. We had made it. When the hill flattened out on the top I could see forward well enough to see a ground guide to the right motioning the Chinook forward. Another man, apparently unaware of the first, was standing to the far left of the nose, also motioning us to him. Picking the man on the left, because I could see him more clearly, I hovered the Chinook forward toward him.

I saw the ground guide reach into the patch pocket of his jungle fatigues and pull out a smoke grenade. He must have remembered his training, i.e., you pop a smoke grenade for helicopters. He did not remember the part about only doing that when the helicopter is in flight, not when they are in a hover. Then he threw the smoke grenade under the front of the aircraft, on my side.

Fascinated, almost like watching a movie, I watched the green smoke completely blot out the little visibility I had. Now, except for being green, the view through the chin window matched the view through the windshield, zero.

"I can't see anything at all. Nothing! You've got it!" I yelled over the intercom, my façade of calm gone.

"I can still see. I can still see! I've got the controls!" the AC yelled back, excited but not yet panicked.

He took the controls as I released them and tried to hold the aircraft steady. I still could not see enough to fly but I felt we were moving. We were, in fact, moving. The aircraft was sliding backwards across the top of the firebase, dragging the generator across the ground under us. It did not feel real somehow. I was back in the movie I was watching as the smoke grenade rolled under the aircraft.

When the AC took the controls, the Chinook had settled low enough that the 6,000-pound generator touched down as we started aft. As we moved backwards, we were dragging the generator across the top of the hill, with the same effect a bulldozer blade would have, i.e. clearing everything in its path. Our flight engineer was talking to us over the internal communication system (ICS), saying things like, "Bring it up, bring it up NOW"!!! but the AC was too occupied with trying to control the aircraft to hear or to respond. When the generator was approaching a bunker full of men trying desperately to stay out of its way, the Chief punched it off (hit the release that disconnects the sling from the cargo hook).

Remove 6,000 pounds from a helicopter without reducing a high power setting and the aircraft will climb. Climb fast, and in this case, since we were already moving backwards, climbing fast and backwards. That's one nice characteristic of tandem rotor helicopters, like the CH-47 and its smaller brother, the CH-46. They fly just as well backwards as they do forwards, since they don't have tail rotors to get in the way .

To us in the cockpit, time stopped. The AC and I looked at each other, opened-mouthed with surprise, shock, I don't know what, but at the moment, neither of us was flying the Chinook. We were, in effect, passengers.

Then, time began again when I saw trees out the windshield where trees should not have been. Nor were the trees level like they should be, but instead they seem to be planted at a 45-degree angle. Instinctively, as had been drilled into us over and over, I remembered flight school instrument training from Fort Rucker, "When all else fails, level the wings, pull power and climb. Get away from the ground," so taking the controls away from the AC, I did just that.

Moving my eyes to the attitude indicator, the gauge that shows whether or not your wings are banked, I rolled the aircraft level and pulled an armload of thrust. I sagged under as much "G" as the aircraft could produce, the rotor speed drooping (slowing down) a little under the load. The trees disappeared back into the whiteness, the airspeed stabilized on the positive side showing that we were moving forward instead of backward, and the vertical speed indicator showed 3,000 feet per minute of climb. Finally, passing through 6,000 feet, 4,000 feet above the top of the mountain we'd started from, we broke through the clouds into clear air. With the white blanket below us and blue sky above, I turned the Chinook to the southeast, so that we would be headed toward water, not mountains, and South Vietnam, not North Vietnam.

It was ten minutes before either of us could speak. I flew and the AC just sat there, looking straight ahead. In the back, the crew chattered as usual. All they had seen was white the entire time and had no idea what had happened in the cockpit.

In a few minutes, we found a hole down through the clouds where green was visible, and we descended through it into normal altitudes where helicopters flew. Then, we returned to the PZ and continued our missions in the drizzle and fog: fuel, food and ammo to the firebases: fuel, food and ammo to the firebases, all day long. The missions must be done. It was still raining when we shut the helicopter down ten hours later in the dark at Liftmaster Pad.

We never spoke of what happened.

Good training with luck and superstition thrown in . . .

## 8

# TRACERS

LAOS ■ MARCH 1971

---

*According to one calculation from the Vietnam Helicopter Pilot's Association, of the 11,827 helicopters deployed to Vietnam, 5,086 or nearly 43% of them were destroyed. Of the 58,272 names on the Vietnam Memorial Wall, 4,914 are helicopter pilots and crewmen.*

---

They start out so small and soft-looking, tracers do. Tiny little glowing green lights, they drift slowly up from the ground, almost lazy as they rise. Then suddenly, they speed up as they get close to you. They speed up and get bigger and bigger. You try not to look at them—you must concentrate on your flying—but you cannot help it, you look. And, as you look, you know that there are four or five bullets between each of the tracers coming for you. When the NVA fired mortars at you while you were dropping off a load on a firebase, it never seemed personal. The mortar crew was just doing their job, dropping the rounds down the tube and both you and they knew that there was very little chance that they would actually hit you. Tracers are different. The gunners are trying to kill *YOU* personally.

The numbers of aircraft involved in Operation Lam Son 719, the incursion into Laos in February and March, 1971, reminded all of us involved of what it must have been like in England during WWII. Literally hundreds of helicopters flying in every direction, C-130s streaming into the runway at Khe Sanh, attack jets passing over on their way to bomb NVA positions along the Ho Chi Minh trail. There were more aircraft visible at any given moment than any of us had ever seen at one time.

While many of the helicopters involved in Lam Son 719 were based 15 miles to the east of Laos at Khe Sanh, after the first day of the incursion, we Chinook pilots commuted from Phu Bai, about an hour away, every morning because there just wasn't room for five Chinook companies there.

We would takeoff before sunrise and be at the PZs in time to pick up our pre-assigned missions. Some missions were single ship, others required flights of aircraft bringing in external loads of ammo or water or fuel or food quickly, one after another.

On the evening before the first South Vietnamese troops crossed the border into Laos, every inch of turf at Khe Sanh was covered with helicopters, mostly UH-1H Hueys, AH-1G Cobra gunships, and OH-6A LOACHs (popular name for the Light Observation Helicopter). Because our Chinooks just took up too much room, the plan was for us remain overnight (RON) at Firebase Vandergrift in the valley east of Khe Sanh, about ten miles away.

I had been an AC for several months now. Since I was the only trained flight instructor in the company at the time, the Ops O wanted to move me into the IP position soon. He wanted me to have more total flight time before I stepped up, so I usually had the longest missions. Not necessarily the most dangerous ones, but usually the longest ones. Because my missions ran long that day, I was late getting up to Vandergrift, in fact mine was the last aircraft to arrive before it got dark.

To reduce the possibility of mid-air collisions, we were instructed to follow the only road from Vietnam to Laos, QL9, west from the low lands into the mountains. Once past the Rockpile, an almost vertical rock formation and scene of major combat for the Marines a few years earlier, we would turn south for a straight shot into the PSP ramp at Vandergrift. As I made the turn at the Rockpile, I saw a flash from the hillside next to us and as I turned my head toward it, I saw a streak of smoke.

"That looked like a rocket," I remarked to my copilot. Then I saw more flashes and as I looked away from the hillside and toward Vandergrift, I could see the result of the 122 MM Soviet Katyusha rockets as they impacted around the base, red flashes turning quickly into black smoke above their impact point. I quickly added power and put the Chinook into a climb as I turned away from Vandergrift. As I orbited at 6,000 feet to the east of Vandergrift, I could also see helicopters that had shut down for the night already turning up as quickly as they could, blades turning to a blur as the rotors reached speed. In less than two minutes from the first rocket impact, the first of the helicopters was lifting off to get clear of the incoming fire. Fortunately, the rockets were as inaccurate as the mortars because the NVA could not use the proper launchers, so all the helos got off without being hit. Over the squadron FM radio frequency came the call for all of us to return to Phu Bai. All those helicopters in the relatively small area of Vandergrift were just too tempting a target. We would leave Liftmaster Pad early the next morning to join the fight.

The next morning after taking off before sunrise, eight Chinooks from Playtex flew into Khe Sanh per the revised plan. We all shut down for a mass mission brief by 101st Division Intel for the at least one hundred other aircrews that would support the Army of the Republic of Vietnam (ARVN) troops as they crossed the border into Laos. There were so many aircraft involved in the mission that only the aircraft commanders went to the briefing. Copilots would stay with the aircraft and have them "cocked," ready for immediate start, in the event of a scramble takeoff like the one at Vandergrift the night before.

We knew our individual missions, but the general commanding the operation wanted us to know the situation on the ground. For once, we would have an overview of what the situation was. Intel briefed us that the NVA had this division here, this regiment here, and that division there. These were not VC guerillas; these were regular NVA troops, probably over 20,000 strong. They were equipped as Soviet divisions of the 1950's had been, complete with tanks and artillery. They had light machine guns, heavy machine guns, anti-aircraft machine guns, anti-aircraft artillery in 37mm and 61mm. We could expect fierce contact. As the Intel officer spoke and pointed to the enemy positions on the large area map, I never saw so many pilots go so quiet before or since.

When the briefing was over I returned to my Chinook. My crew of four gathered around, curious about what had been said. Rather than tell them immediately, I just said, "Eat your lunch right now."

"But, sir," my flight engineer replied, "we've only got one bag lunch and no C-rats and it's going to be a long day."

"Trust me," I said, "Eat it right now." My reasoning was that we would quite probably be shot down. If we survived, it might be a very long time before we could get back to friendly lines and get more food. Better to eat it now than lose it in the crash. As we ate, I spread out my map on the cabin deck and told them what Intel had told me. They were very quiet as I talked. The door gunner quickly finished his lunch and started re-checking the M-60D machine guns on each door.

At launch time, all eight Chinooks were ready to go. One after the other we lifted off, moved over to the PZ, picked up our loads and flew into Laos in trail formation, one Chinook following the other at about two minute intervals. Nothing happened that day, nothing at all. It could have been a mission at Fort Rucker back in Alabama. The NVA just watched. They wanted to see what we were going to do. The second day they watched too.

On the third day, the shit hit the fan. In the following six weeks of the operation, 107 helicopters were destroyed and another 600 were damaged. Some units had nearly all new pilots and aircraft at the end, but our resources were so deep in 1971 that even with those losses, there were still 600 helicopters engaged when Lam Son 719 ended.

Now, three weeks after that first briefing, we were taking an ARVN artillery battery 21 miles into Laos, our furthest out firebase yet. By now Khe Sanh had so many helicopters, around 300–400 at any given moment, that we Chinooks had been told to land at another base closer to the border, Fire Support Base (FSB) Airborne, to keep real estate on Khe Sanh free.

I was not supposed to be flying because the next day I was scheduled to go on two week's leave back to the states. After my flight with the Air America pilot, I walked from the airbase out into town to the North West Orient Airline office and booked my flight from Da Nang to Saigon and then on to Nashville, Tennessee, for 5 March 1971. The war showed no signs of ending and we did not know if any big operations were coming up, so there was no objection to my going from anyone in my chain of command. Even with the chaos of Lam Son 719, no one objected to my going. The war was going to continue and I would be pulling more than my share when I got back anyway.

On the evening of 3 March, the Ops O said to me, "Since you're going to be off for three weeks how about you fly tomorrow and give someone else a rest?" I readily agreed and now was headed into Laos again on 4 March.

As had become the routine, we had taken off before daylight from Phu

Bai to get to Khe Sanh in time to get the mission briefing. We did not have to refuel at Khe Sanh because we had taken on enough extra the night before to cover the flight time from Phu Bai, so we flew directly to FSB Airborne and shut down. The operations officer from the 159th Assault Support Helicopter Battalion (ASHB), our next higher headquarters, was already there waiting for us.

The first mission of the day was simple: insert an artillery battery into the new firebase so that it could provide fire to cover the ARVNs operating further out as they tried to cut the Ho Chi Minh trail. The brief was also simple—pick up the guns and ammo, fly to LZ and set them down where the ground guides direct. If you get shot down, try to land at this spot or this spot or this spot. If you see one of your brother aircraft go down, do not attempt to rescue them. The mission must be completed as planned. No one will come to get you until the mission is over, but it shouldn't be too long. After that first mission, we would all be given individual tasks that did not require all eight aircraft at once.

We would take all eight 105 howitzers in the ARVN artillery unit in one lift. Each load would be mounted on a double sling, with the lower load the ammunition and the upper the 105 howitzers. When we came over the load, the gun and its ammunition would be sitting side by side. We would hookup the sling, climb straight up until the upper load, the howitzer, was off the ground and then slide over until the gun was directly over the ammo. We would then lift higher until the second, lower load was off the ground. When we arrived at the LZ, we would sit the lower load, the ammo, down first and then slide to the side to set the gun down next to the ammo. The idea was that the crew would be able to bring the gun into action almost immediately. Sometimes the gun crew would get onboard the helicopter before we picked up the load and ride to the LZ with us. When they rode with us, we would put the ammo down, the gun down, and then land and let them out to commence firing. This time they did not need to ride because they were already there, having been flown in by Hueys earlier to prepare the gun positions before the howitzers arrived.

I was to be Chalk 2 (Chalk is an Army term indicating your position in a formation flight. Chalk 2 is the next aircraft behind the lead) in the flight of eight Chinooks. We lifted off one by one at about two minute intervals. I could see lead picking up his load as I headed inbound, but just as I was about to start my approach, a flight of Hueys crossed in front of me and I had to turn away. The Chinook that was originally supposed to be Chalk 3 became Chalk 2 and moved in to take my load to keep the process moving smoothly. I became Chalk 3 and, in turn, picked up the gun and ammo that was supposed to be his load. Lead flew in a wide circle to the east of the border as he climbed to an initial 4,000 feet. We all fell in behind him in a very loose trail formation, climbing to match his altitude. When lead saw the last aircraft pick up its load, he turned toward Laos with the seven of us following.

Laos did not look any different from Vietnam. Both were jungle, with mountains on each side of QL9. Around Khe Sanh, both sides of the border were equally scared by bomb and artillery craters. Even so, it seemed as if the air inside the Chinook changed when we crossed the invisible line between the two countries. The gunners became visibly tenser, as they looked out over the barrels of their M60D machine guns. In every aircraft, the pilot not at the controls moved his hands closer to the cyclic and collective so that, should the other pilot be killed, he could take over instantly. Everyone onboard looked around more intently even though the odds of seeing the NVA were very small. The NVA were good at using camouflage and the forest hid them completely. They knew all too well that what can be seen can be killed, like a Chinook flying at 90 knots with a double sling load beneath it.

But they would have to work to kill us while we were en route to the new firebase. As we headed toward Laos, we were steadily climbing to get above small arms range. We kept going until we were past light machine gun range too, but a helicopter cannot fly high enough to avoid anti-aircraft fire from M-1939 37mm and/or the S-60 60mm guns. Our only counter to these weapons was to tune our NDB (Non-Directional Beacon, a homing radio that allows the pilot to fly to a navigation beacon or a commercial AM radio station) to the lowest band and lowest frequency. If the NVA used the Soviet radar that came with these weapons, you would hear a "buzzzz, buzz" sound over the Automatic Direction Finder (ADF) radio. While this did not mean they were tracing you, it did mean that they were painting you on their scope. Upon hearing the sounds, we were to change altitude and airspeed immediately. We were told that the radars were very good in azimuth, but poor in determining range.

That was the theory anyway . . .

The NVA tried not to use the radar, though. They didn't use it because we had jets in the air constantly over the battle area that could detect and lock onto the radar signal. As soon as they did, a homing beam-rider missile would be on its way to take the radar out. The NVA could counter that by moving the radar away from the gun, but that made it easier for our aircraft to see their position. So, instead of using radar, they aimed the guns by sight. Both the M-1939 and the S-60 fired a five-round clip and had a practical rate of fire of around 60 rounds per minute, any one round more than enough to take out a Chinook flying at 90 knots. Or any other helicopter, for that matter . . .

Picture a WWII movie: The B-17s and B-24s are on a thousand-plane raid on some German target. As they approach the coast of France, they see the flak boxes start to appear in front of them, puffs of black smoke marking each shell burst. The Germans are not aiming at individual aircraft, instead they are shooting within a defined space that the bombers must fly through. The shells are set to explode at a given altitude and send their shrapnel out to shred the bomber's aluminum skin and take it out of the sky. The aircrews see the flak, but fly on anyway because the mission must be done. If they are hit, they have multiple engines, and if they are too badly damaged, they have parachutes.

Now picture Laos in 1971. Your helicopter is so slow: it is for all intents and purposes stopped in the sky, at least to the NVA gunner. There is no need for a flak box, they have all the time they need to aim at individual aircraft. Besides, their logistics system is no match for the one the German's had. Every round of ammunition must be carried down the Ho Chi Minh Trail, under attack from our aircraft the entire time so they must not waste them. The NVA do not have the capability the German's had to determine the altitude their targets are flying, so they guess when they set the shells, if they don't have proximity fuses. When the gunners fire, the helicopter crews see the flak, just as their fathers and uncles did over France and Germany, but their helicopters are a frail collection of single-point failures, anyone of which can bring it down out of control or tear it apart in flight. The helicopter crews don't have parachutes . . .

We continued to climb until we reached 6,000 feet, about 4,000 feet above the valley floor where QL9 ran. An AK-47's 7.62mm round could not hit us at this altitude, nor could a 12.7mm machine gun round. Well, 4,000 feet is past the tracer burnout range of a 12.7 but the bullet keeps coming for a while after that. Of course if they weren't shooting from the valley floor, but from the hills on each side, we would be well within range. If they had a 14.7mm heavy machine gun, we would be within range wherever they were shooting from, likewise from the 37mm and 60mm.

Lam Son 719 was a surreal time for helicopter aircrews. Back at Fort Wolters and Fort Rucker when we were learning to fly, we occasionally would see a massed flight of helicopters, but here the crewmen were constantly calling, "Flight of 12 Hueys at 3 o'clock crossing right to left," "Flight of four Cobras 8 o'clock and passing on the left," "Flight of six Hueys at 11 o'clock," "Chinook with an external Huey at 2 o'clock." There were more helicopters in the air than any of us had ever seen at one time, with more on the ground waiting for their next mission and still more in the fuel pits or waiting for fuel. Today was no exception, with helicopters streaming to and from Laos, to and from the lowlands, headed out to mountaintops to drop off observers, bring food or ammo—helicopters everywhere.

March 4, 1971, was not a calm day on the radios. On the guard (emergency) channel someone's aircraft was being shot down and the pilot was screaming "Mayday, mayday, mayday." Also on guard, a flight of B-52's was calling "Arc light, arc light, arc light," followed by the lat/long where they were dropping their 500 pounders. Everyone had to know where the bombs were going to come down because the shock wave alone would take your helicopter out of the sky if you were too close. On regular radio channel, someone was talking to a flight of helicopters, giving directions and not getting a reply because they were on Playtex's frequency, not their own. On the fox mike, the Pathfinders on the firebase with the ARVN artillery unit were calling out instructions to helicopters as they brought the loads in. At least my crew was quiet on the intercom.

Just after we crossed the border, we could see the tracers coming up at the two aircraft in front of us, green and soft in the morning sky. They were coming from the valley floor, but we had no Cobras or Huey gunships with us to provide fire suppression, so all we could do was fly on at 90 knots with our howitzers and ammo swinging below us. My crew could see that the tracers were coming at us too, but in the cockpit we couldn't see anything except the glowing, growing green dots coming up at the leading helicopters, a string of green beads coming up from the darker green forest. We said not a word—nothing to say.

The ADF started "buzz, buzz, buzzzz."

The aircraft shuddered, a huge hole appeared in my windshield right in front of me, and I was hit by something in the face, on my neck, on my right upper arm and I slammed back into the seat.

Then the ICS added to the noise of the radios.

"SIR, SIR, Are you alright SIR, SIR," my right door gunner screamed over the ICS. He had been looking up through the cockpit when the 12.7mm round came through. He saw the hole appear and saw me jerk backwards in my seat. He was sure that it hit me squarely in the face.

I knew that something had hit me, but there was no pain, not yet anyway. I did an involuntary "full and free" check, like we did with the flight controls before starting the engines to make sure all my parts were still working—arms, hands, feet—all there, all still working. The aircraft was still under control too, cyclic, thrust, and rudders all functioning normally, but then there was hot red fluid hitting the top of my helmet and running down my back. Red fluid is hydraulic fluid. Without hydraulics, the flight boost systems, the flight controls lock and you sit helpless until the aircraft impacts the ground or comes apart in flight.

After I wiped the broken Plexiglas off my helmet visor, I realized that if I had not had the visor down, the sharp fragments of glass and steel would have blinded me. Both my pilot and I were staring hard at the master caution panel, the big square panel of small lights on the dash, one light for every critical system, with caution lights that tell you a system is failing or is out of limits—but none were lit. Chinooks have two flight boost systems. Though the pressure gauges that sat side by side are within normal limits, the red fluid was hitting me on the head and back. Then the master caution light, the big one on the top of the dash, came on along with the smaller capsule light marked "Hyd #1," and the number 1 flight boost gauge dropped to zero, and the red fluid kept coming out on top of my helmet. Is boost #2 also hit and bleeding the last of its fluid too? How long until the flight controls lock?

As I saw the gauge go to zero pressure, and squeezing with my right index finger on the trigger switch, I yelled into the ICS, "I'm going to pickle, I'm going to pickle" (slang for jettison the load), but I was squeezing the ICS switch so hard I was transmitting over the radio, adding to all the other voices on the radios. I was trying to tell my flight engineer to get away from the cargo hook so it would not swing up and hit him in the face when the load fell away, but he could not hear me. He saw the tracers coming through the hellhole and at the same time, saw a flak burst just below our aircraft, very near the load of ammo. When the aircraft rocked as I flinched from the bullet through the windshield, he knew we were being hit. He immediately jumped up from the stretcher he had been laying on to work the load and ran to the rear of the aircraft to check the aft transmission area for damage. As he jumped up, he inadvertently unplugged his helmet long cord and could no longer hear the ICS. But then it would not have mattered even if he had been plugged in, because I was transmitting, not talking over the ICS and he never listened to the radios.

When the flight engineer did not reply immediately, I pushed the pickle button anyway. We could not get down quickly with the load under us. The hook opened and the howitzer and ammunition fell away from 4,000 feet above the ground. As the hook opened, I could feel the helicopter shudder and begin to climb rapidly as 8,000 pounds of weight on the aircraft was removed. To get on the ground as soon as possible, I pushed the thrust all the way down to enter autorotation and shoved the nose over so far that the trees below filled the windshield. If the controls locked, it wouldn't matter if we were in a dive, it would just shorten the time we had to think about it before we died.

In our dive, the speed built quickly to the point where the aircraft was shaking and vibrating so hard I couldn't read the airspeed indicator or any of the other instruments any more. Velocity Never Exceed (VNE), was 170 knots on a Chinook and I was quite probably exceeding it, but we had to get her on the ground before the controls quit working. Now all that mattered was to save my crew, if I could.

Then time stopped.

The old cliché that your life passes before your eyes did not happen. It just seemed like everything just stopped. My mind was clear, no regrets, no "if only." It just held the question, stated quite clearly and calmly, "Is this what it's like right before you die?" I never got the answer because

Time started up again.

The trees began to get very big in the windshield, so I started a pullout, trying to hold the "G" force down as much as possible. When I looked at the airspeed indicator, it was passing through 160 knots on the way back to a more normal approach speed, but it would still be a very fast approach and an approach to the ground instead of a hover.

On the ground, on the ground, get it on the ground! I had to get it on the ground before all the hydraulic fluid was gone and the controls froze.

Without conscious thought, all the training at Fort Wolters came back to me. All those times the instructor had cut the throttle on the OH-23, leaving me frantically looking for a spot to autorotate to, had paid off, as the Army knew it would. Even though there was a sea of jungle below us, as I entered the dive, I had automatically set the Chinook up for a landing in a clear area not too far from an ARVN base. The LZ looked raw, as if it had been prepared recently, but it was too far from the ARVN's perimeter to be their primary helo pad. As I flared the Chinook to lose speed for touchdown, I saw that the LZ I had picked held the crashed remains of a Huey in the northern third of the cleared area. This LZ had been hot once, but we were committed to the landing. The Huey was totaled but it was upright so maybe the crew got out. I hoped they did.

I picked a touch-down point as far away from the broken Huey as I could so that we could avoid blowing up loose parts that might go into our rotor blades. Seconds later, I slammed the Chinook onto the ground, aft wheels first, hard but upright with the flight controls still working.

Within seconds of the wheels touching down, the flight engineer had the ramp down and all three crewmen were running from the aircraft, each carrying an M-60D machine gun. Normally, the Chinook had two door guns, but today, the flight engineer, for some reason he didn't really understand, sent the crew chief and gunner back to the armory to pick up two more M-60s and a case of ammunition. As I shut the aircraft down, I could see one of the crewmen establishing a fighting position out in front of us, placing his M-60 where he could cover the most ground. The NVA had certainly seen us going down and could well be headed toward us right now, provided, of course, that they weren't here already. My copilot jumped out of his seat and as he left the aircraft, grabbed the remaining M-60s lying on the cabin deck and joined the perimeter defense while I finished shutting the aircraft down.

Shutting down my Chinook on March 4, 1971 was very simple—I just pulled the condition levers to "Stop" and turned the fuel and battery switches to off, not bothering to start the APU, completely ignoring the shutdown checklist. We made it to the ground without the controls locking, why push it now? I unstrapped and climbed out of the cockpit quickly while the rotor blades spun down to a stop. Before I left the cockpit, I stopped for a few seconds to stare straight ahead. The bullet hole in the windshield was directly in front of where my face had been. If I had been leaning forward, or the gunner had fired a second sooner or later, it would have hit me in the forehead. I couldn't see a hole where the bullet had continued into the forward pylon, but it must have done so to take out one of the flight boosts. I ran out the open ramp and quickly surveyed the area to see where my crewmen were.

We were maybe a quarter to a half mile from the ARVN base but it was unlikely they would come over to provide security. They were quite probably too worried about their own security to consider us. My four crewmen had gone to more or less the corners of the LZ, loaded their weapons and were ready to fire. I quickly grabbed two ammo cans of 200 rounds each from the case and carried them to the closest fighting position. The door gunner had just taken the single belt he had in his weapon when he ran out of the Chinook. He also had his M-16 over his shoulder and a .38 on his belt. I got another two cans to the other gunner and two more to my copilot. A quick weapons count showed we had four M-60D machine guns, three M-16s, four .38 pistols, one .45 M1911A1 automatic pistol, and one M-3 grease gun with a silencer, my personal weapon. We had somewhere over 5,000 rounds of ammo.

I bought the grease gun off one of our company dopers. As I was walking through the company area one day, I saw puffs of dirt coming up in front of me and froze in place. Someone was shooting but I was not hearing the shots. Looking at the puffs, I saw they were following a rat running hard for cover under one of the hootches. Looking for the source of the puffs, I saw a soldier with the grease gun holding the trigger down as he tracked the rat. When he emptied the magazine, I walked over to him and said, "How would you like to sell me that weapon?" He replied, "Sure, man, $20." I gave him the $20 and the grease gun was mine. I did not ask him where he got it. My thought was that I would only use a weapon if I had been shot down and was doing escape and evasion (E&E) to get back to friendly lines. If I had to shoot someone, I would only do it if they were close and would prefer no one else hear me doing it. Besides, the M-3 uses the .45 round and I was already carrying an M-1911A1 pistol, also .45 and 100 rounds of .45 ammo in two boxes in the pockets of my survival vest.

Standing outside the aircraft, it occurred to me that I had not made an emergency radio call. I had not made a "Mayday" call because of the oldest order of precedence when flying: Aviate, fly the aircraft; Navigate, take it to where you are going; and, last, if you have time, Communicate. I controlled the aircraft and found a landing zone big enough to handle it, taking care of the first two in the correct order. There was really no need to make any radio calls since we had been briefed on what to do when we went down. Besides, many aircraft had seen me go down and we knew that no one would come for us until the mission was complete anyway.

Since the NVA had not immediately attacked, I called the flight engineer over. He was not hurt from either the explosion below our aircraft or the cargo hook swinging up when I pickled the load. He and I went to the Chinook to see how badly it had been damaged. Leaving his machine gun in place on our defense perimeter, he came over to me. The wounds to my face and arm were obviously not serious. Though I was still bleeding ten minutes after the hit, I was still functioning. The hydraulic fluid was still burning through my soaked shirt and the holes in my face, neck and arm, so I took off the shirt and T-shirt and threw them back inside the cabin. Leaving my bullet bouncer on the ground I put my survival vest back on. The blood had stopped coming from my upper right arm, leaving just a caked area of blood and hydraulic fluid. My face was still bleeding but not to the point where it interfered with what I wanted to do. I was still numb from the impact of the shrapnel, so there was no pain—in fact, instead of feeling pain I just felt angry, very angry. The flight engineer wanted to put bandages from the aircraft's first aid kit over the wounds but I told him no, just check out the aircraft to see if we can takeoff and get the hell out of there.

The flight engineer clambered onto the top of Playtex 820 and opened up the forward panels to see how much damage had been done. As he was doing that, I walked around the aircraft to see what other damage we had. I counted four bullet holes and more damage to the belly, probably from an S-60 round. One of the bullet holes was through the spar of one of the forward rotor blades.

The flight engineer called me to the top of the aircraft so that I could look into the forward pylon. The Chinook has an upper dual flight boost hydraulic actuator, the system that actually moves the rotor head and controls the aircraft. The "dual boost" part means that the two sides are independent of each other; lose one and the controls still function perfectly, but by necessity, the dual boost is one unit with the actuators side-by-side. The upper dual boost actuator is a major single-point failure, so the Army had Boeing put a piece of armor plate in front of it to protect it. Sticking in the number one boost side of the actuator was a 12.7mm armor piecing machine gun round. It had gone between the armor and the actuator and hit the number one side squarely on. Fortunately for us we had been above tracer burnout range, so the bullet had little energy left when it hit the aircraft. Had we been lower, instead of poking a hole in the actuator, the bullet might have taken it completely off, leaving us to fall out of control until the Chinook came apart or hit the ground. But it didn't take the actuator off. The flight engineer pulled the bullet out and handed me part of the jacket. He kept the core for himself: after all, it was his aircraft.

Between the shot out actuator and the holes in the blades, I decided that 820 was not flyable, at least until maintenance looked at it and changed the damaged parts out for new ones. Besides the shot out number one flight boost, the hole in the blade spar could well result in blade failure, another fatal single-point failure. We would either be picked up by helicopter, as per the brief, or, if that didn't happen soon, we would make our way to the ARNV base and wait for rescue. If all else failed, we would escape and evade (E&E) our way back to Vietnam on foot. I took my survival radio out of my vest and turned it on. The survival radio could handle "guard" and any other UHF frequency you dialed up, so I turned it to guard to listen in on what was happening beyond our LZ. Looking at the sky while I worked on the radio, I saw a Huey headed in our direction, apparently on approach to our location.

"Huey coming for downed Chinook, LZ is cold" I called over the survival radio.

"Roger, get your crew together for pickup," the Huey pilot replied.

As the Huey got closer I recognized the emblem painted on its nose, it was the 101st Aviation group commander's aircraft. The colonel commanded all 600 of the 101st's aircraft. He must have been up flying over the battlefield, watching the fight, and must have seen us go down. When he was satisfied that the mission was going to be completed with the remaining aircraft, he came back to get us. I called my crew back together. The excess ammo we put back inside 820 so that it could either be rescued when the aircraft was recovered or destroyed along with the Chinook, if that should be the command decision. We stacked the machine guns, the KY 28, survival ammo can, and our flight gear close to where the Huey had set up to land, while we waited.

Before he came into the LZ, the colonel did a wide circle over the zone, looking for NVA. Satisfied that the LZ was indeed cold, he landed with the Huey blowing up dust in a reassuring cloud. We waited outside the rotor disk until the Huey crew chief waved us over. I sent my crew in first. I would be the last one onboard. As my crew climbed into the aircraft, I looked up at the Huey's cockpit. I could see the colonel looking back at me—me, shirtless, with a survival vest on, with blood all down my arm and face and red hydraulic fluid all over me and the grease gun with the silencer slung over my shoulder. His visor was down so I couldn't see his face, but he shook his head and gave me what looked like a rueful smile.

After a final look at 820, I climbed in the back of the Huey and parked myself on the right side, next to the door gunner. I was getting madder by the second. Mad that the NVA shot my Chinook, mad that I was hit, just mad. I wanted to shoot something, someone, shoot the man who shot me. I hoped that the 105 howitzer and the 4,000 pounds of ammo we dropped at least hit the NVA who shot me. I leaned out the door of the Huey, grease gun locked and loaded, but there was nothing except green jungle and the scars from bombing and artillery fire and the red line dirt marking highway QL9 heading back to Khe Sanh from Laos. After a while, I sat back in the red webbing of the troop seat and watched the world go by as the Huey took us back to Khe Sanh. We had been on the ground for about 15 minutes. It had been 20 minutes since we were hit.

The numbness from my wounds began to wear off as the adrenaline came down. By the time we got to Khe Sanh, 20 minutes later, I was extremely tired and hurting in several places. My anger was gone too, replaced by thoughts of how I was going to explain the wounds to my wife in a few days when I returned to Fort Campbell for two weeks of leave in the middle of the war.

After we landed at the medevac pad just off the main runway at Khe Sanh, an ambulance was there to pick me up, but the Huey crew chief motioned for me to wait while they shut down. I waited just outside the rotor disk until the colonel unstrapped and, climbing out the right door, walked up to me. He looked at the blood and hydraulic fluid covering me, placed his hand on my shoulder and said, "You did good, son. Now go get that looked at." As he walked away he looked back at me again, shirtless, blood stained with the grease gun hanging from my shoulder, shook his head and gave a small laugh.

I walked into the hospital tent at a slow time for them. Very few wounded were there, so they had plenty of time to deal with me. Because I was walking and talking without any problem they had me fill out my own toe tag, the marker the military uses to identify the wounded and the dead. After cleaning me up, I sat on a table for an hour or two while they picked pieces of glass and metal out of me. The doctor told me that the ones he couldn't remove would work their way out in time. There were no big holes, just a lot of little ones and bruises on my arm, neck, and face. The doctor told me that he was putting big bandages on me because Khe Sanh was a very dusty place. When I got back to my base I could remove them, take a shower, put on some cream he gave me and replace the bandages with band-aids. Since my shirt was gone, someone gave me a T-shirt to put on for the trip back to my company.

My crew was waiting for me outside when the doctor finished about an hour later. We all smiled at each other, glad to be alive, as we waited for one of our company aircraft to pick us up and take us back to Phu Bai. The colonel had called Playtex Ops on the radio to tell them we were OK and where to pick us up. An hour later, one of our Chinooks landed and we boarded for the trip back. Four hours after we were hit, we were back at Liftmaster Pad, being greeted by a crowd of our relieved friends waiting on the ramp.

The Ops O met me as I climbed down from the crew door on the Chinook. The blood and hydraulic fluid were gone but the bandages covered most of my arm and shoulder, with more on my face and neck. He turned pale and said, "I'm sorry, man. I didn't know this would happen."

I said, "I know. I'll be alright, but I just want to be alone right now, OK?"

He nodded as I walked slowly toward my hootch. Once inside, I pulled all the bandages off and after running the wringer washing machine full of hot water, I put it on drain cycle so that it would pump the water to the shower. After stepping into the bathtub, I stood under the water and enjoyed the nice long, hot shower. I dried off and put on band-aides where the bandages had been. After putting on a clean flight suit I walked over to the Club. The Ops O was sitting at the bar as I came in.

"Hi, guys," I said as the Ops O looked around. He went from being glum to being mad in a second. "You son-of-a-bitch," he yelled, but the anger became happiness as it occurred to him that while I was wounded, I was not hurt as bad as it looked when I stepped off the aircraft.

The next day I went on leave, traveling to Fort Campbell, Kentucky via Saigon, Hong Kong, and Tokyo. Three days later I was explaining the bruises and holes in my face, neck, and arm to my wife. Two weeks after that, I was back at Khe Shahn helping to pull the last of the ARVNs out of Laos as Lam Son 719 came to an inglorious end.

My final memory of that battle is of an NVA mortar round hitting a 5,000 gallon gasoline tanker truck parked less than 100 yards in front of me as I was landing just outside Khe Sanh on that last day. As the fireball rose in front of me, I jerked the Chinook back into a full-power climb. It missed us entirely.

Luck and superstition again . . .

# 9

# ARMY NIGHT FLIGHT
## I CORPS, VIETNAM ■ APRIL 1971

---

*When there was no moon, or if an overcast hid the moon and stars, Vietnam's I Corps got very dark—very, very dark. There are no city lights in the jungle, no stream of cars with headlights marking a road, no lights from farmhouses here and there like back home, there is just darkness. Coastal lowland, rolling country leading to the jungle mountains, it was all the same, just darkness. One crew was always on standby at night, just in case something unanticipated arose; they could look forward to flying into that darkness if the call came.*

---

When the word came to launch the standby, we aircrew, pilots and enlisted men alike, projected what we thought was an air of calm, like all who fly do. We tried to be cool in the face of whatever came, like all men, from those just out of their teens to those in their late 70's; I never heard anyone admit to fear, but it was there when we went out at night. I never heard it but I saw it, in them and in me, too.

Action had been heavy in the A Shau Valley for the last several days. The artillery, 105mm's and 155mm's ("dime nickel" and "penny nickel nickel" in Army aviator-speak) in their positions in the mountaintop firebases had been firing nearly continuously. All three companies from my aviation battalion, Playtex, my company, and our sister Chinook companies, Varsity and the Pachyderms, had been hauling fuel, food, and water, but mostly 8,000 pound pallets of artillery shells to them constantly as they fired their guns west and north against the North Vietnamese forces there. But now one base, Fire Support Base (FSB) Rifle, call sign for tonight "Alpha Kilo One," located on a ridgeline overlooking the A Shau, had used nearly all its ammo in the non-stop fire missions and was calling for more. They had not called for resupply earlier when it was still daylight because it looked like things were settling down and they would have enough ammo to last the night.

They were wrong. Things had not settled down, but instead, steadily intensified, leaving the gunners sleepless, exhausted, and nearly deaf as they served their weapons, shell after shell going down range into the valley. The men on the firebases did not like resupply at night any more than we did, because, in addition to the work of stacking the shells and breaking down the pallets, they had to have light to position the ammo and store it. Lights gave the NVA something to shoot at, i.e., us bringing the ammo in and the grunts moving it. As noted by many soldiers, it is one thing to shoot and quite another to be shot at.

We had preflighted the aircraft before it got dark and were ready when the call came at 0100 hours. The three crewmen—the flight engineer, crew chief and door gunner—were already aboard the aircraft, since they always slept onboard the Boeing Hilton when their helicopter was on standby. The sky was pitch black; even after our eyes adapted to the dark, we could not see the outline of Gia Li Mountain less than one mile away from the end of Liftmaster Pad's short runway. The red glow of the cockpit lights did not reduce the feeling of helplessness that you get sometimes when you are about to do something you really do not want to do but that you know you must do anyway.

That feeling was always one of detachment for me. A feeling that it was not real and would pass because something would happen that would keep you from having to do it. Maybe the aircraft would break or they would change their mind and not need the ammo after all. Funny how over the years, in situations like this, that feeling never changed, it always came back. And the mission was never canceled, so no matter how you felt about the dark, you went out into it. The missions must be done.

On climb out, I finally could see Gia Li Mountain, but only because of the lights from Camp Eagle behind it. To the west and north of Eagle where the big mountains were, and where FSB Rifle was, I could only see blackness. Our position lights, the red and green sidelights and white tail-light that make us visible to other aircraft, were on, as was our top rotating beacon. We never used the bottom red rotating beacon, figuring it made us too visible to the NVA and would not keep other aircraft from flying into us anyway. Although the lights, red on the right, green on the left, and white in the back, gave the enemy something to shoot at, we presented no better target than we did in the daylight. Since we were flying a Chinook, we were a big, slow target day or night. But, at night, without lights (particularly the red rotating beacon), you were invisible to other aircraft, making the possibility of a mid-air collision very real and guaranteed fatal to all concerned.

I made the takeoff as the AC nearly always did—the AC has to make sure everything is working OK, as a copilot might miss something—and turned the aircraft north. We climbed out following along the lights of QL1, the main north-south highway in Vietnam, to about 3,000 feet above ground level (AGL), well above the effective range of small arms and light machine-gun fire. The bullets could get that high but had little energy left and were no longer accurate, so we did not particularly fear them. We could see the lights of Hue City, the old imperial Vietnamese capital, then moved toward the mountains. Rural electric co-ops had yet to come to I Corps, nor were they likely to until the war was over, if ever. In the dark, there was nothing visible to navigate to, except the radio beacon at Camp Evans. Our ADF was working and we found Evans without any trouble. Under the glare of our landing lights, hook-up of the load was routine and 20 minutes after we had lifted off from Phu Bai, we were climbing out toward the blackness of the mountains to the west.

I had briefed the copilot and crew what to do many times and all of us had flown this mission at least a few times, so we should not have been scared, but we were; at least I was. The mountains ahead of us went up to around 6,000 feet above sea level, so I continued to climb until I reached 10,000 feet. That altitude alone was enough to be scary for helicopter pilots. We almost never flew this high above the ground because of the problems with getting on the ground should your aircraft catch fire or one of the transmissions begin to fail. Helicopters do not carry parachutes and can be made to descend only so fast. What is the time between failure onset and catastrophic failure? Between the time something goes wrong, and the time you ride the out-of-control helicopter all the way down, thinking whatever thoughts come to you in your last moments.

As I've said before, it's not the death part that worries many pilots, it's having time to think about death while falling. The books do not say how fast you can make a helicopter descend without losing control. Putting the aircraft into a dive that exceeds VNE, like I did in Laos, is not recommended. Typically the fastest way to lose altitude quickly is to put the aircraft into a slip by cross controlling the rudders and the stick, but how fast does it fall that way? Maybe it's minutes, maybe it's seconds until you reach the ground, but either way, it's a long time to think about it.

I listened while my copilot called the artillery ("arty") clearance frequency so that we would not inadvertently fly through "friendly" fire. Although they laid out a route for us that was supposed to keep us clear, we had little faith in it. This lack of confidence was not from any feeling that the "arty" guys had it in for us, but came from the fact that, try as they might, the clearance agency was always wrong. We didn't believe them because every day we would get routes and fly them only to arrive at the LZ to find guns blazing away, though pointing in a different direction from that which we were given. Eventually we became philosophical about it. Even an artillery shell is a little bullet in a big sky, so the odds of being hit inadvertently by a "friendly" shell were so small that it was not worth the worry. There were too many other things that could kill you . . .

Still, like putting your pistol between your legs and the door guns on our aircraft, arty clearance served a little psychological protection. You believed that the .45 added some armor. You believed the M-60D machine gun on each side of your aircraft would suppress enemy fire. You believed the clearance would keep you from flying down a gun-target line. You knew in your heart that none of these did much, but you believe anyway. The arty clearance was no help tonight, though, because they said everyone was quiet with no fire missions currently in effect. Except, of course, for the H&I (harassment and interdiction) missions. That was where the arty guys on the firebases pointed their guns—in the general direction of the bad guys, firing blind, all just to keep Charlie on his toes. You never knew where those rounds went, but, again, it is a big sky and in that context, even artillery rounds are little bullets.

Our aircraft had no navigation system except for the ADF we had used to find Camp Evans, but the ADF was of no use in finding a firebase in the mountains in the dark, since the firebase did not have one of the portable radio beacons that transmit the signal that the ADF receives. Even if it did, the ADF was way too inaccurate to use in the mountains where a few feet's distance could put you into the trees or cliff face. Our highly developed map reading skills were of no use either, since we could not see to navigate, nor did our memory of how the terrain looked around FSB Rifle help since it too was not exact enough to trust your life and the lives of your crew in the darkness. Blackness below us was the same blackness wherever we looked, left, right, up, down, as we flew toward the area of the firebase.

To find the firebase on its mountaintop, we called the Air Force radar unit that covered all of I Corps and into the southern part North Vietnam and gave them its name and our location. After they picked our Chinook up on radar, they gave us a vector to the firebase. While I flew and talked to the Air Force air traffic controller, my copilot called the grunts on FSB Rifle to tell them we were on our way.

After 15 minutes, the Air Force controller said simply, "Playtex One Two, you're over them now."

Below us, the earth was the same black as the sky, nothing to differentiate one from the other. Time to talk to the grunts and get their exact location.

"Alpha Kilo One, this is Playtex One Two. We've got a load for you. Turn on a light," I called.

"Playtex, Kilo One, we hear you above us, but negative on the light. Wind is light from the north."

I understood. If they turn on a light, the NVA will shoot at it, and by definition, at them. Now they must understand.

"Alpha Kilo One, Playtex. You want this load, turn on a light. We cannot find you otherwise. No light, we take it back."

Silence from the ground. Then, in the sea of black below us, my right gunner calls over the intercom, "Green light, two o'clock low!"

Swapping my vision from the flight instruments to the outside, I catch a glimpse of the light below and call over the FM, "Green." From the ground comes, "Confirm green."

I try to remember where the mountains are from the map and from the many hours I have flown here, but I can't. It's just black below us, above us, to the sides of us. I put the Chinook into a box pattern on a course that I think will keep us clear of the mountains. As I start the descent, I hear the Air Force radar operator saying the same words the FAA controller said when the U-8 started down into the Smoky Mountains two years before, "Losing you in the ground clutter. Give a call out- bound and we'll vector you home." Like the FAA controller, the Air Force controller didn't say good luck or anything like that, not because he was superstitious, but just because it was not cool for him or for us. Better death than uncoolness.

I planned a steep approach angle instead of the normal shallower one, coming down at a 15-degree angle instead of the usual 5-degrees. We were light on fuel so the weight wouldn't be a problem and it would keep us higher and out of the NVA's range longer; might also keep us from hitting a mountain too. Without being told, my copilot turned off our red, green, and white position lights and our top rotating beacon as we started down from 10,000 feet. No jets down among these mountains in the dark to fly into you, so why give the NVA a target?

It's called pucker factor. It's the involuntary tightening of your rectum when the tension gets high, like when you know you may be headed directly into a rock wall, invisible in the darkness, and knowing that you do it anyway because that is what has to be done if the mission is to be done. The mission must be done. Your rectum gets so small and puckered that we said you couldn't drive a broom straw up it with a sledgehammer. The standard joke was that it took half an hour to get the seat cushion out of your ass you were so puckered. At the same time, your right hand grips the cyclic stick so hard, we said it was like you were trying to squeeze the black out of the plastic. Sometimes afterwards, your forearm would hurt, your legs would go stiff on the rudders, and your teeth would clinch.

Concentration is also there with the pucker factor. The noise of the helicopter disappears. The radios go silent. All that happens is that your eyes go back and forth over the instruments on the Chinook's dash—from the flight instruments, attitude indicator, altitude, airspeed, attitude, altitude, airspeed—to an outside green light on the ground, back inside to attitude, altitude, airspeed. Wings level, altitude decreasing toward the height of the firebase, no radar altimeter in C model Chinooks so you hope your barometric altimeter is close to being set right, airspeed coming back toward zero, but you keep it above 20 so you won't lose translational lift and get caught behind the power curve trying to hover out of ground effect in the mountains with 8,000 pounds of ammo swinging below you. In the background you might hear some mumbling over the ICS as the copilot calls airspeed for you and landing check complete, but your world is attitude, altitude, airspeed, attitude, altitude, airspeed until at last you can stand it no more because the landing zone must be coming up fast, so you call for the landing light and then the world is lit in blinding white light and you see the barbed wire around the firebase and the man with the flashlight waving you forward. You also hear the yells over the radio as the pathfinder calls for you to kill the light before the mortars start, but you don't because mortars may not come, and if you lose the light a crash right in the middle of all these men will not come out well for anyone.

"Down 10, 5, load's on the ground, load's released. Cleared to go," your flight engineer calls, and the landing light goes off as you pull up the thrust lever, adding lots of power and climb out, attitude, altitude, airspeed. Attitude wings level with a little nose down to gain speed, attitude increasing rapidly to get your aircraft back above 6,000 feet and those invisible mountains, airspeed increasing toward 120 knots for the trip home. Green, red, and white back on, Anti-collision lights back on as you climb back to where the jets are.

It takes about 15 minutes after you reach cruising altitude and the Air Force is directing you home for the pucker factor to decrease enough to let the seat cushion start coming out from between the cheeks of your ass, just like the joke says. It's only a thirty-minute flight back to Lift Master Pad, but you have to refuel at Camp Eagle on the way so that the aircraft will be ready to fly in the morning.

Finished, you lift off and in a few minutes you are on the ground back at your base. After shutting down in the revetment at Liftmaster, you find you are so tired you can barely climb out of the seat. You sit there for a few minutes gathering your stuff and trying to show nothing but cool. After that few minutes, you climb out of the cockpit and go through the companion way back into the main cabin. Everyone is too tired to give a shit about cool and besides, you can barely see each other in the dark.

The night is nearly over for you but not for the enlisted crew. They start the process of turning the aircraft around, doing the maintenance checks, getting it ready for its next missions in the morning. You are supposed to post-flight but you are too tired, so you walk back across the PSP to the gate out onto the company street without stopping. The crew will catch any problems. Once you clear the wire around Liftmaster Pad, you stop at the barrel buried in the ground at a 60-degree angle. You pull out your .45, drop the magazine, and pull back the slide to clear it. Then you dry fire it into the drum just to make sure it really is empty before you pick up the ammo can with the survival gear and the KY28 and walk on to Ops to turn it all in and to find out what's next for you. No missions tomorrow, or at least not tomorrow morning. Sleep would be good now.

# 10

# FLARES

## I CORPS, VIETNAM ■ JUNE 1971

---

*The preferred method of delivering flares was artillery, and with the coverage of I Corps in 1971 nearly everything was within reach. After artillery, the Air Force C-130s flying out of Da Nang were called. They had a lot of fuel and a lot of flares so they could provide coverage for quite a while. Sometimes neither the artillery nor the C-130s were available and the Chinooks took up the mission.*

---

You see your name on the mission sheet as "night flare ship standby" and know two things—you can't drink that day and you will spend the day and night hoping that nothing will happen that would cause you to have to fly. You hope it so much that you almost begin to pray that it will be a quiet night and that nothing will happen until tomorrow in the daylight. But each time you get night flare ship standby, somehow you feel that that night will not be quiet, and as you preflight your aircraft in the late afternoon, you try and do an extra careful job, not that it matters much. Your aircraft isn't the problem—the dark is the problem.

Flare ship standby flew out of Camp Evans, 40 miles north of Phu Bai. Before dark you would take your bird up there, and after refueling at Evan's "crash pad" (so called because of its slope which made your front wheels touch down first instead of the back ones, resulting in a less than graceful touch down) to max fuel instead of the usual 4,800 pounds, you would shut down on the helicopter pad over by the Tactical Operations Center (TOC).

Before you came to Camp Evans, the crew would have already removed the beam that the cargo hook hangs from in the center of the hellhole and replaced it with a square cover that fit the opening exactly. A two-foot long tube a little bigger around than a flare is fitted to the center of the cover. Directly over the tube the crew has installed a wire with a six-inch metal ring on its bottom end. The crew will attach the flare's arming wire, which acts like the pin on a hand grenade, only after the flare has been manually placed in the tube. When the crewman releases the flare, it falls through the tube and away from the aircraft. The arming wire remains attached to the ring, thus as with a hand grenade, the pin is pulled and after the pre-set time has passed the flare's parachute will open and the flare will ignite. The crew then loaded the pallet of flares that would be used to provide the illumination for the night, usually around 48 three-foot long aluminum cylinders.

The AC always goes into the TOC and waits. The crew had the aircraft "cocked"—the checklist done up to APU start, so that no time would be wasted when the call for illumination came from the grunts. When they need flares they need them NOW. Then you waited. Most nights that's all you did, wait. Sleep if you could. Look at the maps and the friendly troop positions and the positions where Intel thought the NVA were. Look at the pile of Soviet bloc weapons in the corner, captured somewhere and now just sitting there in the TOC. They would never be souvenirs to bring home because some of them were automatics. On some of the AK-47's you could see the holes where pellets from a Clamor mine had hit them. One AK had its stock mostly rotted away by the jungle damp, but if you looked down the barrel and worked the action it was apparent that the weapon would still fire if asked to.

But mostly you waited—and waited—and waited: hoping that the call would not come and yet, at the same time, bored to the point where you wanted something, anything, to happen.

Then a radio call from Division Ops, a grunt patrol could hear Viet-namese voices and movement, but they couldn't see where they came from. Flares. Flares would let them fix the enemy for destruction by the artillery or machine guns. No artillery or C-130s available tonight. Here are the coordinates, takeoff now!

You run to the aircraft down the dark path, yelling as you go and by the time you climb in the back over the slick ramp, the APU is running and the red lights are glowing and oh, shit is it dark out there beyond the wire . . .

By the time you are strapped in and have your helmet on, the copilot has the engines running and the blades turning and you take the controls, and as the flight engineer says "Ready in the back, clear to lift" you are pulling up on the thrust lever and climbing into the dark, dark, dark. As you clear the wire around Camp Evans, all you see are the red instruments on your dash as you climb toward the invisible mountains to the west and north.

The Air Force radar is up tonight and over the UHF radio, you give them the grid coordinates where you are headed, where the grunts need the flares NOW. They vector you in that direction as you continue to climb until you hit 10,000 feet, the standard operating procedure (SOP), drop altitude, 4,000 feet above the highest mountain in I Corps. Leveling off at 10,000 there is still no horizon except along the coast where there are city and town lights—clouds above you and darkness everywhere—cold up there too and you close your window against the wind blowing in. Then you are in further darkness as your aircraft enters the clouds and only the red glow of your flight instruments keeps you oriented to know up from down, right from left. The copilot turns off the upper red anti-collision lights so the red glare does not distract you. The words and directions of the Air Force controller keep you moving toward the coordinates of the grunts that need your flares.

At this stage of your flying career, you don't have much instrument flight time since Army flight school concentrated on getting the pilots to the war as quickly as possible, so you concentrate hard on the instruments, scanning back and forth across the red gauges, attitude, altitude, airspeed, heading, attitude, altitude, airspeed, attitude, altitude, airspeed. Attitude means your wings are level, you are climbing, not diving in the blackness below. There is no autopilot in this Chinook so you must concentrate attitude, altitude, airspeed because a few seconds loss of concentration and you could be out of control and that cannot happen because the men in the back trust you to bring them back from this mission; you are the aircraft commander, the AC.

Your copilot calls the grunts on the fox mike, asking for the situation on the ground and they whisper back. The NVA are near and they cannot talk much or very loudly without giving themselves away. In response to their whisper, your copilot whispers back, but they cannot hear him so he switches back to normal volume. His voice is cool, always cool, knowing that you are listening to him, the crew is listening to him, the grunts are listening and he cannot be anything but cool least it upset the crew, the grunts, and diminishes him in their eyes. In his eyes too . . .

For once the flight engineer, the Chief, is listening to the radios too and when he knows the aircraft is close to tonight's destination, he gets the crew up and ready to start dropping the flares. Behind you, on the cabin side of the companionway, he pulls the black curtain they have hung over the opening closed so that they can use the bright white cabin lights without blinding the pilots. You cannot see what they are doing, but you know that they have removed the plastic covers from the tops of the first group of flares. The flares will not be, must not be, cannot be, armed until they are in the tube, ready for drop. One man will lift the flare and another will guide it into the tube and together they will hold it there while the timing settings are adjusted on the top. During the process, should anything go wrong, they just let go of it and the flare falls harmlessly away from the aircraft. God help us all if one ever goes off inside the cabin. The burning magnesium will eat a hole right through the cabin deck and set everything close to it on fire as it goes through the flooring.

You have the grunts' position in grid coordinates as close as they can give it to you, and the Air Force radar controller begins to vector you in a race track pattern over it. The controller has the winds aloft forecast and moves you a little north so that the flares will move south on their parachutes over the grunts' position for as long as possible instead of drifting uselessly away. You tell the Chief to drop two so that the grunts can see if you are in position to give them the light they need. As he calls "Two away," you brace for the flash of light that comes when they go off in the clouds. The flash never comes. The flares did not light.

"Check your settings and drop three more," you tell the Chief, and moments later he calls them gone. Still no flash, but the grunts below report loud crashes and thuds around them. The flares are falling straight to the ground without their parachutes opening.

The grunts are calling for flares more urgently now. The impact of the unlit flares has the NVA excited. Something is going on but they don't know what. You tell the Chief to just start throwing flares out, hoping you will run out of the bad batch of flares and into a batch that is not defective.

He has ten more out the chute before you tell him to hold. You know you are into a good lot by the dim flashes below you in the clouds. The grunts report it looks like full daylight around them. The NVA have gone, their voices faded as the flares turn the darkness into temporary light. No more flares are required for this mission. Just as the NVA have gone, now so have the clouds and when you look up from attitude, altitude, and airspeed, you see you are in open skies, stars and a faint, faint moon above.

You call back to battalion to tell them you are on your way home, but they tell you to hold, another mission is coming and if you still have flares they want you to take it. There are still 25 or more flares back there so you maintain your altitude at 10,000 feet, comfortable now in the clear air, and you ask the Air Force to keep you in your present position until you are directed to where you are needed next. Passing control of the aircraft to the copilot, you light a cigarette and look out the window toward the faint, dark ground below. Up to the north you can see the lights of the coastal villages in North Vietnam. It seems odd—they should be dark against our bombers, like in WWII, you think as you look at what must be the lights of a small town in the far distance. But then we don't bomb coastal villages and towns, just jungle and military positions. Do we?

On the ground there is a flash, then another and another. Artillery impacting. How odd that it should be hitting there in the lowlands so close to what your map shows as friendly positions. You switch the fox mike to the arty clearance agency and ask who's firing and where it's going. No one is shooting, they tell you, so you give them the location of the impacting rounds as close as you can figure it. Still they insist no one is shooting, yet you see more flashes below you. Arty clearance again tells you it isn't us shooting.

Looking to the north across the DMZ, you see a faint flash and you count until you see the flash on the ground below you. North Vietnamese artillery is shooting into the south. You've waited a long time for this. Digging through the papers in your helmet bag, you find the one you need and then pull the signal operating instructions (SOI) from the pocket in your bullet bouncer and find the frequency for the long range 175's howitzers at their firebase near Dong Ha.

"Oscar Kilo One, Playtex One Two, fire mission over."

A moment of silence from the artillery, they've never had a Chinook call in a fire mission before. They ask you to authenticate who you are by using the code letters in the SOI, and when they are satisfied that you are who you say you are, they give you the artilleryman's reply, "Playtex One Two, Oscar Kilo One, fire mission out."

Your heart starts beating faster as you prepare to adjust the long-range guns against the enemy positions. With each radio, you call in the sequence you must go through to adjust artillery fire and hope no one stops you. When you talk to artillery, headquarters at each level is always listening and can abort the mission with a word. But also when you talk to artillery, silence is consent, and silence remains except for you and the gunners calling back and forth.

"Counter-battery fire," you tell them, and you can almost hear the passion in the artilleryman's voice as he answers you. Cannon against cannon, maybe for the first time in this war. Their 175's will rip the old Soviet guns the NVA are firing into twisted hot metal bits as soon as the rounds arrive on target.

As you near the end of the call for fire checklist, maybe 30 seconds from the first rounds headed down range, things change. Out of the black sky, over the enemy gun position in North Vietnam, comes a bright red stream of tracers, like a fire hose spraying red water. An AC-130 Specter gunship has found the enemy and is playing their 20mm Gatling guns over them, maybe their onboard 105mm gun too. On the ground below the invisible Air Force aircraft, you can see little flashes in the blackness. The big flashes to the north have stopped. You tell the artillery what happened and they "roger." You go off their frequency and return to standing by, waiting in orbit at 10,000 feet. To the north, where the flashes came from, there is only blackness now. The lights of the small city still twinkle.

You are down to only an hour of fuel remaining when battalion tells you the other mission is canceled and you can come on back to Phu Bai. You are getting tired now and welcome the call. As you fly south, the clouds return and you are inside them again. You take the controls back from the copilot, attitude, altitude, airspeed. Only blackness outside the red glow of your cockpit now and you want badly for this to be over. You are so tired, tired from concentrating on keeping your aircraft in the air, tired from trying to get light to the grunts, tired . . .

The Air Force radar turns you over to Phu Bai radar for a ground controlled approach (GCA) "Playtex, descend to 1000 on heading 180," they call as they line you up for the runway. The calls come, left, right, on course, above glide path, below glide path, left, right, on glide path, on course, approaching decision height and then you are out of the clouds and the runway is in front of you where it should be. "Switch to tower frequency," the GCA controller calls, wishing you good night. Then, as your copilot finishes switching, bright white flashes stream in front of you between you and the runway. *50 cal machine gun* and blood pumping, you pull in an armload of thrust and shoot back into the now sheltering clouds, climbing as hard as the aircraft can climb.

"Tower, Playtex One Two, you've got a 50 cal right off the end of your runway," you scream into the radio.

Silence for a moment, then, "Playtex One Two, tower, those are the approach lights."

A few more moments of silence and then again from the tower, "One Two, would you like another approach?"

Your copilot switches the radio back to GCA and you shoot the second approach until you can see the ground, ignoring the flashing strobes this time, and when you see the ground, you break off approach and fly visually the ten minutes back to Liftmaster Pad a couple miles away and end tonight's mission.

After you taxi the Chinook back into the revetment, you start the shutdown checklist. When the rotor blades finally stop and the APU comes off line, you realize you are too tired to get out of the cockpit and you sit there in the seat in the early morning light for a few minutes until you feel you can climb out on your own. You hope no one notices, but you see the flight engineer watching you. He knows the tiredness you feel, and he knows not to say anything about it. You did the mission and brought them all back and that's all that matters right now. It is nearly dawn as you walk away from the aircraft toward Ops to turn in your KY-28 and blood chits. Your fellow pilots are preflighting their Chinooks in the dark. Soon the Playtex aircraft will be lifting off into the morning sun for their day's missions.

## 11

# NAPALM
### NORTHERN I CORPS, VIETNAM ■ JULY 1971

---

*Youth is a wonderful thing. Before you actually recognize that you are not immortal, you do things that in retrospect were so incredibly stupid you wonder, what were you thinking? Then you realize you weren't thinking at all. Orders were orders and you just did the missions. The missions must be done.*

---

One of my fellow Playtex ACs rode along on a napalm drop with his 8mm movie camera with a zoom lens. In the back of the Chinook, he lay on the deck next to the flight engineer, looking down through the hellhole at the load of red drums swinging in the net below the aircraft and the green forest below them. As the Chinook began its drop run, he aimed the camera at the load, focusing on one barrel marked with a slash of white paint. When the cargo hook opened, and the front of the sling released and the drums fell away, he kept his camera focused on that one barrel as it separated from the others in their fall. Beside him, the flight engineer threw a smoke grenade after the red barrels, purple smoke against the green jungle, but the smoke was only in frame for a second as he continued to follow the barrel going down. As the chosen red barrel fell, the AC worked the zoom to keep it large in frame—red barrel filling the view with blurry green forest around the edges. Then the red barrel disappeared into the green. Two, maybe three seconds later, the green disappeared into red orange flame and as he zoomed out, the view became green around the red orange, then black gray coming up from the red orange. Then he released the camera trigger and the view went all black.

Mostly we dropped napalm to clear out mines and booby traps the NVA planted around firebases, trails, and landing zones. Napalm was, at best, a temporary solution; the vegetation grew back so fast that it was hard to tell what had been burned after two weeks had passed. The mines and booby traps grew back fast too. Mostly we dropped napalm to clear mines and booby traps, but not always.

The Chemical Corps made the napalm we dropped and commanded the drop missions. The formula they used was probably not the one used by the big company famous for its napalm, but it worked. One of the RLOs ("real live officers," lieutenants, captains, etc., as opposed to warrant officers) told me that they just put powdered laundry detergent in with the mogas (motor gasoline) in the red 55-gallon drums so that the mogas would jell. Jellies stick to things better than liquids and burn longer.

Fifteen of the red drums would be filled and placed in a cargo net. Our usual pickup zone (PZ) for the napalm missions was the Chemical Corps pad at Camp Evans, 30 miles north of Phu Bai. When we came into the pad at Camp Evans to hookup the load, the rigger would attach the sling to our aircraft with two donuts so that when we released, by pushing the pickle switch (the sling load release button, the normal way we let go of external loads), only the front of the sling would let go. The fifteen drums would spill out while the net remained attached for the crew to drag inside the aircraft. Save the net for reuse since cargo nets are expensive. Red 55-gallon drums full of jellied gasoline are cheap.

After the load fell away, the pilot would hold the aircraft steady at 70 knots or so while the crew pulled the net in, all the while thinking about how the slow Chinook was giving the NVA time to set up their firing solution to take the aircraft out of the sky.

The mission was simple. We would fly into the PZ, line up with the load designated by the hook-up man's up-raised arm, and lower the aircraft to about 25 feet above the ground while bringing the load under our nose. As we came over the load, the hook-up man would raise the donuts, the nylon ring on the end of the sling, and try to hit the hook as soon as possible, always risking shock from the build up of static electricity or getting hit by the aircraft or by the hook.

"Load's in sight. Load's coming under the nose," I called as I eased the Chinook forward slowly.

The flight engineer would reply, "Load's in sight. Forward ten, five, three. Hold your forward. Down ten, five, three. Load's being hooked. Load's hooked. Up slow. Tensions coming on the sling. Steady. Back five.

Steady. Up. Up. Load's off five, ten, twenty—clear to go."

I would climb out slowly, holding the transition to forward flight as smoothly as possible so as not to set the load swinging. The drums had a large surface area for their weight and could be unstable. As we passed 200 feet, I would tell the copilot to "safe" the hook. He would move the switch on the overhead console back from the "arm" position to the "safe" position so that we would not accidentally release the load before it was time. Top speed with napalm was 90 knots, by company standard operating procedures (SOP), the same as any external load. I would hold 90 until beginning the drop run and then slow to 70 for the actual drop. I climbed to 3,000 feet, our usual cruise altitude, above accurate small arms fire range and at the limit of accurate fire from the heavier .51 anti-aircraft machine guns, but they were rare. None had been reported recently where we were going today. So, at 90 knots and 3,000 feet, I would fly the big helicopter to the area for the drop with fifteen 55-gallon drums of napalm swinging below me, and on final approach would descend to our drop altitude of 1,500 feet.

Just like the pickup of the load at Camp Evans, the actual drop was not usually difficult. Sometimes a LOACH would mark the targets for us with a smoke grenade, but usually it would just be the Chemical Corps officer pointing at a place on a map and then at a place on the ground. With the target in sight, we would turn toward it from down-wind so that the red drums would fall closer to where we wanted them. Flying into the wind at 70 knots, I would watch for the load to pass under the nose and appear again between the rudders. At my command, the copilot would arm the hook by pushing the overhead switch forward. When the load reached the hydraulic line between the rudders that we used for reference, I would push the pickle switch with my right little finger and call "pickle" over the ICS. In the back the hook opened, the front of the net released, and the red drums began their fall. They tumbled toward the green earth, red drums spinning and tumbling end over end, red, red, green earth, red.

The flight engineer lay on his belly on the stretcher from where he watched the red drums as they swung beneath the Chinook. He would be holding a smoke grenade, and as the sling opened, he would pull the pin. As the red drums began their fall, he would count, "one thousand one, one thousand two, one thousand three" and on the third beat he would throw the smoke grenade down through the hellhole after the red spinning drums and toward the green earth.

The impact of the fall would rupture the red drums among the green forest, sending the jellied gasoline in a wide splashing arc, the gasoline fumes rising very quickly to meet the burning smoke grenade arriving three seconds after the drums hit. No more red drum, red drum, green forest, but now just a brighter red with orange in it, flame red, and then black smoke turning gray as it rose above the green forest.

If you knew you were going to be shot at or even thought it possible, the drop would be from much higher, 1,500 feet or more to stay above the small arms or light machine-gun fire looking for the napalm drums swinging below your aircraft. Accuracy was not too important in either case. Napalm, as dropped from Chinooks, was an "area" weapon, not a "point" weapon like a rocket would be. Smoke grenades would not work from 1,500 feet; dropping from that height, more often than not, they missed hitting the fumes of the napalm. Instead, the Cobras that came with you on hot missions would play their miniguns over the ruptured drums— 1,500 rounds a minute and every fifth round a tracer. There would be a stream of red, like water from a garden hose, into the green forest and then red orange and black gray over the green.

Today we would be shot at. It was easy to tell. The mission was clearing mines near the DMZ, always NVA there, and because of that, the mission sheet told me I would have two Cobras for cover and a LOACH to mark targets for my two Chinooks. We knew we would be shot at. We were not picking up at Evans, but at another base further north and closer to the DMZ, which would reduce turnaround times between loads.

At the appointed time, all five aircraft arrived at the PZ, actually a small landing zone (LZ) named after a Marine killed near here three years ago. Both Chinooks and the LOACH landed while the Cobras circled overhead. The Chemical Corps captain that was commanding the mission came onboard and reviewed what we were going to do. We didn't shut down the helicopters for a brief since all of us had done this many times before, so we left our copilots holding the controls while the ACs walked over to the captain to hear what he had to say. After confirming what I already knew with the captain—mines and booby trap clearance today, probably NVA in the area—I called for the first load. The other Chinook would take the second, and after two loads each, we would all fly the 20 miles back to Quang Tri for fuel and to let the Cobras and LOACH refuel/rearm.

With the load hooked, I climbed out for the target area, near the Rock Pile, a singular pillar of rock that stood in a valley between the first row of mountains before you got to the high plateau leading to Laos. Two years before, the Marines had seen heavy fighting around the Rock Pile and now it was the Army's turn. QL9, the main east-west road, wound beneath me as the Chinook and its red drums swinging below flew past. Dash two, the second Chinook would pick up its load and follow in five minutes. As I passed over the first ridgeline, a grunt called me over the fox mike, "Hook over the Rock Pile, Alpha Zulu One Three, over." He sounded excited, upset, not the usual flat tone.

For a brief second I wondered how he got our frequency, but quickly figured that if he had an SOI it wouldn't be hard, considering there are only three Chinook companies in I Corps. You just call on all three until someone answers.

"Zulu One Three, Playtex One Two, go ahead," I called in my best bored aviator voice. Death before loss of cool.

"Playtex, One Three, We're pinned down by NVA about a mile north of the Rock Pile. Can you send those Cobras with you over to help us out, over?"

Looking off to the northwest, I could see smoke on the other side of the rocks below. Concentrating on the source of the smoke, as we got closer I could see small flashes from weapons and tracers from a ragged line of armored personnel carriers (APCs), firing their machine guns to the north, and there among the vehicles, a red flash with black smoke rising after it. Then, a streak from the north toward the APCs and a flash from one of them—probably a rocket propelled grenade, an RPG.

The Chemical Corps captain had a headset on, but couldn't hear the fox mike, so I briefed him over the ICS on what the grunts were telling me about their urgent request for fire support. Pulling my map from its place next to my seat, I pointed out to him that the area where the NVA fire was coming from was a free-fire zone. We could kill anything that moved there, people, animals, trees, anything. Anyone and anything were all NVA in a free-fire zone. Even the earth itself was the enemy in a free-fire zone.

The captain approved the mission change, and I told the grunts they would have more than Cobras coming. The grunt acknowledged, his voice under control now. The LOACH pilot and the Cobras had been monitoring the exchange. The LOACH pilot sounded near ecstasy at the thought that he would be marking targets other than just the forest canopy.

"One Three, One Two. They got anything heavy? They got .51's?," I asked the grunts.

"Negative, One Two," he replied. "We've seen nothing heavier than AK's and RPGs. Maybe an RPK (a Soviet light machine gun), but no .51's or tracers."

Still, we would drop from 3,000 feet, I decided. Maybe the NVA were just sandbagging while they waited for the helicopters that always came when the grunts called. Maybe the grunts didn't tell us, afraid we would go away and tell them to call for artillery support instead. The drop would be from 3,000 feet so that if they did have hidden machine guns, one of their tracers would not hit the red drums of jellied gasoline hanging below us and put the red and black smoke over the streaked green of my Chinook, leaving just a black smear in the sky as the pieces of ruined aluminum rained down on the darker green of the forest below. It would be 3,000 feet for the drop, not lower.

The Cobras knew what to do without a word being said, and sprinted ahead, lead Cobra pulling in front of Chalk Two Chinook. Far below, just above the trees, I could see the little green LOACH weaving and sprinting just above the darker green trees. Even though they are slower than Chinooks or Cobras, LOACHs always looked much faster down there, darting about just above the trees.

The LOACH pilot was talking to the grunts on the fox mike and the grunts were firing red tracers into the area where the enemy was, to make them easier for him to find. Suddenly I saw a yellow smoke grenade come from his aircraft, and I watched as it hit the ground in one patch of jungle no different from any other. The LOACH jerked away and back toward the grunts and their APCs, as the LOACH pilot called for me to put the napalm right on the smoke.

Lead Cobra rolled in on the target ahead of me, firing 2.75mm folding-fin aerial rockets (FFARs), and 7.72mm minigun rounds streamed red from his nose turret toward the green below. As he broke hard right just above the trees, Chalk Two Cobra was in rockets and miniguns, both slamming into the green to protect lead as he pulled away. As he pulled away, I was in, 70 knots level flight, not the diving 140 knots of the slim Cobras, but a fat Chinook with fifteen 55-gallon drums of napalm swinging below me in their red barrels, red over the green.

The yellow smoke of the target marker was gone now, but the smoke from the rockets marked the area clear enough for my napalm. Unlike the Cobras, I was flying parallel to the grunts instead of over them, trying to keep down any possibility that the load might hit them instead of the NVA; it needed to spread out linearly over the NVA, killing more of them with the load if possible. The patch of black smoke and green forest I picked for a release point moved under my nose, and then appeared in my chin bubble.

Pickle. A small jerk as the sling opens and the drums begin their fall.

Hold course and speed while the crew drags the sling into the aircraft through the hellhole. Behind me, I can hear the lead Cobra calling in hot. This time we did not drop a smoke grenade to light off the napalm. The lead Cobras FFARs would do that after the fumes had time to spread out enough. Miniguns and 2.75mm FFAR and red, red black into the green.

The sling inside now, I push the nose over and add power speeding up to 140 knots and back to the PZ for another load. Behind me I can hear Chalk Two Chinook talking to the grunts and the LOACH as he moves to drop his load. I hear the grunts telling them the first load missed. The NVA is still firing, heavier if anything, pissed that the helicopters came and they had no heavy weapons to reach us at 3,000 feet. Brave men, the NVA, to face napalm, the miniguns and 2.75mm FFAR and the grunt's .50's—brave men.

Fifteen minutes later, I am inbound again, another fifteen 55-gallon red drums swinging below my aircraft. Both loads have missed and the NVA are still attacking. I see much smoke from the first two drops now as I get within five miles. The Cobras are shooting less now, saving their remaining rockets and minigun ammo to light off the red drums. After my run, they will have to refuel and rearm, and the grunts will have to call for artillery until we get back. Brave men, the grunts, but they are fighting other brave men.

As I start my second run, I see the LOACH, low and fast right above the trees. I see him slow over the target, frustrated with our misses, dropping a smoke grenade right on top of the NVA troops. This time the LOACH seems to wobble in the air for a moment, then it falls spinning among the green trees, hacking into them as it goes down. I can see bits of rotor blade fly into the air. No black gray smoke, no orange red flame, the LOACH was just gone into the green.

I turn my Chinook to the right, away from the unknown situation to give things time to settle down. As I turn, I see two tiny figures, the pilot and the gunner from Little Bird running away from the green woods that hold the crash site across an open area. I see them running, running and I see tracers pouring from the American positions down into the woods, covering the two figures as they run. Both Cobras are diving now, spraying the woods with their remaining red streams of tracers. When I complete the 360 turn, the running figures are no longer visible, they must have made the lines safely. Or they are down wounded or dead among the green brush.

A breathless voice on the fox mike says, "Playtex One Two, Little Bird. I went right down in the middle of the bastards. They were dodging pieces of my rotor blades. Drop right on the LOACH! Drop right on the LOACH!" There was no attempt at pilot cool in his voice, just a 19-year-old exhilarated at surviving, at being alive. Once again a LOACH had crashed without killing the crew, a characteristic that truly made it a beloved aircraft.

I complete the turn, and as I line up the Chinook with the target, I see the LOACH's fuselage lying on its side, light green aircraft on dark green jungle as the last wisps of purple smoke from Little Bird's grenade dissipate. As the aircraft wreckage passes under the top of the dash, I tense, ready to push the pickle switch when it appears between the rudders.

Pickle now.

Unseen to me, the front of the sling releases, the cargo net opens and the drums fall, red and red, end over end, spreading out as they drop.

Again, no smoke grenade to light them, we are too high, and the drums are spread too far apart. The red drums hit the earth as the lead Cobra is in hot, his rockets leaving a white line in the sky as the last of his high explosive 2.75mm FFARs hit and explode in the middle of the ruptured red drums in the green trees. White flash from the exploding rockets, then big red orange ball changing to black gray, spreading in a wide area over the LOACH and the thin purple smoke until both are quickly gone from sight.

I circle wide to the right, watching the flames and smoke above the green forest. Then secondary explosions start on the ground around the burning LOACH, small ones when seen from 3,000 feet. Flash, flash, white, red, black gray, among the red orange and bigger black gray. Three, four, now five explosions then they stop, leaving only black smoke.

"You got the motherfuckers! You got the motherfuckers! That's their RPG rounds going off. You got them!" Little Bird yells over the fox mike. I hear the grunts yelling in the background as he speaks, happy or perhaps relieved, yells now that the NVA fire from the tree line had stopped. The NVA soldiers had withdrawn, broken contact with the Americans. Or they were dead, either way, no fire came from the tree line.

As Little Bird spoke on fox mike, the lead Cobra calls me on UHF to tell me that a Huey was inbound to pick up the LOACH pilot and gunner. I would not have to land and carry them back to their base after all. After I talk to the Chemical Corps officer, I call Chalk Two Chinook and tell him to take his load back to the PZ. We would have to re-plan the original mission and start over again. The mines we originally set out to burn were still there and the mission must be done.

Six hours later, the day was done and both Chinook crews are in the Playtex Club. I am closest to the phone when it rings, so I answer.

I identified myself and hear, "Just the man I was looking for. Great job today. Must have been a hell of a show," the battalion operations officer was actually calling for me, another CW2 amongst the many in our battalion, a first, since he normally only talked officially to RLOs.

"Thanks," I reply. "What are you talking about, sir"? We had done ten or more missions that day, including finishing the original napalm drop, and now after 12 hours in the air they had all run together in my mind.

"The napalm drop, asshole." He replies. "You got 18 confirmed KIAs (enemy Killed in Action) and took out a big ammo bunker. The captain you had with you just wrote you up for a Silver Star."

I didn't say a word for a minute. I just sat there thinking about it. When I did speak, I told him it was a crock of shit. The captain just got it wrong and the battalion operations officer should just tear up the recommendation.

Silver Stars are for people who have done brave things. I did nothing brave to deserve a Silver Star that day. It is not brave to sit out of range and kill the enemy with napalm, turning men into unidentifiable things, shrunken and black against the unburned green jungle and gray ash where the flames were. If the green tracers had been reaching up for us and those drums of napalm, it might have been brave, but it is not heroic to kill men who cannot kill you in turn. The brave men were on the ground, trading shot for shot. They are not back in a bar having a beer. They are still out there, out by the Rock Pile waiting for the NVA to attack again.

That is, if we killed anyone at all. The NVA could have just given up and moved away when all the helicopters were overhead and the napalm and streams of red tracers and the rockets began to fall. Maybe killing the LOACH was enough for them. Maybe they just dropped their ammo and moved out of the area. Did anyone actually go to the burned ground and count 18 dead men? Who saw the destroyed bunker? The Chemical Corps officer must have wanted a medal and the only way he could get one was if the aircrew got one, so he wrote us up for one and was waiting for us to write him up for one. Or, he just wrote himself up for one without waiting for us to do it and turned it in to higher headquarters himself.

The battalion Ops O is incredulous as again I tell him that it just isn't true and that he should tear up the write up. He sounded disappointed but agreed to do so.

I read, sometime after this event, that Napoleon understood decorations and medals—that he could get men to fight and die for a piece of colored ribbon. He was right, they will. But some men will also lie for them. In my remaining 22 years of service I arranged to never get another medal . . .

# 12

## LAST 'NAM FLIGHT
### NORTHERN I CORPS AND PHU BAI, VIETNAM ■ AUGUST 1971

---

*In most wars, one of three things happens to the combatants. One: your side wins—or loses—and you eventually get to go home; Two: you are wounded too badly to continue and you are shipped home; Three: you are killed. Not in Vietnam, though. There, all you had to do was survive one year, just 365 days, and you flew home on a big jet airplane while the war continued on.*

---

In our 365 days, we found that mostly we all went through three stages— newbie, confident AC, and burn out. A newbie was too ignorant to know when to be scared and would do anything simply because he did not know any better and besides, ACs were god-like individuals; they were like the flight instructors at Ft. Wolters and Ft. Rucker, and could do no wrong. This stage lasted about two months. The confident AC knew he could do absolutely anything and get away with it because he was 20 or 21 years old and obviously the most skilled and knowledgeable pilot in the company, if not in the Army. He was also invulnerable. This stage started about three months into the 12 and lasted until about month 11. By then the confident AC became the burnout who knew in his heart that everyone was out to kill him; only his skill, his skill alone, could keep him alive and by God, he would do everything himself to keep anyone else from killing him.

The newbie had to be watched to make sure that, like a child, he learned that fire burns and you must not run with sharp objects or play in traffic. The confident AC had to be watched to make sure his ego did not take him past his actual skill level. The burnout had to be watched to keep him fit and alive to return home. We instructor pilots (IP) tried hard to ease that transition between the second stage and the third so that he could keep his pride and maybe recover somewhat before he went home. And so that after a year or so stateside, he could return to the war to do it again.

I reached the third stage in the second week of my twelfth month . . .

We, the operations officer and I, the senior instructor pilot, watched closely as the pilots got close to the end of their tour for signs that they were at the end of their rope. We did this by flying with them sometimes and by flying missions as wingman with them at other times. Even so, sometimes we missed seeing it coming.

"The son of a bitch pulled his pistol on me," the copilot yelled as he banged open the screen door to the Club. "He pulled his fucking gun and threatened to shoot me if I touched the controls."

Leaving my open beer on the bar, I went behind the counter pulled two new ones from the refrigerator and went looking for the AC in question. I found him in his hootch, sitting still and silent in his desk chair with his chicken plate (body armor) and survival vest dropped on the floor beside him. He had tossed his helmet bag onto his bed. His pistol was in its holster lying on the desk where it should have been, and not in his hand, where I feared it might be. He was just looking across the room at nothing. I could see him through the screen, sitting there, just sitting. Without knocking, I went in and pulled his roommate's chair next to his. He didn't even look up as I sat down. I open the two beers with my church key, handed him one and took a pull on the other. They were flat and tasted of tin, but they were cold and had alcohol in them. We drank in silence until they were empty, not talking or even looking at each other. I finished mine first, threw the can into the trash and looked directly at him for the first time since I came in.

"We've got a lot of ACs right now and the number of missions Division is sending us is slowing down. Would you like to stop flying now so that some of the newer ACs can get more flight time?" I asked, leaving him an open door, a way out without having to admit he was burned out.

He looked back at me for the first time since I came into his room and took the offered open door.

"Yes. Yes, I would," he said, his voice tired and the strain apparent.

It turned out that for his last few flights the AC would not let any of the copilots fly or even touch the controls. All day, every day for the last week, for somewhere around eight or more straight hours of flight time per day, the AC had been continually flying the aircraft instead of taking turns with the copilot, as was customary. He was respected for his flying and leadership over this tour and no one had said a word until finally this new copilot put his hands on the controls and said he wanted to fly. At that point the AC pulled out his pistol, pointed it at the copilot's head and told him that if he touched the controls again he would kill him. And he just might have . . .

"Yes. Yes, I would."

I tried to watch myself, but others saw it first. The first week into my twelfth month, and while still at least nominally the company senior IP, I found myself getting fewer missions and the ones I got were the easy ones. No Cobra escorts. No napalm drops. No night re-supplies. Finally I was assigned the aircraft recovery standby, usually the lowest tension mission Playtex had.

Aircraft recovery standby consisted of sitting in the battalion Tactical Operations Center (TOC) and waiting for a helicopter—anything smaller than a Chinook, since it usually took a CH-54 Flying Crane to lift a Chinook—to go down somewhere. Aircraft were often shot down, but even more often something simply failed; the pilot might have landed the aircraft in the closest spot available, and it was just too much trouble to fix whatever was wrong with it in the field. When that happened the aircraft recovery standby was called and we would pick up the downed bird and carry it as an external load back to Camp Evans or Phu Bai or Camp Eagle, wherever the unit it belonged to was assigned. No big deal as far as an external lift went, a routine load, one all the ACs had done many, many times.

However, an aircraft going down, whether shot down or merely broken, was a big deal to everyone else. A reinforced platoon of infantry was also on standby, as was a specially trained crew of riggers, the men who prepared the slings necessary to lift the aircraft as an external load. When Division made the decision to recover an aircraft, the infantry platoon would be lifted to the spot by Hueys while the on-call Cobras orbited overhead to provide air cover. Once the landing zone was secured by the grunts, the riggers would be inserted into the LZ by their own Hueys with their gear. If the aircraft was intact and upright, they would rig it for a routine external load. If it went in un-controlled and was more or less in pieces, they might wrap it in a cargo net. The grunts would provide security while the riggers worked. Most of the time, eight out of ten anyway, the birds would just have a mechanical problem that was too hard to fix in the field. With shot down aircraft, Division normally waited until things had cooled down before they called for the Chinook to pick them up. Most times.

The standby Chinook always flew from our home heliport to the spot set aside by the battalion TOC, near the runway at Phu Bai, to wait. The AC went to the bunker to wait for a call while the pilot and crew hung around the bird, sunbathing, writing letters, sleeping. When a mission came, the HAC would get the brief and go out to the bird, ready for whatever the mission required. When the recovery had been made, the duty bird would return to the helipad and wait for the next mission. At dusk, they would fly back to their home heliport, mission complete. No recoveries were done at night, too dangerous all the way around. It was also very rare for a mission to involve hot landing zones; again, too dangerous for the grunts, riggers, hookup men and helicopter crews. Why lose more aircraft when you've already lost one at that spot? So, recovery standby was usually a nice easy mission, requiring some skill but no real nerve, perfect for a soon-to-be burnout.

I was in the TOC, reading a paperback when the first call came in. A Cobra was down on a ridge, close to the Rock Pile, up near the DMZ. Not shot down, but an engine failure, which unfortunately occurred while the crew was shooting it out with an NVA 12.7mm machine gun. Hot zone, but the Cobra crew does a magnificent job of autorotating their powerless helicopter to a very small, clear spot and then, since there is no place to land another helicopter, rides out, draped over the stub wing of their wingman, hanging on to the rocket pods to keep from falling off. Division commanding general (CG) is pissed, not at the crew, but at the thought of losing a Cobra to an engine failure and wants that Cobra back. At the call "Launch the recovery standby," my aircraft will be on its way north very shortly.

I've got my map out, though I knew the area where the bird went down very well. It's a skinny ridge by the looks of the map, with contour lines very close together. More information is coming into the TOC now. The Cobra pilot says he autoed in, was right on top of another couple of NVA digging another gun pit. Reports are coming in from other aircraft about seeing many NVA in the area. F-4's called and will be overhead shortly. Artillery is shooting up the area already. My rectum is puckering as I listen. The recovery plan is simple. They launch the grunt security element in a combat assault to a zone just below the Cobra's position. The grunts will fight their way up to the downed bird if they have to, and secure it for the riggers. Other Cobras are shredding the jungle all around the downed aircraft with their rockets and miniguns as the grunts start their way up. NVA tracers are coming back at them, but it's hard to see where the fire is coming from through the thickness of the jungle trees. The NVA must be rattled since their fire is ineffective; at least so far, it's ineffective.

Before I leave the TOC, I tell a runner to alert my crew while I get as much information as I can. In a few moments I hear the Chinook's APU start up, followed by both engines. "Burn, burn goddamn you, burn," I think to myself, hoping the NVA will light the Cobra up and set off the fuel tanks or the rocket pods before the grunts get there. It doesn't happen. They do light it up, but the Cobra refuses to burn.

The aircraft is completely ready to go as I strap in and brief the crew over the ICS. They know perfectly well where we are going and that it will be hot when we get there. No one runs to the aircraft for a routine recovery. No one says a word, except those few required to get us airborne. "Takeoff checklist complete," says the copilot. "Ready in back," says the flight engineer, and I am climbing out, turning north as I go. The copilot knows better than to ask if he can fly, not this time. Thirty minutes later, at 6,000 feet altitude, I can see the black smoke on the green ridge still ten miles away to the north. It's a pretty day for I Corps, blue sky above green mountains, puffy clouds up above us, all the way into North Vietnam fifteen miles away.

As we get closer, I see new smoke coming from flashes on the hillside. Artillery? No, then I see the F-4 pulling off target and his wingman rolling in. Jets, Cobras, artillery, all for one downed Cobra. My flight engineer came up front, something he rarely did, to watch the action through the cockpit windows. I looked over at him but neither of us said a word and after a few moments he returned to his position in the cabin and lay down on his stretcher, ready to make the hookup.

As we flew toward the smoke, I told the crew all I knew. The Cobra had an engine failure while engaging an anti-aircraft machine gun position.

It had just refueled and re-armed so it was heavy. We had 6,000 pounds of fuel when we took off and would have around 5,000 when we got there, which made us heavy. It would take everything we had to lift it from the ridge where it rested.

As we got to within five miles, I could see the F-4s departing the area. Now the Cobras and their LOACH were working the area, talking to each other, calm and relaxed as they did their mission—major cool points for all of them.

"Little Bird, Gun One, you got a 12.7mm tracking you from your three o'clock."

"Gun One, Little Bird, don't see him. Can you do something about that?"

In the distance, I could see a Cobra rolling in and the streaks of his 2.75mm FFAR as they went toward the green hillside, then an orange flash and another, then gray smoke among the green of the forest.

"Gun One, Little Bird. I see him now. You got him. Want me to pick up the gun?"

"Little Bird, Gun One. Nah, leave it, It's bound to be fucked up anyway."

Pucker. I'm puckering, sucking the seat cushion up my ass, my hand is trying to crush the cyclic grip, and my legs are stiff against the rudder pedals. I take a deep breath to try to relax my hand, my legs. My Chinook is not a little LOACH dancing above the trees and dodging .50's until the Cobras can kill the NVA gun crews. My Chinook is big and slow and ungainly, particularly when it has a broken Cobra swinging on a sling below it. I am an easy target for the machine gunners. Pucker. But I force myself to breathe deeply again and exhale slowly and relax my right hand on the cyclic and my legs on the rudders. The pucker remains, diminished, but still there. My right arm is starting to ache from squeezing the cyclic.

I knew how high up the mountain the Cobra was when they gave me its position, but now it comes home to me. It's nearly 4,000 feet above sea level on a narrow ridge. The day is hot, the wind is light, my aircraft is heavy with fuel. Lifting this load is going to be close to all the aircraft can do and close to all I can do.

As we approach, I can see three Hueys orbiting to the east, over the lowlands. They had brought in the riggers and the infantry security and will pick them up after I get the Cobra out. The two Cobras that took out the 12.7mm machine gun are above the pickup zone. Two more Cobras are orbiting to the north, ready to come in when the first section runs low on rockets or 7.62mm minigun rounds. I cannot see the LOACH, but he's there right above the trees, searching for more 12.7mm's.

I can see the downed Cobra now and can see the hookup man standing on top of it, holding the donut up as he waits for my Chinook to come overhead. For a second I think about who has less fear of death, the LOACH pilot presenting himself as a target so the Cobras can come down to kill the NVA, or the hookup man, standing there high against the sky, a target for all as he holds the donut high.

"Load coming under," I call.

"Load in sight, forward ten," my flight engineer replies.

I see nothing now but the pickup. I am the Chinook. It takes no conscious actions on my part to make the machine do what I want it to do, to go where I want it to go. It is almost like I am outside the aircraft watching as it comes over the load.

"Forward five, four, three, hold your forward. Load's hooked, up twenty. Slowly, tension's coming on the sling. Sling's tight. Up twenty. Hold you forward, up, up. Load's off. Jesus, it's shot up. Hold your forward. Up ten. Steady," the flight engineer calls, but I am looking at the torque as I hold the aircraft over the ridge. It is taking everything this aircraft has and I have not yet lifted the broken Cobra the twenty feet we need to get it to clear the trees around the zone. The Chinook's engines can produce no more. If I pull more thrust, rotor speed will drop, maybe to the point where the aircraft settles into the ground, with the dragging Cobra pulling it down in a crash.

When stressed, pilots seem to go into a zone of relative time. In your mind, events stop, or at least slow way down. You can step back mentally and view things from different angles. In my moment of relative time, I considered what to do. Put the Cobra back down and fly away to burn off a thousand pounds of fuel? No, that would mean leaving the grunts on the hill to hold the position for another 30 minutes, maybe enough time for the NVA to kill some of them. Maybe enough time to get another machine gun into place to kill my fat, slow Chinook with its ungainly load swinging below it, sky-lighted above the ridge.

Relative time ends and real time returns to normal speed and I pull the thrust lever up rapidly to use all the power I have to get the load above the trees before my rotor turns droop and I settle the aircraft back down to the ground. At the same time, as we climb out, burning up the momentum from the last of the added thrust, I push the nose of my Chinook over and we dive down the mountain, the Cobra swinging below us just barely clearing the trees as we fall down the mountainside. Everything the Chinook has is now applied. There is no power left. My crew does not talk or maybe they do, but I don't hear.

Fly. I need to get enough speed so that I can fly with the load. Fly. I am trading altitude for airspeed to get there and I must get there, say at least sixty knots, before I have no more altitude left to trade. We stay just above the green tops of the trees in our dive down the mountain, our external load Cobra probably too close to the treetops. God, don't let it snag in the treetops. Flying now. Flying, vibrating and shaking now, but flying. With our speed, we no longer require all the power the Chinook has to stay in the air, but I don't reduce it. I want to get away. The Chinook is flying and now it smoothes out as we end our dive down the mountainside and begin to climb, climb above the altitude where the NVA can hit us with small arms and then even above the altitude where they can hit us with machine guns, as we pass through 5,000 feet out over the low lands.

"Load's riding steady," I hear the flight engineer call as I climb the aircraft and its load away from the smoke of battle behind us. The riggers have done a good job. The drogue chute is steadying the Cobra and keeping its nose more or less straight with my Chinook as we cruise southeast at 90 knots. Looking off to starboard, I see the Huey's that were waiting for us to clear, now headed in to pick up the grunts and riggers waiting in the zone.

"Nice job, Playtex," someone calls over the UHF or fox mike, but I know better. I risked my crew unnecessarily to recover a shot-to-pieces hulk of an aircraft. But that was the mission and the mission must be done.

Thirty minutes later, I drop the Cobra at Camp Evans. We fly on back south to Camp Eagle to refuel and then back toward the battalion TOC to wait for the next load. But as I report inbound from refueling, the TOC releases us to return to Playtex and Liftmaster Pad. Darkness is too close now for another recovery so we can go back home and call it a day.

Suddenly I am tired, very tired. I realize I have flown every minute since we took off from battalion three hours ago and my right hand and arm hurt from squeezing the cyclic grip. My copilot never said a word about wanting to take the controls.

Tired. The voices of my crew seem distant as we go through the shutdown checklist. As the APU comes off line, and the blades slowly spin to a stop, shut down is complete, the aircraft now secure in its steel revetment. I look out through my window to see the other company IP and the Ops O standing outside the rotor disk watching the blades slow to a stop, dipping close to the PSP (pierced steel planking) as they complete their final turns. Gathering my gear, I climb out of the aircraft and walk over to them.

"Would you like to quit flying now?"

"Yes. Yes, I would."

Yes, yes, I would. On August 7, 1971 my combat missions in Vietnam were done. I never flew a Chinook again.

# FLYING LIFE TWO

## THE NATIONAL GUARD
## 1972–1975

*The US Army was nearly destroyed by 1972. Drugs, the unend-ing war in Vietnam, and the growing fight against it at home—all of it came together to bring morale to a very, very low level. I came back from Vietnam gung-ho in 1971, a budding lifer, but within a year I requested release from active duty so that I could go to college full time. A former active duty Army aviator, now a student at the University of Kentucky, suggested I join the National Guard while I was going to school like he had done. I would still get to fly and the extra money would help. He told me that the Kentucky State Aviation Officer, a colonel, was coming down to Ft. Campbell and I should talk to him. I leaped at the chance and called the colonel. He agreed to meet, so I picked him up at the airfield and took him to lunch at the Officer's Club. He invited me to Frankfort to see their operation, so a week later I went to the Boone National Guard Center for an interview. After we talked, the colonel said, "Let's go flying." I declined on the grounds that I did not have flight gear, but he said it would not be a problem. So, in civilian clothes with only a flight helmet, I started up a UH-1H and we took it around the traffic pattern for an hour. He liked my flying and I was formally invited to join the Kentucky Army National Guard as a CW2. I accepted immediately.*

## 13

# TRUCK STRIKE
### BOWLING GREEN, KENTUCKY ■ JANUARY 1973

---

*"2113th Transportation Company, you call—we haul. We got 2-bys, 4-bys, and them great big mothers that bend in the middle and the brakes go SHUUUU." (My company's standard telephone greeting, circa 1975)*

---

When the call came from a fellow student at the University of Kentucky, a National Guard captain when he wasn't studying accounting, I could not believe it was real. I knew him as a friend, and while I knew he was a captain in the Guard, I didn't think of him as a "Captain" like the RLO (Real Live Officers, as opposed to warrant officers) captains I had known when I was on active duty in the Army. He was just a fellow student and friend that I flew with now and then.

"They're calling us up. Report ASAP to the Aviation Center for your assignment." he said.

"Right. How about you kiss my ass instead? I haven't got time for this shit, I got a big test tomorrow," I replied and hung up.

The phone rang again, in just as long as it took to re-dial it.

"Look, man, I'm not kidding. Call them, if you don't believe me. You are supposed to bring clothes, money and whatever else you think you will need for a one week deployment somewhere in the state."

"No shit?"

"No shit."

It only took a few minutes to call my wife at work and the two professors from tomorrow's scheduled classes with the news. Instructions were left with my wife to call the remaining teachers. The RON call ("remain overnight" call, made so that all would know you actually made it to wherever it was you were going) would come from wherever and whenever the night ended.

The drive to Frankfort, the base of all Army National Guard aircraft in Kentucky, in my red Pinto was faster than usual, not that I could be fast under any circumstance in a 1600CC 1972 Pinto. Somewhere, I had read that a Guardsman called to active duty could not be arrested except for a felony, so I used the opportunity to see just how fast the Pinto could go. The answer was not very. In fact, it was hard to tell I was going for max speed—even on the interstate in the days of 70 MPH speed limits and 80 MPH drivers—when my red, gas-tank exploding model Pinto would only do 83 no matter how long I kept my foot to the floor. Had I passed a state trooper, I doubt he would have even bothered to stop me.

At the Boone Aviation Center, many of the other pilots, 20 or 25 of them, were already there. The pilots talked excitedly about the truck strike and where they were going to be assigned, while the commanders gathered around maps and talked about who should go where. All were excited to be back in action as opposed to their normal civilian lives, even if the "action" was going to be routine flying, not combat. I found 35 cents in my pocket and bought a soft drink from the machine while waiting for some order to come from the full time Guard officers who were in charge of us "weekend warriors" milling around the room. Finally the RLO's conference broke up and a sheet of paper listing aircrews, aircraft assignments, and deployment destinations was taped to the whiteboard in the front of the room.

"OK, here's the deal," the colonel started, "As you know there's a truck strike going on. Some truckers are blocking gas stations, others are slowing down traffic, and some people are attacking trucks on the roads. Sometimes it's rocks thrown from overpasses, sometimes it's shots fired. We've had reports of both, so the governor has decided to call us up to provide air surveillance of the roads. You are not to attempt to interfere with whatever is going on. You will each be assigned a state trooper to ride with you. He will have a police radio, since they operate on different frequencies than we do and *he*, I say again, *HE*, will call any trouble in to the closest police unit. You keep the helicopter in position for the trooper to observe what is happening but far enough away to keep from getting shot. I realize nearly all of you are Vietnam vets and this must seem like a bit of a joke after that, but wouldn't it be really stupid to get killed here in Kentucky after the war is over?"

We all nodded in agreement, but I could see a bit of a light in the eyes of a couple of the old LOACH pilots. I had flown cargo helicopters during the war, and did not want anyone shooting at me then and certainly did not want anyone shooting at me now.

Scanning the aircraft assignments posted on the board, I saw that I had drawn an OH-58A Jet Ranger and since I was the senior pilot in the crew, I would be the AC and another CW2, the copilot. Our flying assignment was to patrol a triangular stretch of interstate highway in the western part of Kentucky from sunrise to sunset starting first thing tomorrow morning. We were to be billeted at a Holiday Inn located just outside Bowling Green, home of Western Kentucky University and General Motor's Corvette plant. After a quick preflight of our Jet Ranger, we took off into the cold, gray Frankfort afternoon. Since I was the AC, I did the first takeoff, like all ACs do. Got to make sure the helicopter is working as it's supposed to.

As we were climbing out, my copilot, said, "Would you mind stopping by my Mom's place. I don't have any money."

I looked over at him in the left seat of the cockpit in amazement. It had to be a joke, but by the look on his face I realized that he was serious. How could anyone go on an active duty mission like this without any money was a mystery to me, but that pretty much was him. I knew he was a student at the University of Kentucky, like me, but he was not married and so was apparently less concerned about money and things like that. Since I did not have enough money to support two of us, I saw little choice.

"Sure. Where does your Mom live"? I asked, trying to keep the sarcasm out of my voice.

"She lives south of Louisville, right on our route," he said while holding a chart under my nose.

The town he indicated was indeed not far off our route. He assured me that the backyard of his mother's house was plenty big enough for a Jet Ranger. When we arrived there 15 minutes later, I agreed that his mom's back yard was indeed a big enough landing zone for a 58. I landed the helicopter a ways back from the house so as not to blow things around and he un-strapped, opened the door, and trotted up to the back door.

He must have called ahead before we took off because an older woman was waiting there at the back door as we landed. She gave him a hug as he came up, and then she disappeared into the house. I could see the neighbors coming out into their backyards to see what was going on, wondering if anyone was calling the police about the helicopter making all that noise out back. A few moments after she went inside, the woman was back and handed my copilot some money. Trotting back to the aircraft, he strapped in and we were off to Bowling Green again. Normal operations for the 1970's National Guard.

It was dark by the time we finally landed at Bowling Green's airport. After I called back to Frankfort with our RON and to confirm nothing had changed in our mission instructions, we caught the fixed base operator's (FBO) aircrew van over to the Holiday Inn. The FBO would pick us up again in the morning about an hour before dawn.

Everyone in the motel lobby stared at our flight suits and helmet bags as we checked in, curious but not asking questions. Unpacking only took a few minutes and still in our flight suits, we went to the motel restaurant for dinner. We could have changed clothes, but as a Guard pilot you don't get to walk around in a flight suit very much and they do get attention, always positive in Kentucky and the south in general.

Even if the Commonwealth of Kentucky was buying our dinner, we didn't order too much. The saved TDY money could be better spent back home in our real lives as students, as would the extra pay for every day this mission continued. After dinner we went to the bar for a drink, as is usual when you are TDY ("TDY" is a government term meaning detached duty away from your home station. The Marines and Navy sometimes call it "TAD" for Temporary Additional Duty, which is also translated as "Traveling Around Drunk"), and as usual, going to the bar was a mistake. There in the bar was a group of "West-by-God-Virginians," all older women (since both of us were less than 25 years old, about everyone was an "older" person), in town for a meeting of some sort. As soon as they saw the flight suits, they wanted to buy us drinks, among other things.

By 10:30 PM, I was beat and a little bit wobbly from free drinks. It had been a long day and free beer or no, I was not used to drinking late into the evening and still making a dawn launch. I told my copilot I was going back to our room and rack out (sleep). He said he would stay for "just a little while longer."

Sometime later, loud noises in the motel room woke me up, loud noises followed by bright light. I opened my eyes to see that my copilot had thrown open the curtains on the picture window. He was standing there, framed in the plate glass facing the parking lot, stark naked. His arms where stretched out to the sides like he was making wings.

"What the fuck are you doing"? I asked, very sleepy, but rapidly becoming awake and becoming very angry.

"Hot. It's hot in here. I need some air," he replied.

"That Goddamn window doesn't open. And close the fucking curtains," I shouted.

He was in no condition to argue or do much of anything else and began fumbling to close the curtains. Before the light was gone I looked at the clock and saw 1:30 AM. He opened the door before he hit the bed so he could have his cold air. I closed it as soon as he went to sleep, about 30 seconds later.

At 5:00 our wake-up call came from wherever wake-up calls come from. I figured it would be best if I went ahead and took a shower before trying to get my copilot out of bed. When I did, he came up easier than I thought he would and was ready to go in short order.

The FBO van was there and ready to go when we got to the lobby. We managed to get a roll and some coffee from the buffet to take with us but my copilot pitched his roll out the window as we pulled out of the parking lot.

When we got to the airport, our state trooper was waiting for us in his cruiser. We shook hands and he came inside with me as I checked the weather at the Flight Service Station. While I talked clouds and visibility, he called his police command center in Frankfort to confirm the mission was on. He was excited about flying instead of driving all day and writing speeding tickets. The weather was overcast but fine for the kind of flying we would be doing, low and slow observation work. While I was inside, my copilot preflighted the helicopter.

With the state trooper and his radio strapped in the back seat of the OH-58, we lifted on schedule in the gray light. I hovered the aircraft out for takeoff since my copilot was looking a little pale. With the control tower's permission, I did not bother with the runway, but instead took off from the taxiway across the grass toward the airport fence and headed out toward the Interstate Highway we would patrol. We could just see the beginnings of daylight as we climbed out from the airport. We saw nothing significant for the first 20 minutes of flight along the highway, except cars on the interstate and trucks parked at rest stops, but then my copilot began pointing violently at the ground.

I thought he saw a sniper or some sort of ambush on the side of the road, so I pitched the nose of the Jet Ranger sharply up about 30 degrees and began a split-S type maneuver, a "return to target" we called it, a rapid turn accomplished by pitching the nose of the aircraft up and rotating it sharply to the right before pushing the nose down toward the ground, so we could get back around, keeping the target in sight the entire time. As I banked the aircraft hard in the tight turn, I saw my copilot suddenly put his hand to his mouth.

No ambush, no sniper—my copilot was sick from too much "West-By-God-Virginian" beer.

As quickly as I had turned the aircraft into the return-to-target, I rolled it wings-level, and lowering the collective, headed for a rapid landing in a pasture beside the road. Too late. At least he threw up straight-ahead; projectile vomiting, I think best describes it, covering the windshield and dash on his side, and luckily for him, not covering me. The smell in the small cockpit nearly made me vomit too, but I slid open the small window in my door to get to the cold outside air and kicked right rudder enough to get air blowing through my door and carry the smell out his side.

By going direct instead of following the road, we were back at Bowling Green Airport in 10 minutes. No words were said by the trooper or me or the copilot until we were on the ground.

"You son-of-a-bitch, clean up the goddamn aircraft. When it is clean and doesn't smell any more we will go flying again," I told him as calmly as I could. If a pilot gets air sick, *he* cleans it up, so I did not offer to help him.

The trooper went back inside to the FBO's ready room with me and drank coffee and talked as if nothing had happened, expressing no interest at all in the copilot. The thought occurred to me that had my copilot been driving a car, the trooper would have been very interested indeed in his blood alcohol level. Forty-five minutes later the copilot came in and said we were ready to go. To try to make things better he had refueled the aircraft, and so, without another word we went out to the bird and took-off again.

The day passed without incident. No snipers, no ambushes, just three refueling stops and six hours of flight time up and down the interstate. He did not get sick again. We returned to Bowling Green just as the sun was setting.

After having a hamburger in the motel bar, we watched the Nashville evening news on the television.

"The Kentucky National Guard is patrolling Interstate 75 today as the truck strike continues," the announcer said, while showing a picture of a much larger Army Huey from Fort Campbell, instead of our Kentucky National Guard OH-58. The mistake was obvious to anyone who knew anything, since the Huey had a big "101st Airborne" sticker on its nose, while our Jet Ranger had even bigger "Kentucky Army National Guard" stickers on both cockpit doors.

"I wonder why they did that," I said. "Our Jet Ranger was parked right next to that Huey when they were filming."

"Well," my copilot replied, "I was cleaning up our aircraft when they were getting ready to film. The smell made me sick again, so just as they started to roll the film I had to throw up. I was leaning up against the side of the aircraft, puking, and they just moved the camera over to the next aircraft on down the line."

After two more uneventful days of patrolling without "West-by-God-Virginians" in the bar at night, we flew back to Frankfort, turned in the helicopter, and changed back into college students again.

Sleep well, America. The Guard is awake tonight.

# 14

# NATIONAL GUARD NIGHT FLIGHT
## CINCINNATI, OHIO ■ DECEMBER 1973

*Just because you are a weekend warrior, you are not released from the obligations of all Army Aviators when it comes to instrument flight check rides and annual minimum flight times. But sometimes, as a weekend warrior, you get to reflect on things in ways you may not have expected.*

So much instrument time and so much nighttime as well, not to mention the total flight time you are supposed to get, have a way of sneaking up on you when the end of the year rolls around. It's not that you don't want to fly, you love to fly, but you've got a family, a job, you're a student, and it just sneaks up on you. One day, near the end of the year, the technician from Operations at the Aviation Facility calls and tells you, "Son, you are two hours short on your night time."

It is December 27. The weather, while not cold enough for icing here on the surface of the airfield, is too cold to take a helicopter up into the clouds where there will certainly be ice. Even if there wasn't ice, you couldn't take the helicopter up there because Frankfort only has non-precision approaches and the clouds are too low for that kind of instrument approach. But in any case, Huey's can't take ice, so here in a hover at the Boone National Guard Center at Frankfort Airport with the temperature just above freezing, at least you can technically "fly," since a hover means that the aircraft is not in contact with the ground and is "flying."

But you do feel like an idiot. Why didn't you pay more attention to how much nighttime you'd accumulated over the past year so that you could at least get higher than these 3 feet? It is too late now, so here you are, hovering a helicopter around Frankfort's airport, rain leaking through a poor windshield seal onto your left leg on the 27th of December. At least this Huey has a working bleed air heater so you are not cold as well as wet, like you would have been back when you were flying OH-13Es.

*Other National Guard night flights come back to you, like the time the year before when four aircrews decided to take their Hueys and do some nighttime formation flying. We would all takeoff in formation and fly a loose cruise up to Cincinnati's general aviation airport, Lunken Airport, refuel, get a cup of coffee at the snack bar, check weather, and fly back. It would be a loose cruise, what some jokingly called a "nuclear formation" because the aircraft were so far apart that an atomic weapon wouldn't get you all. We had been excellent formation pilots once, or at least thought we were back in Vietnam, but that was a long time ago. Now we were students, office workers, family men and weekend warriors instead of cocky CWOs (chief warrant officers).*

*The trip up to Cincinnati was an uneventful night flight, no weather to speak of, just high scattered clouds and lots of lights on the ground, unlike the dark of Vietnam's jungle. Being who we were now, we were all rusty enough at formation flying that we didn't get too close to each other, so there was no high tension to the flight. Lead knew better than to make any sharp turns and no one wanted to show off since that would not be cool. Once, over-lapping rotor blades coming into hot zones had been "normal," but not now. Now everyone stayed at least four rotor diameters away from the next aircraft. After 45 minutes of wandering our way north, Lead called Lunken tower, "flight of four Hueys five miles south for landing." Tower cleared us to land and one after another we hovered off the runway onto a dark, empty ramp. In the daylight we would have been a sensation for the civilians at the airport—four military helicopters on the ramp where war machines were rarely, if ever, seen—but at night at a general aviation airport, there is usually no one to see you.*

*The terminal building at Lunken, Cincinnati's main airport, was dark and appeared deserted. We all shut down our Hueys and as a group, walked toward the weather office and snack bar inside the main building. As we walked the 100 yards or so, one of the pilots decided he could not wait to get inside to relieve himself, so stopping on the ramp, he un-zipped and proceeded. We all waited a moment for him to finish and then continued as a group.*

*The first men through the terminal door more or less just stopped barely inside. As the rest of us came in, we were met with the sight of a fancy restaurant inside the terminal, just to the right of the door we had just entered. Every table appeared full, people dressed for a night out, food and wine bottles and candles lit and sparkling on the tables, but no one was talking or drinking. Every head was looking directly at us.*

*I looked past the faces turned our way, back through the window out toward the ramp. The glass was clear enough to see through the window from the inside to the outside, but from the ramp the glass was too dark to see from the outside to the inside. The four helicopters parked on the ramp were clearly visible. There, also clearly visible, about half way between the Hueys and the restaurant, was a large dark puddle on the ramp blacktop. No one said a word, but the offending pilot stepped forward and keeping a straight face, took a small bow, and with that, we all proceeded to the weather office and our briefing for the return flight.*

*When we went back to the aircraft past the restaurant we all looked straight ahead but I did notice that the voices from the tables trailed off as we passed. Maintain cool, always, and pretend that nothing happened. Pilots are usually good at that.*

---

But that was last year and I have to meet minimums this year. Now it's December 27th and I have to fly tonight because the Aviation Facility is closed after tonight until after New Year's Day, so it's fly now or explain to a flight disposition board why I could not manage to do something as simple as get a few hours of nighttime flight in an entire year. Fortunately, I was not alone. My copilot, also a UK student, was in the exact same situation. He only needed one hour but had agreed to stay with me for the entire two hours. He could have said no and I could have been totally by myself for an hour, bouncing a Huey up and down with a sandbag in the left seat to bring it up to the minimum cockpit weight of 240 pounds.

I drove over from Lexington to Frankfort in the rain, thinking black thoughts the entire 40-minute trip. Just blow the two hours off and bluff through the disposition board. Sit in the office for two hours, drink coffee and pencil whip it (just write the time in the log book instead of flying it). No, I would do none of these things. I would hover the God-damned Huey for two hours in the rain. It was my fault I did not get the time so it was now my responsibility to get it.

I am wet from preflighting in the rain. I am pissed off because it is raining and December 27th and I want to be home with my family. I start the aircraft under the red map lights and relax some as I feel the rotor blades start turning as the engine lights off. The Huey is rocking its familiar rhythm as I bring it up to full RPM, taking me back to all my other flights in this model helicopter. The Huey's sounds fill the world outside my helmet, the high-pitched sounds of the engine turbines and the transmission as the RPM increases, the thump of the rotor blades. The cockpit turns a deep red as I adjust the instrument lights to the level I need, their red lamps glowing dim on the gray dash.

Checklist complete, I turn on both the landing light and searchlight as I lift the aircraft into a three-foot hover. No large "beat" to indicate that the rotor blades are out of balance, no strange vibrations or sounds either—the aircraft is ready to fly. Adding a little collective pitch and a little left rudder as I slightly lower the nose, I move the aircraft out onto the taxiway and hover toward the runway. Frankfort is an uncontrolled field so there is no ground control or tower to talk to, and since the weather is just too bad to fly in, tonight we have it to ourselves.

Before moving onto the airport's single runway for takeoff, I would make a blind call over the common VHF radio frequency so that any other aircraft coming in to land would know we were there. I hold off making the call since I am not going to take the runway just yet. I stop just short of the runway and slide the Huey left over the grass on the far side of the runway lights. After a moment, I land the aircraft and turn the controls over to the other pilot.

My copilot spends 15 minutes picking the aircraft up to a hover, turning on the spot using the rudder pedals, hovering forward, hovering backwards, sliding left, sliding right, landing, picking up to a hover. The rain continues to fall, our windshield wipers doing their usual miserable job of removing it even with the rotor blades slicing the rain into smaller drops. The OAT (outside air temperature) gauge shows 10 degrees centigrade, still too warm for ice here in a hover, but still too cold to go any higher into the sky. The bleed air heater pulls hot air from the engine to provide warmth inside the aircraft. After 15 minutes, it has brought the cockpit temperature up to something comfortable and is drying my wet flight jacket. Only an hour and a half to go.

As we take turns hovering the Huey around, my thoughts drift in boredom to how the controls work on helicopters. The cyclic controls had exactly the same function on the CH-47Cs that I flew in Vietnam two years ago and the UH-1H I was flying tonight, smart on the Army's part, since all rotary-wing aviators are qualified in Huey's. This makes it easier to transition from utility Hueys to cargo Chinooks. The coolie hat on the cyclic works the electric trim in pitch and roll. The top left button releases the springs that hold the cyclic in place.

Through my right flight glove, the cyclic grip feels smooth and natural, its buttons and the trim switch coolie hat switch is right where they should be for easy use; right where I learned they would always be on this model aircraft. My index finger can squeeze the switch on the back of the cyclic to the first detent for ICS, the intercom, and on to the second detent to transmit over the communications radios. My little finger rests on the pickle switch that would release the external load if we had one.

My thumb can move the coolie hat to fine trim the cyclic to whatever position I want to select so that the cyclic will stay there without input from the pilot. You don't have to use the trim, but if you don't, you need either to hold it against the springs or use the top left button to release the trim entirely, which you would do for gross control position changes. In combat, particularly when going into a hot zone, the pilot at the controls always trims the stick for level or climbing flight and holds it against the springs for the landing. He does this so that if he is shot and no longer controlling the helicopter, it will start upward and the other pilot will have a chance to get on the controls before it hits the ground.

That's the theory anyway . . .

Hueys have a handy set of two red levers on the lower back of the pilot's armored seats. Pull them both up and the seat rotates backwards so that the shot pilot can be removed from the seat in flight. Handy, that . . .

My thoughts come back to flying. Hover forward, hover backwards, set down on the skids, lift up to three feet again—another hour and fifteen minutes to go. The rain is still falling. The windshield wipers continue their sweep.

While my right hand works the cyclic, my left hand has the collective pitch lever. On the forward end of the collective is a small box with the beep trim switch and the landing and searchlight switches. The beep trim button is what the pilot uses to set the computer that holds the engine at a particular RPM. On a Huey, it is normally 6,600 RPM, a speed that is neither the rotor speed nor the speed of the compressor in the turbine engine, it's just a number on the gauge that provides a reference for the pilot to know all is well. Some helicopters show the actual rotor speed, like a Chinook, but not the Huey. The thumb part of the glove that works the beep button is often the first part of the glove to wear out, at least for C model Chinook pilots since you have to often beep one or the other of the engines up or down to keep them matched. Not on a Huey though, only one engine on a Huey, so set it at 6,600 RPM and leave it to the computer to keep it there.

When you try to pull more power than the engine can produce, the rotor speed decreases, you "droop turns." Sometimes helicopter's "normal" rotor speed, the one you routinely use for flying, is just a bit above the ideal RPM. That way, when you droop turns, you are actually going toward a more efficient RPM and may be able to gain a momentary advantage. All pilots know it is only momentary and to continue to droop will inevitably result in a loss of altitude. Lose enough rotor RPM and the helicopter will quit flying. If the engine quits you've got less than three seconds to get the collective down or your rotor speed will droop so low that you cannot recover. As the instructors said back at Fort Wolters, at that point your rotor blades, your wings, have stalled completely and your craft has all the aerodynamic properties of a footlocker.

The collective has a coolie hat too; only instead of cyclic trim this coolie hat controls the direction of the searchlight. Huey's have two lights, the landing light which is fixed in position, pointing more down than forward, and the search light, which the pilot can move to see some particular area better. Back at Fort Rucker we were taught to put the searchlight at about a 45 degree angle before takeoff so that if the engine quits you can turn on both the landing and searchlight and use the searchlight to see what's in front of you as you flare the aircraft to break your rate of descent. At that point the nose is way up and you should be able to see with the landing light.

Gallows humor says that in the event of a complete loss of engine power at night, the pilot should turn on both the landing and searchlights.

If he does not like what he sees, he should turn them off.

The throttle on helicopters like the UH-1H and the OH-58A is a twist grip, the same as a motorcycle throttle, only backwards. This caused minor problems for new student pilots back at Fort Wolters but everyone soon got over it. The Huey throttle has a detent that prevents the pilot from completely closing it inadvertently and unintentionally shutting the engine down. To start the Huey you first roll the throttle all the way on, then back it off to the detent, push the release button and move the throttle to just below the detent before you pull the starter trigger. The reason for this is that all sorts of bad things can happen when you start a helicopter.

The first is a hot start. In a hot start, instead a rising normally, the engine temperature shoots way past the normal range and can quickly damage the engine or even give you an engine fire. To counter it, you close the throttle and motor the engine without fuel to suck in air and cool it down.

In some aircraft the next possible problem is a "quick start." In this situation, instead of the engine turning up normally, a rather slow orderly process, the engine immediately goes to full power. This time the danger is to the entire drive train; engine, transmission, tail rotor drive shaft, 42 degree gear box, 90 degree gear box, etc. Again the procedure is to close the throttle and remove fuel from the engine.

---

*My armed helicopter flight instructor at Fort Rucker had an abbreviated procedure for starting the Huey. He was an old UH-1C "Charlie Model" gunship pilot between tours in Vietnam and had apparently lost all fear of death. Maybe he thought that death was waiting for him back in Vietnam and nothing would kill him in Alabama, I don't know because WOCs didn't ask instructors things like that. Instructors were gods and gods would not let you down.*

*His preflight consisted of comparing the number he wrote in ink on the web of his left hand with the number in big orange letters on the side of the helicopter. If they matched, he untied the aircraft and climbed in. His checklist did not consist of the normal 25 or 30 items, instead it was: seat belt on, helmet and gloves on, then battery on, fuel on, throttle full open then closed to the detent and moved just below it. He would yell out the open door, "CLEAR," warning anyone close to the aircraft he was starting it and pull the start trigger. When the igniters (think of them as sparkplugs used for lighting off a turbine) began their electrical "snap, snap, span" he would smile and look like the happiest man in the world. As soon as the engine started winding up he would roll the throttle full on, and while adjusting the beep to bring it to 6,600 RPM he would turn on the radios, slam the door closed and call for taxi, checklists be damned.*

---

The throttle setting on the Huey is completely different from the Kiowa, the OH-58A or Jet Ranger in its civil version, which we also flew here in the Guard. On the 58, you start with the throttle closed and wind it up when the engine reaches a certain RPM. It is easy to see that a pilot has forgotten which aircraft he is flying and uses the Huey procedure on the Kiowa. There is a roar and a ball of flame when the engine lights off, instead of the steadily increasing whine of the turbine. No damage, no foul, most of the time.

I turn the controls back over to the other pilot. It is again his turn to hover around the field for a while. Just to do something different, he lowers the nose and begins a takeoff run over the grass paralleling the runway. The rain hits harder against the windshield as we gather speed, increasing the drip on my leg from the bad seal. He holds the aircraft ten feet off the ground as we pass the shudder of translational lift. As the end of the field approaches, he goes into a slight side flare to slow the aircraft without the danger of sticking the tail rotor into the ground. Stable in a hover now, he pedal turns the aircraft 180 degrees and does it again headed in the opposite direction. The wind appears to be calm so it doesn't really matter which direction we takeoff. Thirty minutes to go.

The rudder petals adjust back and forth using a knob on the deck of the helicopter in front of the cyclic. A Huey's rudder petals are substantial metal things with "Bell," the company that manufactured them, in raised letters on them. In American and British helicopters, the rotors turn counterclockwise when you add power, while in French and Russian helicopters they turn clockwise. Why? Beats me, but they do. For the pilot, the difference is that in American single rotor helicopters, you add left rudder when you lift up. In the Russian and French helicopters, you add right. Of course, to an experienced pilot it makes no difference since they only add what rudder is required, i.e. if the wind is strong enough from the right you might add right rudder instead of left when you lift to a hover. Fifteen minutes to go.

It is still raining and windshield wipers still slide back and forth across the Plexiglas. I am thinking of the first time I ever sat in a Huey cockpit. Back at Fort Rucker, in the summer of 1969, we were about to finish up our instrument training in the TH-13T Sioux and start our transition to the Huey. We were strongly encouraged to learn the start checklist before we actually got to the flying part of training so that the instructors would not have to waste time on trivia and could move into the actual flying part. We were told to go to one of the three main heliports at Fort Rucker and dry practice, that is go through the start checklist without actually moving any of the switches, of course. I was sitting in the cockpit of a D model Huey dutifully dry practicing when a maintenance contractor came up and asked me to start her up. He needed to check something and the aircraft had to be running to do the check. Part of me wanted so badly to fire that Huey up, but I didn't do it. I was too close to finishing up to risk damaging a Huey and getting washed out.

When you washed out of flight school in 1969, they handed you a rifle and sent you to the rice paddies. And that was no theory . . .

Ten minutes to go. I hover the aircraft back into the National Guard compound still holding a standard three-foot hover. We fudge the last five minutes and shut it down. The rain is still falling as we sit and watch the rotor slow to a stop. The Huey doesn't have rotor brake so we "help" it slow down by adding full left rudder, putting pitch on the tail rotor blades to use up a little of the energy left as the rotor blades slow to a stop. I climb out of the cockpit into the rain and throw the rope end of the blade tie-down strap over the forward stopped blade and pull it down so that I can put the metal hook in the ring on the end of the blade. I walk the blade around the aircraft until I can tie the rope end to the tail boom. My copilot joins me as I am finishing up and we walk back over to Operations to close out the aircraft log book for this flight and my flying for the year.

One hour later I am back home in Lexington and am again a student. My flight suit is still damp as I climb out of my car.

Private Bob Curtis during basic training at Fort Polk, Loisiana, 1968.

Curtis as a Warrant Officer Candidate (WOC), Fort Wolters, Texas, 1969.

WOC Curtis with an OH-23D "Raven" at Fort Wolters, Texas, 1969.

CW2 Curtis
with CH-47C
in revetment at
Camp Evans,
Vietnam, 1971.

CH-47C carrying 500 gallons of fuel or water bladders (aka Elephant Nuts), Camp Eagle, Vietnam, 1971.

UH-1H shot down in Laos, one of 107 helicopters lost during Lam Son 719, 1971.

Battle damage to Playtex 820 flown by CW2 Curtis, March 4, 1971.

Curtis with silenced M3 grease gun, 1971.

CH-47C with 8,000 pounds of 105mm artillery ammunition, Camp Eagle, RVN, 1971.

Gravity hot refueling a CH-47C, RVN, 1971.

An M-60 gunner's view over RVN, 1971.

CH-47F ready for night flight on the deck of the USS *Guam,* 1989. *Photo courtesy of David Libbey*

CW2 Curtis in the cockpit of a CH-47, August, 1971.

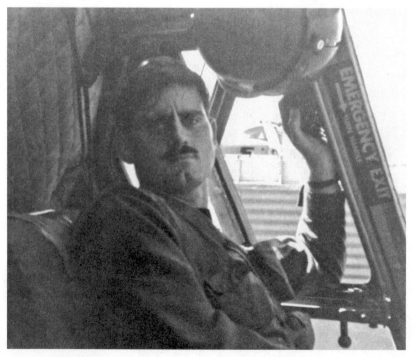

Clearing a site for a fire support base in
Northern I Corps, Vietnam, via napalm, 1971.

CW2 Curtis
with Kentucky
National Guard
UH-1H, 1973.

Bob Curtis and
his son, Master
Rob Curtis,
with an OH-
58A Kiowa at
Bluegrass Field,
Lexington,
Kentucky,
1974.

Captain Bob Curtis in an HMM-264 CH-46F Sea Knight, France, 1986.

In Sardinia, 1986.

HMM-264 CH-46F Sea Knights on the deck of the USS *Guam,* 1977.

Major Bob Curtis, 2nd from right, in front of a CH-46E, Morocco, 1988.

Curtis with an 846 Squadron Sea King MK IV, Northern Norway, 1984.

Sea King MC IV over northern Norway, 1985.

*Left:* 846 Squadron Sea King MK IVs over Somerset, UK, 1983.

*Bottom left:* HMS *Illustrious,* Lisbon, Portugal, 1984.

*Bottom right:* HMS *Fearless* in Balsfjord, Norway, 1985.

846 Squadron Sea King MK IVs off the coast of Cornwall, Captain
Bob Curtis' last flight with the Royal Navy Junglies, 1985.

Major Robert
Curtis, onboard
the USS *Nassau*,
1987.

# 15

# TORNADOS

## FRANKFORT, KENTUCKY ■ APRIL 1974

---

*That April, a vast swath of violent weather swept across the eastern US from Alabama all the way north to Ohio. There were so many tornadoes that the exact number has never been determined. Many people lost their homes, some their lives. In all of the states with extensive damage, the National Guard was called out to help with relief and recovery.*

*What folks don't always realize is that the Guardsmen are just as affected by the storms as they are, but the Guardsmen sign up to be available to help and help they do, even if it's in ways they cannot imagine beforehand.*

---

At home in my townhouse in Lexington, the tornadoes that destroyed homes across all those states, including a big swath of Kentucky and Ohio, were terrifying. It turned dark as the power went off, except for the lightning flashes and the roar of the wind. The three of us, my wife, my son and I, huddled in the downstairs bathroom against the possibility of flying glass, but we were spared any damage at all. The path of the tornados was west of Lexington and well away from us. A short time after the storms passed, while the power was still off, the phone rang; I was called up again by the National Guard, this time not as a pilot but as an officer to support the disaster relief effort.

The situation was still tense at home. My son was four and had never seen anything like this, and he was terrified, but since the storms were past, real worry was no longer necessary. I put on my fatigue uniform instead of my flight suit and packed three days' worth of clothes, including a flight suit and the rest of my flight gear, just in case they needed some flying done. Within 15 minutes of the phone call, I was headed toward Frankfort. The trip was only about 30 miles by the Interstate and should have only taken about 40 minutes tops, but it took over an hour this time. I dodged all kinds of debris in the road, including at least one dead cow, before I pulled into the Boone National Guard Center parking lot. This time it was the armory building, not the aviation facility.

There was a crowd inside the building around the armory door, men in uniform smoking and waiting for orders. As I walked up, one of the sergeants was ordering them into formation, making order out of chaos like NCOs (Non-Commissioned Officers) always do. "First platoon, FALL IN. Dress right, DRESS." I almost felt the pull to fall in myself, but remembered I was here to lead this time, not follow.

As I walked, I saw a colonel I knew slightly, not an aviator, in the center of a group of officers. He seemed to be in charge, so I reported in, coming to attention in front of him and saluting. "Sir, Mr. Curtis reporting for duty."

"Mr. Curtis, here's what I want you to do. Take that platoon of men and report to the Civil Defense Director in the basement of the State Capitol Building. Do whatever he wants you to. I will send rations and relief personnel tomorrow morning but it is important that you get there quickly. Call me at this number if you need anything, such as more resources than you have. And, Curtis, stop by the arms room and pick up your pistol before you go. Remember your rules of engagement before you shoot anyone."

Pistol? Shoot someone? Ah, this is real, not another National Guard exercise. What are the rules of engagement, exactly?

The military issue .38 caliber Smith & Wesson came with a holster and a box of ammunition. I loaded it because I believe if you are a soldier and have a weapon, it should always be loaded. Then I found my NCOIC (Non-Commissioned Officer In Charge) and asked if he knew the rules of engagement and if he'd briefed our soldiers on them. As I expected he had. The rules were simple, shoot only to preserve life, period. No one was to shoot to protect property from looting, only to protect life—theirs or someone else's.

The NCOIC, a staff sergeant, was not from my company, confirming to me that I was in charge—not because I was a well-known infantry leader, but because they knew I was a student and would be readily available for call up. No, I was just a helicopter pilot who was easy to get into position.

Well, that and apparently I was one of the few officers that had a working telephone after the storm.

The staff sergeant called the men to attention. "Sir, the platoon is ready to move," he reported while saluting me. Very smartly done for a National Guard unit, so I knew he had done active service, a fact confirmed by the yellow and black 1st Cavalry patch on his right shoulder. Like me, he was another Vietnam vet picking up some spare money by serving in the Guard.

He had a jeep for the two of us and a duce and a half (two and a half ton truck) for the men waiting for us before I even arrived, so I returned his salute and said, "Very well, Staff Sergeant. Let's get started."

He ordered the men into the duce and a half and he and I climbed into the jeep, me riding shotgun. The last time I was in the lead vehicle of a convoy we were returning from the annual rifle range qualification at Fort Knox. That time it was cold in the open jeep, so I got in my sleeping bag in the front seat and stayed there until we got back to Frankfort. Not very military perhaps, but warm nonetheless. The jeep driver jerked the vehicle a little as we started off, probably because he, like me, was excited at the prospect of leading a real, albeit small, convoy of troops through Frankfort in the midst of the storm's wreckage.

When our small convoy left the Boone National Guard Center compound, I felt a real sense of military reasonability, something I had not felt since I left the active duty Army. Real troops, live ammunition, in the middle of Frankfort, Kentucky, the state Capitol, led by a helicopter pilot who had never commanded troops before, armed or not.

The feeling of excitement continued when we pulled up in front of the Capitol Building fifteen minutes later. I remembered coming here with my parents and grandparents when I was little. My grandfather was absolutely fascinated with the Floral Clock, but it was not visible from our parking area. We left a lower ranking sergeant in charge while the staff sergeant and I hurried down the ornate stairs to the basement of the building where the Civil Defense Office was located.

Recognizing the Civil Defense Director from his picture on the office wall, I positioned myself in front of him, came to attention, saluted and said, "Mr. Curtis reporting for duty, sir. I have a platoon of 20 men with me. What are your orders, sir?"

The Director looked harried and very tired already. He replied, "Great to see you, Curtis. Look, there are lots of people wandering around in here that are not supposed to be here. They are interfering with my staff's ability to get things done. What I want you to do is simple: keep everyone that does not have a badge that looks like this out of this end of the basement."

I saluted again and got to work. The platoon sergeant and I pulled the fire evacuation diagram from the basement wall and used it to determine where to deploy our men in the hallways leading to the Civil Defense Office. He would work out a rotation of time on duty and brief me on it after he had the first men positioned. I would take the position closest to the front door of the Civil Defense Office and he would relieve me after two hours. The men would rotate once an hour because they would be standing, like sentries always do. I was the officer, so of course I would be sitting.

There was an empty office, or at least one with no one in it right now, just down the hall from the Civil Defense Office. Seeing a small table there, I pulled it into the hall and rolled out a chair to make myself comfortable. I took off my helmet and replaced it with a soft cover, a military version of a baseball hat with my wings and a CW2 bar sown on the front. A soldier always wears some kind of cover when armed, and after all, my .38 was not only on my hip, but was also loaded, the first time I had been armed since I left Vietnam. As I started my first hour of duty, the sun was up and office workers were arriving.

I had not been sitting there at my post for ten minutes when a dignified woman of middle years started to walk past me. She had no badge around her neck.

"Halt," I cried, trying to sound official. "I am sorry, Ma'am, but I am afraid you can't go in there right now. The Civil Defense Director has ordered that we keep all Non-Civil Defense personnel out of there this morning, so I'm afraid I can't let you into this corridor unless you have a Civil Defense badge."

She stopped in her tracks, incredulous that someone would interrupt her purposeful, and obviously important, walk. By the way she looked at me, I could see that this lady got her way more often than she did not.

"Young man," she replied, "I work for (name redacted—forgotten, actually, apparently a powerful state politician)."

I was unimpressed. "Ma'am, I don't care who you work for. I am a weekend warrior and not political person at all. My orders are to keep anyone who does not have the proper badge out of this corridor and I intend to do just that."

"You don't understand," she said more forcefully this time. "The lady's room is just down there around the corner on this corridor. The next one is up three flights of stairs."

"No, Ma'am, I'm afraid that you do not understand." I said. "The Civil Defense Director has ordered that we keep everyone except properly identified people out of this corridor so that his folks can handle the tornado situation. Since you are not part of Civil Defense, you cannot enter."

Red faced, she turned without another word and headed the other direction. She may have been the first, but she was certainly not the last, to try to bluster past my sentry post. Encounters of this type grew ever more heated and continued all morning as more and more people arrived for work. By mid-morning I was ready to request a machine gun and some claymore mines to fight them off.

"Get back, GET BACK!!! I will fire if you do not retreat!!!!!"

It seems that my fate as a former combat helicopter pilot, honorably wounded in battle during the Vietnam War, was to go down fighting in the basement of the Kentucky State Capitol Building while fending off women intent on getting to the bathroom.

After two days, the need to keep all but emergency workers out was over and we were relieved. Our little convoy went back to the armory where I turned the pistol and ammunition back in to the arms room. I went back to being a student and the route to the lady's room was opened again.

Just like in Vietnam, we withdrew and in the end they won.

A week later, I was called up again, this time for only one day as a pilot, not a security officer. I reported to Frankfort, this time without the rush and drama. One of our Hueys had been fitted out with a VIP kit: leather seat covers, fancy headsets, etc., and had been washed sparkling clean, or at least as sparkling as flat green aircraft paint gets. Our mission was to fly to Somerset, Kentucky, about 40 minutes away, where we would pick up the state governor and the adjutant general, an Air Force major general who was in charge of the Kentucky's Army and Air National Guard, and fly them on a tour of the path of one of the tornados so that they could observe the damage.

The damage throughout Kentucky and some of the neighboring states had been severe. Even our facility in Frankfort had been badly damaged. One of our helicopters had its greenhouse windows above the cockpit smashed and several others had dents in their fuselage tops from the hail. As soon as the storm had passed by the Aviation Facility, one of the full time technician pilots had fired up an undamaged Huey and took off following the storm to try to give additional warning as to where the tornado was headed.

Our flight down to Somerset was uneventful. It was a lovely, sunny day, but even on takeoff you could see widespread damage, starting right there in Frankfort. As we flew south, the paths of the storms were only too clear: trees, houses and barns smashed where the funnels had skipped along the ground. An hour after takeoff, we were on the ground in Somerset and, as the first order of business, had the Huey refueled so that we could give them 90 minutes of flight time, should the VIPs want it.

I walked over to the small terminal building to report we were ready to go. It was easy to spot the governor. He was the one amid the crowd of tobacco chewing farmers, laughing about something I could not hear. Upon seeing the general I stopped, came to attention, saluted, and reported we were ready to go.

The general laughed, probably at the fact that I had still retained some of my regular Army habits and had not yet truly become a guardsman, and then he returned my salute. The general and I knew each other from the three times I flew him from Frankfort back to his home town in western Kentucky. He was an Air Guard F-101 pilot, not a helo pilot like me. I, of course, let him fly the Jet Ranger we were traveling in and, of course, the closer we got to the ground the faster he wanted to go until at last, I had to take the controls, least he over torque the aircraft and damage the transmission. Hard to convince a jet guy that the helicopter is not going to stall and fall from the sky if you get it below 100 knots.

Beyond flying together, he remembered me because being not only a National Guard general, but also a former leader of both the Kentucky House and Senate, he had the successful politician's gift for names. Perhaps he also remembered the time when a group of Kentucky National Guard pilots retired to a bar owned by one of us there in Frankfort after night flying. We were all in flight suits, completely against the rules, but instead of reprimanding us he smiled and said, "have a drink on me, boys." He was in a flight suit too and I don't think he was supposed to be there either.

Being a politician was a real asset if you were to make high rank in the Guard. As we heard it, the general, in addition to being a former leader of both legislative bodies, was also a lieutenant colonel in the Air Guard when the governor jumped him three ranks from 0-5 (lieutenant colonel) to 0-8 (major general), by appointing him adjutant general of the state. As we understood it then, the US Air Force didn't recognize his new rank outside the state, but promoted him one rank a year, until at last his federal rank equaled his state rank.

Pushing through the small crowd in the terminal, the general spoke to the governor and they both turned toward the door. The governor hadn't quite made it all the way out the door when he stopped, turned again, and spoke to the small group of farmers standing around him.

"Say," the governor said, "Would any of you boys like to go flying with me in this here helicopter?"

"Why sure, Governor," said four of them nearly in unison and out they trooped with the governor toward the Huey.

When you have been called to state active duty, the governor is the commander in chief, just like the president is with the active duty forces and, within the limits of law, can do whatever he wants with those forces. If he wanted to take some tobacco chewing civilians with him on a tour of the damage, there was no reason why he could not.

I suppose I could have refused on the grounds that there weren't enough seats in the Huey to comfortably take that many passengers—most of the normal forward-facing, red nylon troop seats had been removed to install the two VIP red leather seats—but the governor wanted to take them and that was that. The governor and the general got the nice seats and the rest were crowded into the remaining troop seats on the side. We started up the aircraft and took off to see the damage. After takeoff, I looked back in time to see one of the famers spill tobacco juice from the spit can he was carrying on the deck of the Huey. Never mind, it will wash out. This aircraft was a UH-1D that had been converted to a UH-1H by adding a bigger engine along with a few other changes. It too was a Vietnam vet, and though it did not have any visible patched bullet holes like a lot of the aircraft did, it probably had far worse than tobacco juice spilled inside.

I hovered out to the runway and lowered the nose while pulling power. The Huey was lightly loaded, the wind directly on the nose, and so we were rapidly through translational lift and climbed quickly up to 500 feet. I was careful not to maneuver it too hard. The general was a pilot and accustomed to much harder turns than the Huey could make, but the governor and the farmers were not. No need to make anyone air sick, particularly with Kentucky's one and only VIP kit installed.

It wasn't hard to find the path of the tornado from 500 feet above ground—trees down, barns smashed, houses torn apart, all just a few miles from the airport. It looked like what I saw around Khe Sanh in Vietnam after the artillery and 500-pound bombs had done their work, only here it was in a line, not the more random destruction of war. Then we saw the unexpected among the ruins: the tornado had gone right through a whiskey distillery warehouse. Casks of bourbon were spread out across the fields all around the ruined warehouse for a distance of what looked to be at least a hundred yards.

The general looked over at the governor and said, "You know Governor, if we throw these farmers out we can get one of those barrels in this helicopter."

The governor replied instantly, "Shit, General, if I throw you out too, me and the crew can get two of those barrels in here. Haa, Haa, Ha!"

Although we were supposed to be keeping our minds on flying and not the VIP's conversation both my copilot and I started to laugh. Then the general joined in, but the farmers did not have headsets and could not hear the ICS, so they just looked alarmed as the aircraft rocked a bit as I laughed.

Then in a minute, the view of the destruction of people's lives came back to us and we laughed no more on that flight.

After an hour, we were finished with the tour of the disaster. I dropped the governor, the general, and the farmers off at Somerset. As he walked away from the Huey, the general turned and saluted us. We shut down, refueled again, started up and flew back to Frankfort, hovered into the parking spot, and shut the Huey down for the last time that day. As we walked back toward the Operations section, the ground crew was headed the other way to remove the VIP kit and bring it back to standard H model troop lift configuration. And to wash the tobacco juice off the floor . . .

My state active duty was over and the next day I was a student again.

# 16

# NATIONAL GUARD SUMMERS
## GULF PORT, MISSISSIPPI AND
## FORT EUSTIS, VA ■ JUNE 1974

---

*Normally the National Guard pilots do one weekend a month and two weeks in the summertime, summer camp, active duty, plus 24 AFTPs (Authorized Flight Training Periods). The AFTPs required that you spend four hours on duty and fly at least an hour to get credit (and pay) for a full day's duty. As a student I needed as much active duty as I could get, and if I could get an additional summer camp or an Army school, I would be in clover—two more week's full pay, including flight pay, would go far toward easing the next school semester.*

---

M y two summer camps in 1974 consisted of one real summer camp at Gulf Port, Mississippi, and then two weeks at the Army's Nuclear, Chemical, and Biological Warfare School at Fort Knox, Kentucky. The former was much more fun than the latter.

The actual summer camp would be first, then a two-week break back home before Fort Knox. My National Guard unit flew into Gulf Port, en mass—well, as much as four helicopters, two Hueys and two Kiowas can be called a mass—for our two weeks of active duty. Our National Guard U-6 Beaver, a high wing tail dragger built in Canada by de Havilland, very popular in Alaska and other rough areas, also came down, but since it cruises at 80 knots, it was even slower than our helicopters and so came on its own. The Beaver still beat us to Gulfport; though it was slower, it could hold its 80 knots for nearly six hours and so did not have to stop and refuel after every hour and a half of flight. For us helicopter pilots the flight down to Mississippi was particularly boring—clear weather, a couple fuel of stops and we were there. We did not fly into nearby Kessler Air Force Base but rather into the military half of Gulfport's civilian field a few miles away. Army pilots tend to avoid Air Force bases when they can. The US Air Force is just too different from the US Army for either group to be comfortable around the other when it comes to aviation; in those days it was way too serious. The Seabees had a base at Gulfport as did the Mississippi Air Guard, and we would be sharing it with them for our two weeks.

My billet, my job, in the Army National Guard was the best a young warrant officer could ever have: by billet, I was a pilot. Another WO-1 and I were the only "pilots" in the company, although six of the eight other officers were rated Army aviators. They had jobs like CO (commanding officer), XO (executive officer), shop officers, etc., but my friend and I were "pilots," with the job of flying the two Hueys or the two Kiowas to bring maintainers to aircraft down in the field, pick up parts when required, in the event of war. But in peacetime we only did our job when we flew a couple hours a day to keep our skills up and coincidently, to keep the CO and XO from assigning us other jobs.

At the Gulfport Seabee base, all the officers lived in a row of barracks converted from open squad bay into a series of double rooms. The junior officers, i.e. all the warrant officers, were two to a room, while the senior officers, the captains and our major CO, had private rooms. We two "pilots" were assigned the end room of the building. On the first night, we made an interesting discovery: we had the temperature control for the entire building in our room. We promptly closed off two of the three vents in our ceiling and then turned the dial on the thermostat down as low as it would go. We were just cool enough while the other officers froze all night.

Some mornings we "pilots" would sleep in until the mess hall was closed and miss breakfast. We would then fire up one of the Hueys, taking along whoever could get away from the day's scheduled events, and fly west down the Gulf Coast beaches to New Orleans Lakefront Airport. Lakefront, like Lunken in Cincinnati, had been New Orleans' main airport until air travel and the planes grew too large. Like Lunken, it was now the general aviation airport and also like Lunken, it had a restaurant. We would land, shut the Huey down, and all of us go inside to have a breakfast of biscuits and red eye gravy, New Orleans food fit for kings. Afterwards, we would fly east, low and slow back up the coast to Gulfport doing the beach patrol, waving back at the girls on the sand as we passed. We flew just off shore, low enough to see everyone and everything but not low enough to scare anyone.

Four days into the first week, my fellow "pilot" and I decided we would night fly, only instead of doing it in the evening as usual, we would do it in the morning. We got up at 0230 hours and walked over to the flight line. The OH-58A that we had been assigned was ready to go, so after a short preflight we were hovering out into the night at 0330 hours. Tower told us we were the only ones up and to enjoy ourselves, no need to call for each takeoff and landing. We called anyway and for some reason decided it would be good to use what we fancied a French accent. Tower just ignored us. We flew for two hours, basically until we had used up one load of fuel, and then hovered back in to the parking area and shut down. After finishing up the paperwork we walked over to the mess hall for breakfast. We were up early, so there was no need to fly down to New Orleans this morning, no matter how much fun it was.

We had finished our coffee when the XO walked in.

"Ah, just the man I was looking for. Pack up your gear and get ready to go. I'll send a jeep to bring it over to the flight line. When you are packed I'll see you at Ops," he said to me.

It seemed that the Military Aviation Repair Depot at Pensacola, Florida, had finished re-work on a couple of our Hueys three weeks early and was ready for us to pick them up and remove them from their flight line. Our mission was to fly them from Pensacola back to Frankfort. The XO had another mission for me to follow that one. After dropping off the Huey, I was to pick up an OH-58A and fly it on to Fort Eustis, Virginia where the other half of our company was undergoing training. It was going to be a very long day . . . .

I would be the copilot on the first leg, Gulfport to Pensacola. The AC and I briefed quickly (We are here. We are going there. Done) and after our gear was secured in the back of the OH-58A we started the aircraft and headed out to the east down the coast. After a smooth flight through the morning Gulf Coast haze, we arrived at the Depot an hour and a half later.

What a joy it was to see aircraft coming straight from the depot, before the oil stains from the various usual leaks, before the paint started to need

touchup, before the rotor blades were blasted from sand in landing zones. Even the Huey's interiors looked new, no marks on the dash, no crazing on the windshields or green houses. The new paint even gave them a new car smell. That would be gone by the time we got back to Frankfort, but they would stay beautiful for a month or two before they were just another aircraft on the ramp.

Despite the new aircraft look and smell, we gave these Hueys a very, very detailed preflight. We trusted the depot with our lives, but these aircraft were new to us, unfamiliar, so it was important to get to know them before we headed north. We found only the most minor of discrepancies, nothing that would keep us from flying them. An hour after we started our preflights, we were ready to go. We all wanted to get into Frankfort before dark because it is a long flight in a helicopter from Florida to Kentucky; not by flying standards, perhaps, but sitting in a cockpit for eight plus hours was no longer second nature to us.

I was flying with one of the senior officers in the company, an RLO, long past active duty. He was staying in the Guard as long as he could because Guardsmen, like Reserves, cannot draw retired pay until they reach 60, so why retire before you were forced to? Because my billet was "pilot," I signed for the aircraft and would be AC. The weather was typical southern summer, hot and sticky, with the possibility of afternoon thunderstorms, but suitable for visual flight rules (VFR) operations all the way north, so we filed a VFR flight plan as a flight of three.

We left Pensacola and headed north to our first refueling stop. We were flying H model Hueys, so we had around two hours of fuel, about one hour forty before we got to our visual flight rules (VFR) reserve. Both the D and H models hold 1,400 pounds of jet fuel and for planning purposes, burn 600 pounds per hour, but old pilots always distrust the fuel gauges and subtract 100 pounds for the wife and another 100 pounds for each kid. We all like H's better than the B's of earlier days. The H was longer, with seats for four more passengers, had a bigger, more powerful engine, and best of all, held more fuel. The B was at fuel reserves in one hour and twenty minutes, although that could be stretched if you took it very easy.

The B and L utility models and the C and M model gunships all had the short fuselage and small fuel capacity. Some crew chiefs back in Vietnam carried a foot-long piece of 4X4 lumber with them. When the aircraft went in for fuel, they would jump out and put the 4X4 under the back part of the right skid, tilting the aircraft to the left. This would let them put perhaps another five gallons of fuel in the tank, another few minutes of flying time.

That was the theory anyway . . .

---

*Our first stop was Birmingham, Alabama. I had been through Birmingham before, back when I was on active duty but before Vietnam. That flight too had been a ferry flight. At Fort Campbell, we had only six OH-13E Korean War veterans for helicopters. The Army decided we needed some more aircraft since many young aviators were being stashed there before being sent on to Vietnam. There wasn't enough flight time available for everyone to get the required four hours per month with only six helicopters. All the combat aircraft, i.e. those with turbine engines capable of carrying troops or weapons, were needed overseas, but some training aircraft, TH-13Ts, were available. So in March, 1970 two of us pilots and one maintainer were flown down to Fort Rucker to pick two and bring them up to Fort Campbell.*

*We felt honored to be ferried to the pickup site in the Fort Campbell U-8A, a twin-engine fixed-wing usually reserved for the commanding general's use. In short order, we were there at Cairns Army Airfield, Fort Rucker, Alabama. We stayed in the BOQ (Bachelor Officer's Quarters) there, the very first time I ever stayed in officer quarters and not in a barracks. After we checked into the BOQ, I took a walk down memory lane and visited the Warrant Officer Candidate area where I finished up my initial flight training. Nothing had changed in the six months since I graduated, except of course this time, I was an officer and a rated aviator, not a candidate—a good feeling. Early the next morning we caught a ride out to where our aircraft awaited: Hanchey Army Heliport, the largest airfield in the world devoted strictly to helicopters.*

*I had flown TH-13Ts on instrument training flights out of Hanchey like all the students who went through Fort Rucker did, but I was a student and only flew the aircraft once we had climbed out to altitude for instrument flight procedures training, no takeoffs or landings. The TH-13T had been fitted out with a full instrument flight panel, unlike its older cousin, the OH-13E that had no instruments beyond those for the engine and transmission. The "T"* model even had a side panel that pulled into place so that the student could not cheat by peeking outside the aircraft when he was supposed to be flying strictly by reference to the flight instruments. Instead of looking outside as normal, the student had to perform all maneuvers solely by scanning the attitude indicator, turn needle and ball, and the RMI (Radio Magnetic Indicator— a compass with two needles for navigation radios). Of course everyone tried to peek, pull out panel or not, since as the saying goes, "a single peek is worth a thousand scans"—unless of course you are actually in the clouds and there is nothing to peek at.

The upshot of the TH-13T's cockpit configuration was that unlike the OH-13E, you could not remove the doors when it got hot outside. The air coming in would scatter the papers the student needed to do instrument approaches and might interfere with the screen blocking the outside view, so the only ventilation was a small sliding window in the doors. Of course without the doors, the air would only come in when the aircraft was not in trim, but most students could not maintain good trim for more than a few seconds at a time anyway. So the doors remained on, and in the Fort Rucker, Alabama, summer, the heat was nearly unbearable while you were on the ground. Once a grease pencil, used to write radio frequencies on our kneeboards, melted in my hand, the black grease dripping on my leg.

The maintenance warrant officer at Hanchey shook our hands and said, "There are your aircraft. Get them off my Goddamn ramp."

I was expecting a checkout in the aircraft before being turned loose, but they figured that since we were qualified in OH-13E's, we were qualified in TH-13T's. This was not a good assumption. The OH-13E had flight boost (sort of a hydraulic power steering that makes the controls lighter to move) only on the cyclic, the collective had nothing and was fairly stiff to move. If you let go of the collective it stayed right where you left it. The 13T had flight boost on both. There was no lag when you rolled the throttle in an OH-13E. The TH-13T was turbocharged, i.e. it used exhaust gas to compress air going into the engine for combustion, much better at altitude since power did not decrease, but it had a turbo lag of what seemed to be a half second from the time you first rolled the throttle on until the power started to increase.

Climbing inside the TH-13T, I was assigned as the aircraft commander this time instead of a student. I vividly remembered all those flights six months *before, sweating in the sun while trying to figure out how to make the heli-copter do what I wanted it to do without looking outside. I did not remember how to start it because I had never started one before. I did not remember be-cause students never started the aircraft, the instructor started it, hovered it out, and made the takeoff. When you returned, the instructor made the land-ing and hovered the aircraft back to its parking spot. The student's job was to take over at altitude and complete the instrument maneuvers as directed. For-tunately for me this time, there was a checklist stuck in a side pocket so that I could figure out the starting sequence. It was close enough to the OH-13E that I managed without too much difficulty and got the aircraft started without breaking anything.*

*I was the wingman, Chalk Two, in this flight. The other pilot was far more experienced than I, so he would lead and I would follow. Our aircraft were parked across from each other and I could see him looking my way after we were both completely ready to fly. After a "thumbs up" from me, he made the call to ground control for taxi. We got clearance and started to hover out to the takeoff pad. Not used to the turbo lag, I was up and down like a yo-yo all the way out to the takeoff pad. Pull too much power and start to climb above the proscribed three feet, take it off and nearly settle back to the ground—up and down all the 100 yards to the pad. My face was burning be-cause in my head, I could hear the other pilots and ground personnel laughing. In retrospect, I doubt anyone laughed. I doubt anyone noticed because no one paid any attention to another TH-13T hovering out since they came and went all day, every day.*

*At the takeoff pad, I completed the checklist, at least the OH-13E checklist, never mind I was in a TH-13T. Tower cleared us for takeoff and I added power and began to climb out. Passing through 200 feet, Tower directed us to change to the en route control frequency. I released the collective to reach for the radio dial and found myself in autorotation, headed for the trees directly in front of the aircraft—rapidly headed toward them, the ground coming up fast.*

*I forgot that the TH-13T, unlike the OH-13E, had a fully boosted collec-tive. As noted earlier, let go of the collective on a 13E and the collective does not move. Without the "power steering" effect of the hydraulic system, the col-lective does not move until you move it. Not so on the TH-13T. Unless you friction down the collective (a wheel that lets the pilot adjust the feel of the collective from very light to completely locked), it will fall all the way down as soon as you release it; which is just what it did when I let it go and reached for the radio.*

*It only took a half second for the situation to register in my brain, but before we reached the trees, I had grabbed the collective back and cranked on throttle to get us climbing again. Tower noticed, "H-13 on takeoff, do you have a problem?"*

*"Negative, Tower. Switching frequencies," I replied without too much trembling in my voice. It didn't matter anyway because I had already lost all cool points for this flight. Not a good start to our three-day trip back to Fort Campbell.*

*All was well after that because I tightened the friction on the collective enough that I could move it, but it would not fall on its own.*

*Two other events kept this trip in my mind: the first came after our first refueling stop and RON in Montgomery, Alabama. We could have made it further but we had a late start after signing for and inspecting the aircraft. Also, we did not trust the fuel gauges on the aircraft since neither of us was really qualified in the TH-13T and had no feel for how much fuel it consumed per hour in cruise flight at 75 knots. It is better to do a real world fuel consumption check by seeing how much you burned in cruise, than it is to run out of fuel far from an airfield.*

*After the hour and a half it took to fly the 80 miles from Fort Rucker, we landed at the civil airfield instead of Maxwell AFB, because we were not required to use military bases and generally speaking, in those days, the civilians were friendlier to old, slow Army helicopters than the Air Force was. We hovered over to one of the FBOs—the people that provide fuel and maintenance for civil (and sometimes military) aircraft. As they usually did, the FBO had a pretty girl in a short skirt wave to get our attention and when we headed in her direction, she guided us into a parking spot. FBOs long ago figured out that pilots prefer pretty girls to greasy mechanics when it comes to ground directors. They sell a lot more fuel that way. We were no exception and followed her direction to their ramp. Besides the pretty ground directors, the FBOs also gave S&H Green Stamps (for those too young to remember, the stamps were part of a rewards program between the 1930s and the 1980s), but we weren't allowed to take them—might be considered a bribe.*

*After refueling, we put the covers on the helicopters to bed them down and checked into a motel for the night. The next morning, after preflight and checking weather, we took off on our second leg to Birmingham, Alabama. Our flight path took us directly over the downtown part of Birmingham. As I looked down at the city, I began to nearly panic. At Wolters and Rucker, the instructors taught us what do if your engine quits—how to do an autorotation under nearly all conditions.*

*If you must go into trees, you plan your flare (to provide an initial break to your very rapid rate of descent) high enough that you are just above the treetops when you have used up all that energy. As the airspeed is converted to lift and your fall stops, you level the nose and as you start to build a descent rate again, hold the helicopter steady so that you settle straight down into the trees. As your skids enter the branches pull, all the collective you have to slow your fall. You want to slow the rotor blades as much as possible before the trees take them off and turn them into projectiles.*

*If you must go into water with a dead engine, you jettison the doors on the way down if you can. Then as you approach the surface, do the same procedures you would do for going into trees, only when you touch the water, roll the helicopter to the left so that the blades hit the water and stop, then you can get out without getting hit by them.*

*But how do you autorotate into a city? Pick the building you want to hit and go toward it?*

*Francis Gary Powers, the U-2 pilot shot down over the USSR in the 1950s, faced this decision when years later, the engine on his traffic helicopter quit over a city. He picked the only open area he could reach in autorotation, but when he got close he could see the field was a playground full of children. Rather than risk hurting them, witnesses on the ground said that at the last second, it looked like he pushed the nose of the helicopter straight down. He impacted the ground short of the field. He died with honor.*

*As I cleared the city, the feeling of near-panic passed, but ever after, I avoided cities whenever possible. I didn't want to have to make the decision that Powers did.*

*The second reason I remember this flight is that my first near mid-air collision happened between Birmingham and Nashville. Near Muscle Shoals, I was cruising along at 75 knots and 1,000 feet when I saw a dot on the right side of the bubble, just a tiny black spot really. By the time I got my head turned the 45 degrees from straight ahead to 2 o'clock, I was looking at the underside of a jet fighter as it flashed by in what must have been a 90-degree bank. I read the word "NAVY" painted on the underside of his wings as he went by. He must have seen me a second or two before I saw him, giving him time to take evasive action. I had no time to do anything.*

*Three days and 9.3 flight hours after we left Fort Rucker, we parked the TH-13Ts next to their OH-13E older brothers.*

---

But now, five years later, I was headed north in a flight of three Huey's, freshly rebuilt from the depot, not old, tired TH-13Ts freed from duty as trainers. Instead of smelling of sweat and student fear like the TH-13Ts, the Hueys smelled of new paint and freshness. They also cruised at 110 knots, not 75. We made Birmingham in 1.8 hours. I remembered clearly the feeling of near-panic the last time I flew this way, but the turbine engine in the Huey made the fear recede almost completely away. Turbines don't quit as easily as reciprocating engines. In another 1.4 hours we were landing in Nashville for our second refueling stop. Then, 1.4 hours after Nashville, we were shutting down on our parking spots at the Boone National Guard Center in Frankfort, but the day was not over for me.

I called my wife and told her I would be at Bluegrass Field, Lexington's airport, in an hour and asked her to pick me up. I handed the Huey logbook to the maintenance man and picked up the logbook for the OH-58A, Bureau number 72-21287. I would be flying over to Lexington as soon as I was ready to go. I stowed my bag in the back seat and preflighted the Kiowa in the fading light. Forty-five minutes later, I was hovering out to the runway. Fifteen minutes after that I was landing at Bluegrass, with my wife and son already there waiting for me.

Eighteen clock hours and 8.3 flight hours after I woke up in Gulfport, my day was over. Just like I had been three years before in Vietnam, I was tired, so tired. But the next day, after my son and wife waved goodbye, I flew the OH-58A solo from Lexington, Kentucky, to Fort Eustis, Virginia. Well, not actually Fort Eustis, since we were told not to bring the aircraft into the Army airfields there because there was no ramp space available. Instead, I was to fly into Newport News, the closest civilian field.

I flew across the Appalachians in Kentucky, West Virginia, and Virginia using a road map and the Cincinnati and Washington Sectional Aeronautical Charts since the aircraft had no navigation radios. It was a boring flight since not only did I have no one to talk to, I could not listen to commercial AM radio because the OH-58A did not have an automatic direction finder (ADF). Since I was not in a hurry, I stopped for refueling in Charleston, West Virginia; Roanoke, Virginia; Lynchburg, Virginia; Navy Norfolk, Virginia; and finally at Newport News. I had arrived for the second half of summer camp after 5 hours of flight time on the second day, for a total of 13.3 for the trip from Gulfport, the most flight time I got in two days in my three years as a Kentucky National Guardsman. Four days later, I flew the OH-58A back to Kentucky with only two fuel stops, Lynchburg and Bristol, Tennessee. My sectionals and road map worked fine for navigation aids both going and coming home. Who needs navigation radios when you have these?

Just under one year later, on June 14, 1975, I flew my final flight in an Army aircraft. It was a very old UH-1B, Bureau Number 60-03562, with the big red buzz numbers still on the doors from its days as a student training aircraft at Ft. Rucker, from Ft. Campbell. I was the copilot on the flight back to the Boone National Guard Center because the other pilot wanted to do a fly-by of the house of a girl he had met the night before. His detour meant that we burned more fuel than we should have, so when we landed at Frankfort after 1.9 hours of flight in a helicopter usually only good for 1.5, there were only fumes left in the fuel tank.

National Guard Mission complete. Luck and superstition got me through again.

Ah, youth . . .

# FLYING LIFE THREE

## THE MARINE CORPS
## 1975–1993

*Ever since reading F. Lee Bailey's "The Defense Never Rests" in Vietnam, I wanted to be a lawyer. With high test scores on the law school admission test, I applied to two law schools and was accepted by both. While walking through the Student Center two days before the deadline for accepting an offer, I saw a film clip of military aircraft flying. It was the USMC Officer Selection Officer, looking for recruits. As we talked I thought back to Covington, Kentucky, seven years before. This time there would be no" rice paddies and all the VC I could kill." I would be an officer and aviator. After all, F. Lee Bailey had been a naval aviator before he was a lawyer, so I could do it, too. You are never too old to go to law school, but you can get too old for flying. That evening I asked my wife what she thought about it and when she said flying stories were more interesting than law stories, I knew she was right. I turned down law school and enlisted in the USMC.*

# 17

# NIGHT VISION GOGGLES
## YUMA, ARIZONA ■ AUGUST 1978

---

*To learn tactics and advanced tactics is complicated and requires an extended period of flying with experienced pilots. Once the officer has advanced completely through the syllabus in the squadron, and has shown promise as an instructor, he may be sent to Weapons Tactics Instructor (WTI) School, the most prestigious flying course I ever attended—and the most fun . . .*

---

The second Marine Aviation Weapons and Tactics Instructor class at Marine Weapons and Tactics Squadron-1 (MAWTS-1), conducted at Marine Corps Air Station, Yuma, Arizona in the fall of 1978, was going very well indeed. All the students were very experienced aviators, and aviation support personnel from all portions of Marine Corps air wing had been hand selected for their skill and were to be the future trainers of the Marine Corps tactical pilots and air controllers. As the instructors always told us when they had something particularly difficult in mind for us to do: "we were the cream of the crop—never again would we be as technically and tactically proficient in our aircraft, as Marines, as we would be when we graduated from this course."

But even the cream of the crop can make mistakes.

On the first day of class, the major who was the lead helicopter instructor walked in flanked by two of his assistant instructors. One assistant was ceremoniously carrying a frozen chicken and the other was carrying a feather pillow held out reverently before him in both hands.

"Gentlemen," the chief instructor began, "You will shortly all be issued one of these chickens and a pillow. If by chance, you should happen to hit a saguaro cactus while flying in this course, you will land your helicopter immediately, stuff the chicken in the hole, and cut open the pillow with your survival knife, sprinkle feathers all around, and swear you had a bird strike. Are there any questions about this procedure?"

It seems a student in the last class had hit an endangered cactus, thereby damaging his CH-53 and coincidentally giving away the fact that he was flying lower than allowed, "flat hatting," as it is called in Naval aviation. It has been a problem since the first aircraft got off the ground. It often leads to a situation where the pilot "ties the record for low flying." You can't break the record but when you impact the surface you do tie it, adding your name to the way-too-long list of pilots who died doing something they knew they shouldn't.

Mid-way through the four-week course we went into the main classroom for instruction on "Night Vision Goggles" (NVG). None of us students had ever heard of "Night Vision Goggles" until we got to Yuma, but if they would help us see better for night missions, we were all for them. Every aviator has scary stories about night flight or "night fright," as it was often called, as witnessed by the night firebase resupply and flare drop missions I had flown. One saying went that only bats and twats flew at night, leaving which we were open for discussion. MAWTS-1 had every single pair of NVGs the Marine Corps owned at that time, 20 sets in all.

One rule every soldier must know is that tracers work both ways; that is, you can see where your bullets are going but the enemy can see where they are coming from. The same is true for light sources like flares or searchlights. You may be able to see the enemy using them, but they can see you too. NVGs allowed us to see the enemy, but because they are passive, the enemy could not see the source of what was providing us with vision.

The goggles are passive because they work by amplifying ambient light. The first generation NVGs really needed moonlight, the more the better. Starlight worked somewhat if it was a very clear night, but not very well to see clearly through the lenses. NVGs were not originally developed for flying. The original units were monocular "Starlight" scopes developed for use by snipers in Vietnam. Other original uses included vehicle drivers, sentries, etc., who used the goggles instead of artificial light. The ones we would use were developed for vehicle drivers and had not been modified for us in aircraft.

After a lecture on light frequencies, emergency removal procedures, and how to mount the NVGs on our helmets, the WTI cadre passed out the goggles. They were very heavy, so much so that they had to be counterbalanced to keep you from injuring your neck by just wearing them. The twenty-eight ounces of dead weight hanging on the front of your flight helmet had to be balanced by lead plates hung on the back of your helmet using Velcro attachments. We had to have our helmets modified so that we could strap the goggles on and then snap them down so they wouldn't fall off in flight. The staff stressed how important it was to take good care of them because they were very expensive and delicate; never mind, as they reminded us over and over again, that the few sets they handed out to us were every pair the Marine Corps owned.

As mentioned, the NVGs work by taking existing light and amplifying it. The pilot sees two round images, one for each eye, on what is, in effect, a miniature monochrome green-tinted television screen. The NVGs could be adjusted for diopter and focus. Actually, they had to be adjusted for focus when you wanted to look from outside the aircraft to inside the cockpit. This first generation NVG was "full face," meaning that when they were attached to your helmet you could not see around them, the pilot could only see through them in two circles of green light that provided only 40 degrees of vision. The NVGs also were designed to protect themselves by momentarily shutting down when exposed to too much light, thus preventing tube burnout. More on this later . . .

Our instructors were confident, even though they had barely more experience with NVGs than we did. At least they did what all military aviators always do, and acted cool in the face of a very new procedure, as in "death before embarrassment." As the head of the Helicopter Branch explained, "This is going to be a little harder than usual, but you guys can hack it." We agreed because we were all "hackers" or we wouldn't be there—and because, being aviators ourselves, we too were acting cool.

At the preflight mission briefing, a light should have come on or alarm bells gone off inside our heads when the instructor said, "Normally, you wouldn't want to do this unless the moon was a little higher and brighter." In the Marine Corps, a statement like that almost guarantees something bad is going to happen. It is almost like Marines aren't happy unless there is some pain, physical or psychological, in all events. But the briefing officer again stressed that we were the cream of the crop and could handle it.

That was the theory anyway . . .

My instructor and I had grown to be friends during the time I had been at MAWTS-1. Like me, he had flown in Vietnam, Marine 46s instead of Army 47s, in I Corps, the northern-most part of the country, just like me. He too had lots of total flight time and was very relaxed about the whole WTI thing, be it going one-on-one with fighters, nap-of-the-earth flying, evading missiles, flying on NVGs, whatever. He also had a slight tendency to stutter occasionally, but it was never a problem, since it mostly happened when he was drinking and no matter what, he did not drink and fly.

After going through the normal crew briefing, preflight, and start up, we taxied our CH-46F out to the runway and took off for Laguna Army Airfield, to the northeast of Yuma. I can't say the crew chief and first Mec (mechanic, a crew chief in training) were very happy about it because anything new made them uncomfortable, and the NVGs were definitely new, but they trusted us enough to get in the back of the helicopter and go flying. Or perhaps I should say that they were Marines and did as ordered. In either case, it was full darkness when we landed at Laguna to "goggle up" and get that training "X" in the box. Only the pilots would be on NVGs, since we did not have enough for the crew to wear them too, meaning that even though we might be able to see, the crew had only blackness to look at, yet another thing that made them less than happy. The sky was clear but the moon, forecast to be small and low, was nowhere to be seen as we started our training evolution.

After landing in the sand next to the runway at Laguna, I held the flight controls while the instructor rigged our aircraft. As they told us in ground school training, these early NVGs were very sensitive to certain portions of the light spectrum, particularly the red portion. Unfortunately it was the same red commonly used in aircraft to preserve pilot's night vision, so the red of our normal cockpit lighting would cause the lenses to shut down to protect themselves from overload and burnout. In fact, any bright light in the visual spectrum would shut them down. They warned us in class that if the NVGs were getting too much light, they would show what looked like a test pattern and shut themselves down. When the light source was removed or you looked away from it, the NVGs would come back on in about five seconds.

Five seconds is a very long time when you are close to the ground in a helicopter and cannot see outside the cockpit.

After completing the taping over of all our cockpit lights (a pin hole was left in some of the taped over lights, e.g. the fire warning lights, the master caution lights, etc., so that we would know when they came on and we had an emergency), the instructor put his goggles on. As I watched him, I noticed that it was a moderately "dark" night. Yes, there was finally a moon but it was only a thin sliver, just above the mountains. I hoped this wouldn't be too bad, but had a lot of confidence in my own ability and after all, I had one of those "God-like" instructors in the other seat. He wouldn't let anything bad happen to us.

The instructor took the controls and told me to put my own goggles on. It took me a lot longer than it took him, since I was doing it only for the second time. I finally got them on and was looking out the right cockpit window, trying to adjust them when I saw another CH-46 go past us, just outside our rotors at about what seemed like 40 or 50 knots, flying backwards.

The instructor saw it too and was on the radio immediately, "46 on Luguna, you're drifting backwards. YOU ARE DRIFTING BACKWARDS! You damn near ran us over!" he yelled into the mic. No stutter in his voice that time.

The pilot of the other helo "rogered" our call with only a minor shake in his voice to betray his fear at not knowing where his helicopter was going, and although we could no longer see them, he assured us that they were stabilized. It was another warning we did not pay attention to. If he can't see, what made us think we could? Ah, we're hackers and he isn't. That must be it.

Our crew chief had been listening to the radios and called from the back, "Got them in sight. They're well clear." That helped, but it was not a good start and promised that this would not be an easy flight.

I now had my goggles on and mostly adjusted, and while I could see a green, snowy picture of the world outside the cockpit of the 46, I could not see very much else. I also could not see my hands or the instruments. The green toilet paper tube-like, circular view through the twin lenses of the NVGs was only 40 degrees, not the 180 plus pilots normally have.

The instructor had me get on the controls with him as he pulled the aircraft up into a hover. I felt slightly disoriented as we lifted but followed him through as he moved the cyclic stick and collective. It was strange not being able to see the stick with my peripheral vision as he maneuvered the aircraft. I felt disconnected from normal reality and disoriented. No problem though, I was with an instructor . . .

He did a few hovering turns and then sat the aircraft back down, only bouncing slightly. I could not see well enough to tell if we wobbled or not when we were in a hover. I had adjusted one eye to focus inside the cockpit and one eye to focus out, like they told us in class. Since the man flying had to adjust both eyes out of the cockpit to see where he was going, he could not see any of the instruments to tell how high he was, how fast he was going, how much power he had pulled in, what course he was on, or anything else. The other pilot watched all those with his one eye and called them out to the man at the controls. With the other eye, he would look out the window to make sure they weren't about to fly into another aircraft or a mountain.

That was the theory anyway . . .

The instructor lifted the helicopter into a hover again and when I told him "all green" he nosed the aircraft forward for takeoff. As we climbed out, I called altitudes and airspeeds. In that trip around the traffic pattern, both altitude and airspeed varied to the point where it was like the first time a new flight student tried it in flight school, even though an experienced helicopter aircraft commander (HAC) was flying. After a shaky landing, he passed me the controls and it was my turn. I felt the seat cushion start up my rear end as the pucker factor kicked in.

I was apprehensive, but, by God if he could do it, so could I. After adjusting my goggles so that both eyes were focused outside the aircraft, I took the controls and pulling power, wobbled into hover. I couldn't see my hands or the stick position indicator to see how far back the stick was as I added collective. Until that moment, it had never occurred to me that pilots, or at least helicopter pilots, actually see the position of the flight controls with their peripheral vision and use that as a reference of where they should be for the maneuver.

As we lifted up, I could not tell how high we were, I had no idea if we were in the prescribed 10-foot hover or were at 50 feet or 2 feet. I knew we were drifting in our hover, even though I was using all the experience and skill gained over nine years of helicopter flying to try to keep us steady. I was trying to crush the cyclic grip and my legs were ridged on the pedals. Taking a deep breath and slowly blowing it out, I tried to relax some.

I finally was more or less stabilized in a hover when a car on the outskirts of the airfield turned toward us and his headlights hit the cockpit. As advertised in class, my goggles went blank. No, not really blank, blank. Just as the instructors told us, all I could see was what looked like a green fuzzy test pattern of the sort TV stations used to show when they weren't on the air.

"You've got it. I can't see anything!" I said to the instructor as calmly as I could over the intercom. Death before loss of cool!

The instructor must have been looking away when the car lights hit us because he answered, "I can see. I've got it," and I felt his hands come on the controls. Still looking away from the car, he pedal-turned the helicopter to the left—directly toward the lights of a hanger. My goggles, which had been coming back to normal after being off for five seconds, went blank again.

"Can you see?" he yelled through the intercom. No attempt at cool this time.

"No," I replied immediately.

"Shit," was all he said.

Having no further ideas about what to do, the instructor just put the collective down, removing all power from the aircraft. We hit hard but level, and apparently we had landed on a clear spot, because the helicopter stayed upright. Marine Corps helicopters are designed to land hard on the decks of ships and we tested the design on that landing. From the back, we could hear the crew chief give a sort of primal scream. We could hear him over the aircraft noise. He had no goggles and the night was dark enough for him not to be able to see outside the aircraft, but he could hear us talking on the ICS.

We stayed on the ground, still in goggles, while the crew chief checked the aircraft for damage. We all decided the landing was not as hard as other landings we'd done on pitching ships, because the "crash lights"—passenger compartment emergency lights that automatically come on at 3.5 G (G-force or gravitational force)—had not illuminated. The fact that we were off the runway and in the dirt helped, too; dirt is much softer than cement or steel deck plating. Fortunately, as noted earlier, it was level dirt and did not have a tree growing out of it. No damage, this time . . .

When our hearts were under control, we lifted off to a hover again, still on the NVGs. I managed to takeoff and get it around the pattern, at least as well as the instructor had done. Not much to be proud of, but at least it was something. For much of the time while we were in the air, we could not really tell how high we were, or our course, and we relied instead on the flight engineer to vector us back to the runway as he looked out into the darkness without the "benefit" of goggles. "Come right. Roll out. Left, steady." Our hearts weren't in it though, so after 15 more minutes, we landed, and one at a time, pulled the goggles off. We went home without them, much to everyone's relief.

The next time we went NVG flying the conditions were better, with more moonlight and a darker airfield. Even the "cream of the crop" needed a moon with the first generation of goggles, especially when the goggles were full face, and not the "cut aways" that soon were developed and fielded.

Those first generation NVGs were the very same ones that the pilots were using at Desert One when the MH-53 hit the C-130 in the Iranian desert on 24 April 1980.

Sometimes it seems like luck and superstition does not always work, but for me they did on my first NVG flight. Luck and superstition were still with me on my last NVG flight in 1988 too, but that is another story.

# 18

# MARINE CORPS NIGHT FLIGHT

## USS *GUAM* ■ JUNE 1979

---

*The noise and red-lit instruments are nearly overpowering to
your racing mind. The world seems upright but you just can't
tell by the feeling in your ass when the world consists entirely of
the red glow in the cockpit and blackness outside the windows.
You could be slicing toward the sea in a hard bank or going
backwards or both. Or, everything could be as it was supposed
to be, the aircraft level at 300 feet above the sea and holding
the proper speed.*

*Outside the cockpit, the world is completely black, as black
as if someone had thrown black paint over the windshield and
your eyes were closed and you are screaming to yourself, "Oh
God, I don't want to be here! Let me be somewhere else, anywhere, don't make me try to control this helicopter, let someone
else do it because I can't, I just fucking can't tell up from down,
right from left, the sea from the sky, the noise sounds like the
helicopter is going to tear itself apart in the turn, Oh God," but
you say none of these things. You only stare at the familiar mass
of instruments on the dash and fight the panic within. The rest
of the aircrew has no idea what is going on in your head as you
try to remain in control, except every one of them has felt, or is
right now feeling, the same feelings. Maybe they feel them this
time or maybe they don't, but no one says anything and the helicopter moves in the darkness toward another landing on the
ship.*

---

All living ships have a hum that never stops. But, just like city noise,
when you live aboard, you don't really hear it, especially during the
day; only at night when the other noises are quiet, you discover that it is
there. All Navy ships also lean slightly to one side or the other. The USS

*Guam* listed a couple degrees to starboard but unless you thought about it, you never noticed after you had been on board for a while. Like a pain you have had for years, you don't really feel it any more even if it is always there. We swore the *Guam* was the worst of ships and made up acronyms to match the letters G U A M. "Go UA (unauthorized absence) man." "Give Up And Masturbate." Though truth be told, in retrospect, the *Guam* was a pretty good ship to live aboard and to fly from.

At sea, we speak in code, or actually shorthand, much like the verbal shorthand we use internally among the crew when talking over the radio. Altitudes below 1000 feet are broken down in 100-foot increments called "cherubs"—cherubs three would be 300 feet. One thousand feet and above are called "Angels." The radio frequencies are color coded, i.e., red for the Tower, purple for Center. The actual frequencies may change but the colors remain the same. The ship is "Mother." The TACAN, the radio beacon carried by larger ships, is "our Father." The ship's course is "BRC," short for Base Recover Course. "Buster" means go as fast as you can, and "Pigeons" means the course from the aircraft to its destination. The most important is "State," how much fuel you have left. State is given in "Time to splash," self-explanatory (most pilots subtract a little time as a "fudge factor," say five minutes for the wife, and another five for each child). "Souls" are the number of personnel onboard the aircraft.

The men who work on the deck of a ship also dress in different colored flotation vests, called "shirts" even though they are really vests and matching color "cranials," a protective helmet with built-in sound attenuator cups to protect their hearing. The numerous varieties of shirts allow everyone to see at a glance what a particular person's role is. The yellow-shirted landing signal enlisted (LSE) stands in front of the deck spot where the helicopter is to land and gives hand signals to direct the pilot over the three painted squares where the helicopter's wheels are to go. The LSE also directs the blue-shirted aircraft deck handlers who install/remove the chocks and chains to keep the aircraft from rolling on a moving deck. The men who refuel aircraft wear purple shirts. Medical personnel wear white vests with red crosses on them, while cargo handlers and the men who lead passengers to their helicopter wear plain white shirts. Squadron maintenance personnel wear green shirts. No one ever goes out onto the flight deck during Flight Operations without a cranial and vest, no one.

My squadron had joined the ship a week before as part of a Marine Expeditionary Unit, a MEU—pronounced "mew"—that would provide the landing force for the Sixth Fleet (LF6F) in the Mediterranean for the next six months. Our on-load off the coast of Beauford, North Carolina, was the usual controlled chaos and the usual success. Tonight is the first night that the weather has been even marginally within limits for the practice of night landings or Carrier Qualifications—CQs—required if the squadron is to remain combat-ready.

The aircraft we flew out to the *Guam* all had official names, military names like, the CH-46E "Sea Knight" or the AH-1T "Sea Cobra" or the CH-53D "Sea Stallion." The "Sea" part identified them as Naval, or in this case Marine Corps, aircraft. But, as always their crews called them less lovely, less aggressive names.

The CH-53D Sea Stallion is the "Shitter," shortened from "Shuddering Shithouse," in honor of the normal high level of vibration the bird produced when hovering, taking off, and landing. But the crews often just called it a "Hog," because close in to the deck, fighting the wind bouncing off the island and up over the flight deck it wallows like a hog might do in the mud. Once, a CH-53 wallowed badly enough when attempting to do a normal landing on board the *Guam,* that the pilot hit the scupper (drain channel around the flight deck) with one of his main landing gear wheels hard enough to put a major dent in the scupper's steel wall.

The AH-1T Sea Cobra is a "Snake" to its crews, slim and deadly, but wobbly over the flight deck spot and top heavy for its narrow skids. The missions of Cobra pilots does not involve the constant landings and take-offs that cargo pilots do, so they are sometimes not as proficient. The cargo pilots love to critique the Cobra pilots' landings, particularly when we are flying out of a landing zone in the middle of nowhere.

The CH-46E Sea Knight is a "Frog" or "Phrog" to its crews and nearly everyone else. Sitting on its wheels it seems to be squatting, and when it ground taxies it looks like it is awkwardly trying to hop to the runway. The Frog is not lovely to anyone except its crew.

The UH-1N is just another Huey. All models of the UH-1 series have been called "Hueys" since the original Army models were delivered with

"HU-1" for "helicopter utility model 1" stamped on their rudder pedals. The Huey is the most produced helicopter the United States has built and comes in many models. I flew the A, B, C, D, E, H, K, L, and M models, all single-engine versions.

My Marine composite squadron that embarked on the *Guam* had 12 Phrogs, four Snakes, Four Shitters, and two Hueys, a normal mix for an MEU. The crews that flew the aircraft ranged from twenty-four-year-old lieutenants to the "old man," the lieutenant colonel commanding officer at forty-four.

Just forward of the gray steel wall of the "island," that part of the ship that sticks up above the flight deck on the starboard (right) side, on the 02 level (the level just below the flight deck), the crews gathered for their briefings and debriefings in ready room 2. The lights in the ship's ready room 2 were supposed to be red during Night Ops so that the pilots' eyes would have time to night adapt. But on the *Guam*, half of the lights were out and some of those that were working put out more white than red so the effect was not what was intended. It was just shabby, not like a place where men prepared to go night flying or to combat. In the front of the ready room, the red lights did not work at all so the operations duty officer (ODO) had the whites on so he could see to do his paperwork.

The ready room briefing chairs were covered in gray vinyl and very heavily padded, so that in theory at least, you could wait in comfort for the next mission. They were also like school desks from many years ago, except the chairs had gray metal frames instead of light colored wood and the swing-over side arms were metal too. No way to carve your name into them, but the paint was always missing in places, making them worn looking. When the reclining mechanism worked, the chairs could lean back at a comfortable angle, again so the crews could relax while awaiting their launches, ready to scramble to face the incoming enemy. But like the red-dark adaptation lights, some chairs worked and some didn't.

There were two ready rooms side by side on the 02 (Oh Two) deck, one used by the aircrews and the other by maintenance. Nine rows of eight chairs each with an aisle down the middle determined the seating capacity of the ready rooms. The one used by the aircrew was toward the stern of the ship. In the front of the ready room, toward the center of the ship, was the ODO desk with two telephones, and behind him were the boards, some Plexiglas-covered aluminum sheets, others chalk boards. The boards slid out, one after another to show weather, radio frequencies, aircrews and the aircraft they would fly, and other bits of information the pilots would need for tonight's mission. In front, on the wall near the ceiling, was the 1MC, the ship's loudspeaker system, and the five position speaker that was the ship's entertainment system.

The briefing for night CQs was done at the time listed on the flight schedule, as were the morning briefing and the afternoon briefing. The aircrews did their Naval Air Training and Operating Procedures Standardization Program (NATOPS—sometimes referred to by more senior aviators as "Not Applicable to Old Pilots") briefs, and the first crews went up to the twilight to preflight their aircraft. The entire night CQ briefing process had the air of a Roman Catholic mass; the normal relaxed atmosphere of a daytime mission brief was not there, not for a dark night launch like tonight. The rituals that must be obeyed are the same whether day or night, but the rituals are more solemn at night. At night, they are more than pro forma. Checklists are recited like church hymns learned long ago, and like the hymns, the words the checklist called for were said only by rote, with nearly all meaning gone. And if the pilots did not follow their ritual, they would feel guilty, perhaps without even knowing why. But that did not happen at night, not in the middle of the Atlantic, on a hazy night with moderate visibility and fairly strong winds. This is too real for rote.

Following the prayers in the brief, the crews moved out onto the deck for the second ritual, preflighting the aircraft. Each aircraft panel would be opened, connections tugged on, bearings checked, oil and hydraulic levels checked, and so on until the pilots had checked the entire aircraft. Unlike fixed wing pilots who mostly just walk around to see if the panels are closed, helo crews check and re-check everything, even after the crew chief has checked it all before in even greater detail and signed the bird ready to fly. Helicopters do not have ejection seats and the crew does not have parachutes. Not that they would open anyway since helicopters almost never fly high enough for a parachute to work, so where the helicopter goes, also goes the crew . . .

On the Phrog, the HAC always does the bottom and inside of the aircraft while the copilot does the top. The HAC shines his flashlight into those places nearly invisible in the dim light that a fading day leaves inside the helicopter. Outside, he dodges the chains as he walks around the aircraft clockwise, from the crew door aft, checking the landing gear and fuel tanks and lower parts of the aircraft.

The aluminum helicopter skins are nearly always slick from spilled oil, hydraulic fluid, salt spray, and spots on top of the fuselage are worn shinny from the feet of the crew chiefs and maintenance personnel. Checking the top means the copilot must climb the side of the helicopter using the small, oily foot wells, to the top of the aft pylon, crossing his legs over each other until he is 18 feet above the steel deck. Because the aircraft are parked in the "bone" (the area where aircraft are parked on the deck between flights), with their sterns hanging out past the edge of the deck, the copilot is now 70 feet above the dark sea. Fading light and high winds add a difficulty factor and make it more interesting. After all the appropriate things are examined, pulled, tugged, etc., the panels would be closed up by the crew chief, whose movements are much more smooth than the pilots, with a grace developed from countless trips. Then the crew chief, using a stubby screwdriver, closes the deus fasteners (the large headed screws), securing the panels.

About 15 minutes before launch, the aircraft is moved from the boneyard to one of the spots on the deck. A flight deck crew of four men comes with a yellow tow tractor and hooks the helicopter up, tow bar to helicopter nose wheel. The flight deck crew consists of a tractor driver and a Landing Signal Enlisted person (LSE) or "yellow shirt" (since this is the color designated for this role) who will lead the entire process, and two wing walkers to walk beside the helicopter and signal it is clear of obstacles as it is moved across the deck. One or both of the pilots sit in the cockpit to release the brakes when signaled, and to lock and unlock the nose wheel as the LSE directs. When the aircraft is on the designated spot, the chalks and chains are replaced and the process of preparing for launch continues.

If not already strapped into the cockpit seats, the pilots do so now and begin the third major ritual of each flight, the checklist. Usually the copilot or H2P (helicopter second pilot) calls and the HAC answers, a responsive reading much like the psalms in church services. Light signals from the pilots to the LSE, standing clear of the rotor blades at the 2 o'clock position from the cockpit, are required for each major event, like starting the auxiliary power unit (APU), spreading the blades, starting the engines and engaging rotors. If they don't already have them on when the APU comes on line, the crew puts on their helmets against the noise. If they weren't already, they now all become far more serious about their upcoming task.

Like all military aviators, Marine pilots come in three classes: first—new guys, like the first-cruise lieutenants; second—confident, second or third cruise captains, tactical and proficient, with their reflexes at their sharpest; and third—the older field grade officers, majors and perhaps a few lieutenant colonels, with many cruises under their belts, but not flying as much as they once did, responsibility and age having caught up with them. Their eyes are now behind prescription lenses, maybe even bifocals and their reflexes are slower than ten years ago, not that they would admit it. "Age and treachery beat youth and skill," they say, but they know in their hearts it is often not true.

The first crews would launch into "pinky time." It is that time right after official sunset, a twilight that lets you still see enough to maintain some small level of comfort. Strapped into a sea of cockpit sound—the howling, shaking helicopters—the pilots lift off before it is completely dark. The time between official sunset and true darkness allows the first pilots to get their six landings that are required to keep current for Night Operations. The second and third copilots trade places with the preceding pilots, "hot seating," and go from the semi-red lit ready room into the dim red cockpit, surrounded by complete blackness.

The first launch was usually reserved for two of the three classes of pilots, brand new guys on their first cruise, and field grade officers: the new guys, to make their training as tension-free as possible until they were ready for the hard stuff, and the field grade, because, well, because they were senior. The second and particularly the third—the dark-dark launches—went to the senior lieutenants and captains, the ones theoretically at the peak of their proficiency. The easy early launch in pinky time is called "field grade night," in honor of the more senior officers flying then. The much more difficult dark launches or launches into shitty weather are "company grade night."

I was a captain and left the ready room 15 minutes before my dark-dark launch. This was my third Mediterranean cruise and the 16th year I had been flying helicopters, all of which put me firmly in the second and third launch, "company grade," category. And that is why I left early enough to try and gain some feeling of what the night held before it was my turn to fly.

The interior passageway, leading to the flight deck and on upward to the bridge and control tower, was marked by a shinny stainless steel door, a disguised hatch really. Normally the commodore (in the Navy, the commodore is almost, but not quite, an admiral), who commands the entire LF6F five-ship flotilla, uses this passageway, but because LPH's like the *Guam* are relatively small, there might not be a passage exclusively for his use. Working the wheel that sealed the hatch closed, I opened it and stepped into the red darkness of the ladderwell. Up one level, I came to a black hole that was the way to the flight deck. Feeling my way between the flat black painted aluminum "blackout panels" that kept inside light from projecting into the outside blackness, I found the hatch onto the deck and opened it. Very effective, blackout panels—almost make you think you've gone blind.

As required by all the regulations and rules of the flight deck, not to mention basic common sense, I had on full flight gear, helmet, gloves, survival vest with built-in Mae West floatation vest, steel-toed flight boots, and zippered-up flight suit. The clear, plastic visor on my helmet was down against the wind that blew across the flight deck, and ear cups muffled the sound. I always felt somehow insulated from all the elements in full gear, disassociated from the reality of the deck, almost like watching a movie. The deck itself was awash in the normal vague red glow, marked here and there by the yellow flashlight wands held by the LSEs and the rotating beacons on the wall that show the status of the deck: green for ready, red for foul.

The blast of rotor wash from a landing CH-46E hit me as I opened the hatch and I had to hold on hard to keep from being blown off my feet. When the Frog settled unevenly on the deck, the wind died somewhat, and I stepped out onto the black non-skidded deck and secured the hatch behind me. Carefully staying inside the foul line, the painted white line marking the safe area of the flight deck from the operational area, and avoiding the chains lying on the deck, I walked forward past the Flight Deck Officers' shack to the front bone. I found a spot near a tow tractor to lean on the steel wall of the island and watch Flight Operations.

Only one aircraft was on deck at that time. The steady dim of its position lights, a red glow from the cockpit, and two circles of greenish light from the Phrogs blade tip lights were the only light on the deck besides the dimness of the deck lights. A few red, anti-smash lights, off the port side in the sea of black beyond the red-lit flight deck were visible. No stars, no moon, no horizon, and only a hint of dim ship lights astern—a real "company grade" night, meaning that only the young and experienced need apply. The majors and higher, the "field grade" officers, got the moonlit, cloudless nights.

Another CH-46 followed the LSE's wands into Spot Five, wobbled over the deck, and finally settled onto the spot, more or less on the three-by-two-foot square white boxes painted on the deck that marked where the wheels were supposed to, but often did not, rest. If the wheels were exactly on the spot, there was more than adequate clearance between the rotor blades of the helicopters occupying the spots up and down the flight deck. Because it was so easy to miss the painted spots, the pilots often joked that they marked "weak spots in the deck and should be avoided at all times."

---

*To see the importance of this small clearance, you only have to walk to the area of the* Guam's *deck between spots five and seven and look at the creases in the flight deck steel that still remain from the time, a few years before, when a CH-53D drifted backwards into the turning blades of another Hog. When the first Shitter's tail rotor hit the main rotor blades of the second, it crashed and rolled on its side before spilling out its fuel. Both aircraft burned, their flames lighting off the spilled fuel that ran down the side of the ship into the hanger deck. Men died in the crash and fire but prompt action by the ship's crew kept it from being much worse.*

*Hearing the sound of the crash above them, and seeing burning fuel running down into the hanger deck from the flight deck, the crew responded exactly as trained and attacked the fire before it spread, successfully containing and stopping it. Both aircraft were destroyed and their crews killed, along with several of the deck crew, but the ship and crew were saved. Nearly all traces of the crash were removed years ago, but the faint creases in the deck where the rotor blades first hit remain.*

---

Going for maximum aviator cool, I usually could maintain some semblance of calm when faced with night flight, but tonight was somehow different. The semi-vertigo was still there, and the early trip to the deck was not helping. The second Frog, the one on Spot Five (05), had its position lights on, flashing dim, the signal for chocks and chains to hold the aircraft still on the moving deck so that it could be refueled. Over the moderate roar of the flight deck, I heard the Boss call over the flight deck loud speaker for the next pilot for 05 to man the aircraft. That was me. With the wind pushing from behind, I walked down the slightly listing deck to spot four and the helicopter, feeling the flight suit flap against my legs as I walked.

The second launch pilot was just climbing out the crew door as I arrived at the aircraft. He took the long last step to the flight deck and grabbed my arm before he moved under 05's rotor disk.

"Got a small beat (rotor vibration) but works OK," he yelled over the noise of the aircraft. No mention of how dark it was. No reason to state the obvious.

I lifted my helmet bag up and set it inside the crew door. Grabbing the wire cable that kept the door from bending the hinges, I climbed up the crew steps on the right side of the aircraft, just behind the cockpit and into the red-lit interior of the helicopter. I banged the top of my helmet into the cabin roof. Without my helmet I am 6' 4" and the cabin of a Frog is 6'2" so this was normal, as evidenced by the scrapes and dings on my helmet.

Climbing up into the small passageway from the cabin to the cockpit, I slipped a little on spilled oil or hydraulic fluid on the floor. Putting my left foot on the seat itself, I squeezed into the left seat, trying as hard as possible not to hit the flight controls or the engine controls or the fuel jettison switches. The climb into the seat was always difficult for someone six foot four; even without the flight gear it was a difficult entry, but all pilots try to look graceful getting in because the passengers tended to get nervous if they see the pilot fall down while climbing into the seat. Stiff from the cool flight deck air, I had to struggle a little more than usual, but the HAC in the right seat held his hand over the controls for the auxiliary power plant and fuel jettisons just in case I banged into them.

In at last, I felt for the seat belt and shoulder harness. Finding the ends, I moved my hands to the adjustments and let them out all the way. The last pilot was supposed to do that but had forgotten in his haste to leave the cockpit. No matter, I was too tense to let it bother me much. Strapped in now, I reached back to the space on the right side of the console and got my helmet bag. I put it on the left side of the center console where I could get to it easily in the dark. Pulling the red-lensed flashlight out of my survival vest, I hooked it on the snaps provided so that the red light would shine on the instruments if the helicopter's electrical power failed or for some reason the lights went off.

The other pilot was calm and collected. He had been out from daylight through to darkness and had completely adapted. He knew I wasn't and hadn't, so he said, "I'll do this one, Bob. Just follow along and call everything as briefed." He then reached down and moved the heading bug (small pilot-adjustable indicator on the electronic heading indicator that highlights a particular heading on the compass) on the Attitude Heading Reference System (AHRS—the electronic compass) so that it pointed directly down the deck in on the ship's heading, 170 degrees right now. The ship would hold this heading during Air Operations since it was directly into the wind, making it easier for the pilots to land aboard.

The helicopter aircraft commander (HAC) gave the light signal to pull the chocks and chains. The yellow shirt LSE sent the blue shirt deck crew in to pull them off and then, as they held them up, he ran the wands down each one so that we could physically see that they were all off. If you lift up with a chain still attached, it may cause the helicopter to roll over and beat itself to death on the steel deck. The pilot signaled the count was good and the LSE raised the wands straight up to indicate the aircraft was clear to lift into a hover.

On the LSE's signal to lift with the yellow wands, the HAC called, "Ready in the back?" and when the crew chief replied, "All set," the HAC called, "Three on." I turned the Stability Augmentation System, the SAS, to "both," the Automatic Stability Equipment, the ASE, to "On," and confirmed the speed trims in "Auto" and replied, "Three on." As the LSE lifted the wands, the HAC lifted the aircraft into a smooth hover. I followed along on the controls, but it did not seem real, again it was like I was watching a movie of someone sitting in an aircraft cockpit and doing these things. As he held the Frog over the red-lit deck, I scanned the instruments one last time before the LSE gave us the launch signal with his wands.

Sometimes, if you were heavily loaded, and the wind over the deck was not very strong as you cross the deck edge, you start to settle toward the water. You can feel your aircraft sinking toward the sea but you have nothing left, no more power to pull, and the sea is only 50 feet away. You hold the controls as still as you can to conserve lift and think light thoughts until your aircraft shudders through translational lift and starts to climb and the water is left below. We were empty tonight so that wouldn't happen, we wouldn't settle toward the sea—couldn't happen.

"Gauges check good; holding 60% torque; cleared to go," I called. When the LSE moved his wands in the cleared-for-takeoff signal, the HAC smoothly added power while sliding the aircraft to left, toward the blackness on the other side of the deck. As we cleared the port side of the ship, he pulled in more power and nosed the helicopter forward, committing us to the darkness. He was now flying only on the flight instruments. There was only blackness, deep, deep blackness through the windshield.

"Positive power, positive climb; airspeed off the peg; passing through 30 knots," I called over the intercom.

"Airspeed 40; passing through 100 feet."

"Airspeed 60; passing 200."

"Airspeed approaching 80, 250 feet," I called, continuing the constant drone of crew coordination night flight, particularly night flight over water. The compass showed we were still on the same course as the ship, the heading bug indicator at the 12 o'clock position on the AHRS.

*The upwind turn we were about to make was the most critical part of night CQ's. When pilots turn away from the ship, further into the blackness, they tend to unconsciously push the stick slightly forward putting the aircraft in a shallow dive. Starting from only 300 feet, a dive, no matter how slight, will put the aircraft into the water in seconds. Fifteen Marines died off Onslow Beach in North Carolina when a Frog pilot did just that. Reaching to change a radio frequency with his left hand instead of having the H2P do it, he pushed the stick slightly forward. In a second, the aircraft hit the water. The Marines in the back got tangled up in the seat tie-down straps and drowned as the wreck sank into Onslow Bay.*

---

"Standby for Alt hold," the HAC called back. I already had my hand on the switch.

"300, Alt hold on," I said as I pulled the switch on the center console forward. On the Phrog, there are two kinds of altitude hold, radar and barometric. The barometric hold (baralt) is used over land because the constantly changing altitude of the land below would have the aircraft hunting for the altitude you have set. Over water, the level of the sea is more or less constant, so radar altimeter hold (radalt) can hold you exactly where you want to be.

After I turned the radalt hold on, we both relaxed, just a little, as the automatic control, coupled to our radar altimeter, took control of our power and held us at 300 feet, the traffic pattern altitude. It would hold us wherever we set it by increasing or decreasing power as dictated by where we moved the helicopter's nose to adjust speed. As long as the radalt hold was on, we would have to really screw up to crash into the dark sea below. In fact, it would be nearly impossible.

After a few seconds, the HAC called, "Coming left," over the ICS.

In the back, the crew chief looked out into the blackness and replied, "Clear left."

The HAC rolled the Phrog into a left hand, 15 degrees of bank standard rate turn. I kept my eyes on the flight instruments and called, "Flight instruments look good; twenty degrees to go."

The HAC lead the roll-out by ten degrees and smoothly rolled out on heading, 180 degrees opposite the heading of the ship. The heading bug was now at the 6 o'clock position on the AHRS. The airspeed stayed pretty close to the 80 knots traffic pattern speed we should be holding. Outside, straight ahead and to the right, there was nothing except blackness. I took a look to the right and could dimly see the red glow of the ship's deck and the position lights on the superstructure.

In a few seconds the HAC transmitted, "Tower, 05 is abeam, right seat." When he called "right seat," the tower passed the word to the deck crew and the LSE moved to position himself so that the pilot in the right seat would have the best view of his lighted wands as the aircraft approached the flight deck.

"Roger, 05. Cleared Spot 4. Wind is port 20 at 15," the tower replied.

"Alt hold off, coming left," the HAC called.

"Alt hold is off," I replied as I moved the switch on the center console back. I kept my eyes glued to the instruments as the HAC rolled the aircraft into a standard rate turn of 15 degrees of bank giving us three degrees of heading change per second to the left. He lowered the collective slightly to start us down the 250 feet we had to lose before landing. A fixed-wing carrier pilot told me once that he thought it was insane to do a descending turn from 300 feet at night, but that is the way it's done in helicopters. Concentrate on smooth, slow, carefulness and don't think about the fact that you are seconds from water impact if you screw up.

Port winds at 15 knots meant that the combination of the ship's forward speed and existing wind had created a wind that was 15 degrees off the bow of the ship and would be blowing us toward the ship's superstructure. To keep from hitting the steel wall with our rotors, we would have to get the airspeed down and carefully watch our closure rate to the ship's deck to make sure it was under control and we were not coming too fast. Sometimes if you are too fast, you can do a side flare to lose the speed, but not at night. You might lose sight of the ship if you flare too much.

I called the airspeed and altitude as we came down the glide slope, watching for high rates of descent, "60 knots 200 feet, 50 knots 150 feet . . ." I moved my eyes from the red-lighted dash to the windshield. The dim red patch in the blackness was the ship, coming into view.

"Go visual," I called.

The HAC looked up from his instruments and called, "Deck in sight." It was still more a red glow in the darkness than the distinct lights of a flight deck.

As we closed the remaining distance, the deck seemed to get much bigger than that first dull red glow but still, it remained small compared to the darkness all around. But we did not look at the darkness, we only looked at the red glow. The lighted wands of the LSE came into view as he raised them above his head to show us where he was.

"75 feet, closure looks good," I called.

From the back, the crew chief called, "Over the deck," as we crossed the ship's rail and life rafts on the port side at about 60 feet above the water and 10 feet above the deck.

Watching the wands and judging his position by the dim line of lights built into the flight deck, the HAC stabilized the helicopter, more or less, in a hover over the spot. Although the controls did not appear to move very much, the HAC was working extremely hard. Like always, he was trying to anticipate the movements of the helicopter and counter them before they happened, a process made all the harder by the darkness, wind, and tension of night boat flying. In these moments, you grip the stick so hard your arm aches afterward as you try once again to squeeze the "black stuff out of the plastic" of the cyclic.

As the HAC lowered the collective to put us down, I could see the LSE giving "body English," trying to will our wheels onto the three painted spots. We hit hard, but well within the design limits of the aircraft, as normal a landing as any, especially at night. If you hit too hard, say above 3.5 gee, and the interior "crash" lights come on automatically, there isn't a sign that you have damaged anything, but it's embarrassing nonetheless.

Because we were doing CQ's, the blue shirts did not bring out the chains to tie us down to the deck. The LSE kept his wands crossed and held low, indicating we were to remain on deck until the Tower cleared us. The HAC pushed the collective all the way down, past the normal position to hold the aircraft more firmly on the deck. He turned to me and said, "ASE and SAS off. You've got it."

After turning off the automatic control systems, I took the controls, not sure I was ready to fly but not really having a choice. I knew, as I cleared the deck, the blackness would return but I would not see it, could not see it. All I would see would be the red glow of the instruments in front of me as I concentrated: attitude-altitude-airspeed-heading, attitude-altitude-airspeed-heading; climb, climb to 300 feet; altitude hold on, turn left, roll out, hold heading-hold speed.

"05, We're going to put you in the carrier-controlled approach (CCA—the afloat version of a GCA radar approach) pattern for a few turns," Tower called.

"Roger," I replied. They must be going to turn the ship or maneuver somehow. I would have time to get used to night flying before I had to land. After takeoff, we would climb into the Marshall pattern, one of the three holding patterns oriented around the ship, and hold there until they brought us around for a carrier radar-controlled approach, a CCA, up the stern.

The LSE held one wand up in a "thumbs up" signal. I asked for three on and the HAC reached over and turned on the ASE, SAS, and speed trim auto. "Three on," he replied. From the back the crew chief called, "All set in the back."

The LSE's other wand came on and holding them out to the sides, he raised them in an "up" motion. Holding the stick just slightly back, I lifted the collective up and brought the helicopter into a hover, about ten feet over the deck. The LSE gave a hold sign as he looked toward the bow to make sure there was no other aircraft that we could collide with, and then he gave us the launch signal, pointing his wand off into the darkness.

"Gauges good, cleared to go," the HAC announced.

I applied more power and moved the stick to left. The aircraft started up and sideward at the same time. As we cleared the deck edge, I took out the sideward movement and applied a little forward stick to get us into forward flight. I had put in enough power to get the aircraft rapidly climbing so by the time we reached the end of the deck, we were through 100 feet and our speed was up to 50 knots; attitude-altitude-airspeed-heading. As we approached the bow, the lights of the deck were gone and all was blackness again.

The HAC now made the calls that I made on the first trip around, airspeed, altitude, and so on, but this time the alt hold did not come on when we passed 300 feet. We continued to climb to "Angels one point five," 1500 feet the altitude for the CCA pattern.

"05, switch Purple," the Tower called.

"05, switching."

"Switch Purple," I told the HAC. He already had his hand on the radio switch to change us to the frequency of Center, the ship's air traffic control. The tone indicating that the radio had been changed to the new frequency sounded as he withdrew his hand.

"Up Purple," he said.

Still concentrating on keeping the helicopter at 80 knots airspeed and in the climb, I depressed the ICS to the transmit position and said, "Center 05."

"05, Center. Say state and souls," Center replied.

"Center, 05 is one point zero to splash, three souls on board."

"05, Center. Climb Angels two point zero and proceed to Marshall Three. Report level."

"Center, 05. Roger," I replied.

"Passing 1000, everything looks good," the HAC called.

Center was moving us around to the holding pattern on the starboard side of the ship, a "Marshall," in this case Marshall One in Navy speak. The idea was to sequence us into the pattern so that we would not interfere with the other traffic.

I could feel vertigo building in me as I concentrated on the flight instruments—vertigo and a mild sense of panic. It was a sense of being completely disconnected from reality and dizzy at the same time. I concentrated as hard as I could on the gauges, my eyes moving from altitude to airspeed to rate of climb to attitude to altitude and around again. A side glance at the engine, transmission, and hydraulic gauges to see they were all steady, no impending failures of critical systems, and then back to the flight instruments—attitude-altitude-airspeed heading-attitude-altitude-airspeed-heading.

The voice of the controller called for us to go to Marshall two and I moved the helicopter around the TACAN's line to the new holding point: attitude-altitude-airspeed heading. The vertigo faded as I concentrated on attitude-altitude-airspeed heading. In a few minutes we were in position and we vectored into position for a CCA: attitude-altitude-airspeed-heading. On course, on glide path, on course, on glide path—look up, there is the red glow of the deck lights in the blackness and the yellow wands of the LSE. With a bump, we land on the spot after a wobbly hover, then back up again to complete another five landings. The vertigo is gone.

Finally, after another 30 minutes in the air and the required landings, we get the signal for chocks and chains and then the shutdown signal, the wand across the LSE's throat.

Across the deck and back into the red lights of the ready room. No racing mind now, just a feeling of fatigue and weak legs. I am very, very tired. After the flight's debrief, I walk to my room through the darkened ship. My flight gear is much heavier than it was on the way to the launch. On my bunk is a small brown paper bag, two illegal airline-sized nips of brandy, compliments of our flight surgeon. Rules or no rules, he understands—understands the absolute drain of tonight's flight and the need for the pilots to spool down.

After finishing the second little bottle, I lay back on the bunk in the glow of the red dark adaptation lights above my rack, listening to the sounds of the ship and thinking, "luck and superstition, that's all that lets us cheat death one more time . . ."

## 19

# WIRES
### GREECE ■ AUGUST 1979

---

*Luck and superstition are not always enough; even if you are counting on them, you cannot ever get careless and expect to live to be an old aviator . . .*

---

The northeastern part of Greece is mountainous, like much of the country, and here too, the mountains run down into the sea. Some of them run up to nearly 7,000 feet. The town to the northwest of our operating area had once been called Amphipolis, very appropriate for our amphibious exercise. As the Landing Force for the Sixth Fleet (LF6F), we had been sailing around the Mediterranean Sea for five months, doing those same things, at the same place, that military men have done since the time of the Greeks and Romans, minus all the carnage and pillage of those days. Now we were spending five days puttering around a very small area of Greece trying to keep our skills sharp, just in case we might be needed somewhere.

The practice assault had gone well: half by surface and half by air, plus follow-on training. As the squadron WTI, I had laid out Terrain Flying (TERF) routes that the pilots had been flying for four days. TERF was relatively new in 1978. It was an attempt to take advantage of the helicopter's ability to fly low and out of sight of the enemy; and to legalize something we had always done anyway. Modern weapons had made the statement, "If it can be seen, it will be killed," absolutely true. Shoulder-fired missiles and accurate rapid-fire machine guns were in the hands of virtually everyone now, and the odds of surviving against a prepared enemy were now even lower than they had been in Vietnam.

To keep TERF under control, the Marine Corps had broken it down into three varieties: low-level flight at a constant altitude on the barometric altimeter (generally 150 feet or below) and a constant airspeed; contour-flight at a constant radar altitude with varying airspeed; and nap-of-the-earth (NOE), flight that varied altitude from the surface to fifty feet, and airspeed from a hover to maximum allowable.

All the pilots in the squadron (and probably all pilots in the Marine Corps and Army) had flown at these low levels at one time or another, but most of it was of the illegal kind, "flathatting" in Navy terms. But to survive on the modern battlefield, they would have to really learn how to fly close to the earth without "tying the record for low flying," i.e. actually hitting the ground. That record cannot be broken, but pilots keep on trying; if they could, they would be easy targets for missiles and modern high-speed gun systems.

Generally we only flew NOE in training on military reservations or other areas such as North Carolina's Pocosin Swamps where we could be sure we would not create a nuisance and/or scare the hell out of people, particularly since there weren't any people in those areas. But now, since we would be flying over civilian territory in a foreign country, we would only fly contour here. I had carefully planned and flown each route, slowly, both backwards and forwards, noting the hazards that they presented. In designing low level flying routes, masts, such as radio or television towers, are always a problem; the chief hazard has always been telephone and electric wires. High tension lines are the worst, although even a small telephone line can be fatal to an aircraft. Here in Greece, one set of high tension lines had me particularly worried, a huge set of power lines that crossed a river several miles to the west of our base camp. They came down off a mountain and crossed a river at about 150 feet above the surface of the river, the same altitude that we flew when we flew contour flight. I highlighted this set on the big area map in the operations tent and had the ODO brief each launch on the danger they presented. All pilots were to mark them on their maps too.

We had been there for three days, flying and training as Marines always do. In two more days, we would load all our gear into the helicopters and then be back on the ship. We would then depart for our last port to de-snail, i.e., wash down anything such as agricultural pests trying to hitchhike back to the states, before we headed west across the Atlantic to North Carolina and home. Our six months as LF6F was all but over.

Our base camp was near a small beach with the usual dust and sand, but it was pleasant to be off the ship and living in a tent in the cool Greek spring weather. In the afternoon, a Greek man would bring a bicycle loaded with ice cream in coolers to our base camp. We would buy his wares and eat them looking out at the sea or the mountains. Wine would have been nice, but that was beyond reach this time, bosses looking on and all that.

When we flew, it was nice, too, also pleasant in the Greek spring weather. We saw the remains of ancient Greek temples and cities here and there, columns still standing. And we saw more recent ruins, the abandoned villages that had been left when the people moved to the city or immigrated, possibly to the United States. But more than that, we saw the beauty of the countryside. We saw mountains 6,000 feet high with sheep grazing at the top and small bays, where the water was clear blue as it broke against the rocks. Crossing the top of one of those 6,000 footers at 50 feet above the ground, lower than I should have been, I came face to face with a man herding sheep from horseback. Hard to say who was more surprised when his horse reared as my Phrog rushed past, the cowboy or me? When I last saw him, his horse was rearing and he was holding on, just.

On that third day, I had just come back from my final morning TERF flight and all was right in the world. My lieutenant student had done well, staying more or less on the route I had laid out during the navigation portion of the flight, certainly within standards. When it was his turn to fly while I navigated, he had done well, too. Done well in that he had not scared the living shit out of me even once as he wove in and around our flight path to my called out directions and more or less, kept us at the correct altitude. I signed the bird off as OK, no major gripes with any of the systems, and picked up a "C rat" box for lunch out of the carton in the Ops tent. I walked over to the BOQ tent, sat on a cot and started to open the box, joking as always with the other pilots about student inadequacies, when the operations duty officer (ODO, pronounced OH-doe) came running in, red-faced and excited. To no one in particular, though aimed at the CO sitting on a cot about five feet from me, he said, "A grunt unit just called in and said they saw a helo go down. I lost com with them before they could tell me what kind of helo it was and where they saw it go down. I've been calling and calling but they are not answering"

Four of us including the CO left our lunches and ran with the ODO back to the Ops tent. The flight status board showed that we only had two birds still out after I had returned from my training flight, a Snake and a Phrog. The ODO was on the radio immediately trying to contact them. Just as one of the aircraft replied, we saw the CH-46 in the far distance, near the mountains.

As the ODO began explaining to the airborne CH-46F what the grunts had passed over the radio, I turned to the CO. "Sir, I just brought my bird back. It's up and fueled. I can tear up the yellow sheet I just filled out and be back in the air in five minutes."

"OK," he replied, "Do it, but don't takeoff until I'm on board."

I turned and ran for the CH-46F I had just left. My copilot was right behind me and as we covered the short distance, I was yelling for my crew chief to close the panels he was starting to open in preparation for doing a turn-around inspection for the next aircrew. I told my copilot to get in the back and help the crew close panels or anything else that needed doing. I would start the aircraft by myself and hold the left seat open for the CO. In a couple minutes, I had the aircraft turning and burning, ready to take-off as soon as the CO strapped into the left seat. I talked to the ODO and the other CH-46F on squadron common FM frequency to develop a quick search plan. We agreed to split the area to search for the downed bird; he would take the eastern part of the training area and I would take the western part. As I waited for the CO, the other CH-46F was already on his way to his agreed upon search area.

Even though both the airborne CH-46F and the ODO called over and over again on the fox mike, no word was heard from the Cobra or the grunts who had made the first call.

I could still see the other CH-46 in the distance as the CO climbed into the left seat. As he was finishing strapping in, the other 46 called us.

"Found the site. The grunts are with the aircraft now. I'll orbit over-head the crash. Don't hurry getting here," he said.

With those words we, the crew of my helicopter and the ODO back at the base, knew it was beyond serious. No pilot would orbit the crash site of one of his squadron mates unless there was no point in landing. The CO just looked at me from the left seat as I completed the takeoff checklist without his help and after an "All set aft" from my crew chief, pulled in power to climb out of our base camp LZ. Turning toward the west and the orbiting CH-46F, I did hurry, even if the other pilot had told me not to. I couldn't go slowly, my hands would not let me. As if by themselves, the right one pushed the stick forward and the left pulled up the collective. I could see even on takeoff that the other aircraft was orbiting the power lines over the river I had worried about.

In five minutes we were there, closing at 130 plus knots airspeed. From 500 feet above the ground and several miles away, I could see what had happened. The top-most power line was down where the lines crossed the river, one end dangling in the water and the other still attached to its tower on each side.

"Go on back to base and refuel. Stand by on the ground and I'll call if I want you back here," the CO called over the radio to the other Phrog.

As the other aircraft pulled away, I circled the crash site on a high reconnaissance to pick out a landing spot before beginning an approach. I learned long ago at Fort Wolters how to land in unfamiliar LZs. The proper procedure for landing in uncleared sites is first to do a high recon to get an overview of the area and potential obstacles, followed by a low recon to a wave off, to see if there is anything you missed from higher above. After that, you did a full approach to landing. I was not going to shortcut the procedure, not this time.

From the high recon, 500 feet above the site, I could see below me what remained of the Cobra. The main portion of the fuselage was in the middle of the river. Neither the tail nor the rotor blades was visible. The water looked about chest deep, judging from all the men splashing in it around the wreckage. Apparently they were trying to get the pilots out. Picking a clear spot well back from the crash site, I landed on the western bank with my aircraft facing the wreckage in the river. As our wheels touched, the CO was unstrapping, and as I lowered the collective, he was on his way out of the cockpit. Through the chin bubble, I could see a piece of green metal, oblong and about six inches long, probably a part of the Cobra's skin, under us. I thought to myself that for it to be this far from the wreckage, he must have really been traveling fast when he hit the wire. Looking back through the companionway, I waved my copilot into the seat the CO had just vacated.

*This one was more difficult to handle than most crashes. The senior pilot on-board the crash aircraft, a captain, was not a Cobra pilot. He was a CH-53D pilot taking a "dollar ride" in a Cobra, a tourist on that soft spring Greek day.*

*One year before, in March 1978, the captain had been copilot on a CH-53D during another exercise, this one in Spain, again on an LF6F. As it happened, the CH-53D's mission that spring Spanish afternoon had been to pick me and two other Marines up to take us out for an "escape and evasion" (E&E) training mission.*

*For training purposes, our CH-46F had been "shot down" over hostile territory and we were escaping back to friendly lines. The training was not really for us but for the Navy SEALs (a group of uniquely trained and equipped Navy special operations personnel who operate from, around and in maritime areas—Sea, Air, and Land) who would be picking us up and bringing us back to the ship by rubber boat in the dark. We would find our way to a rendezvous point, leave a pile of rocks stacked in a certain manner for the SEALs to find. They would come to us and basically take us prisoner. After asking a series of questions, taken from our files to make sure we were who we were supposed to be, they would lead us to the boats and take us back out to our ship. This exercise would be quite different from when I was actually shot down in enemy territory in 1971. That time, my crew and I sat behind the aircraft's M60D machine guns until a Huey came to get us.*

*Right after breakfast, we caught a helicopter from the ship to the squadron's base camp LZ down in a valley on the edge of the exercise operations area. We spent the morning discussing what we were going to do as we worked our way across the five or so miles of Spanish desert to the pickup zone (PZ). The mission was supposed to start at 1500 hours but by 1300 hours I was bored with just sitting in the LZ and was ready to get started. The SEAL that was our lane grader (evaluator) was bored too and readily agreed that we might as well get started, so instead of waiting for the CH-53D that was going to fly us out to the "crash" site, I got on the ODO's fox mike and called down a passing CH-46F that was only too willing to take us the ten miles to where we would start.*

*We arrived on a dusty Spanish hilltop in short order and ran from the aircraft to begin our "escape." It was a beautiful, warm, but not hot, spring afternoon. We were feeling good and playing the game as best we could, that is with a little humor thrown in. Since we were close to where the "Spaghetti Westerns" had been filmed, we decided to use the theme from the movie,* The Good, The Bad, and the Ugly *as a challenge and response call—the challenge, "Doddle-duddle-do," the response "Dah-Do-Do." We did our best to sneak across the Spanish desert but after only about 30 minutes, as we rounded a hillside, a woman came out of a house just below us. She had a bag over her shoulder and started walking toward a tied-up mule in front of her adobe house. She must have seen us, because though she did not look directly at the armed, uniformed men trying to hide in the thin brush on the hillside above her, she froze for a minute. Then, moving casually, oh, so casually, she strolled over to the mule, untied it and climbed nimbly into the saddle. As soon as she was settled in, she spurred that mule into what passes for a mule gallop and disappeared down the road in a cloud of dust. Even the SEAL joined us as we all just sat down on the dusty hillside, convulsed with laughter.*

*After that, we moved as unobtrusively as we could to our rendezvous point, seeing no one else on the way. After four hours, we arrived at twilight to find a platoon of Marine grunts sitting right where we were supposed to leave the stack of rocks for the rescuing SEALs to find. Our SEAL left us in hiding and went to find out what the grunts were up to. He returned about ten minutes later.*

*"Why would a CH-53D spin around in circles and throw things out the back?" he asked.*

*My reply was, "Exercise over," as we three "escapees" and the SEAL ran as hard as we could toward the grunt's camp.*

*When I came over the small hill between us and the grunts, I could see the 53 on the ground, still looking like a CH-53D, but with a major airframe change. Instead of being 25 feet or so high, the top of the rotor hub was only about eight feet off the ground. All the rotor blades and the tail rotor blades were still on the upright aircraft but the fuselage was crushed, smashed down. The two main landing gear struts were driven up completely through the structure. One or both fuel tanks had ruptured, leaving the smell of jet fuel heavy in the air, but thankfully, the fuel had not ignited. Inside the CH-53D there were four dead men, crushed by the transmission coming down inside the cabin, but five men had survived, three in the cabin, and both pilots.*

*The CH-53D was supposed to pick us up for the E&E exercise. Since we* weren't there when the aircraft landed, the HAC picked up some backpacks to carry out to the waiting infantrymen instead. Several Marines that had been guarding the packs climbed onboard too. After flying the short distance to the LZ, the pilots brought the 53 into a 100-foot hover to select a good landing spot. Just as they arrived in the hover, the crew chief opened the rear ramp hatch to see the LZ better. As he did, the hatch actuator broke through its mount on the inside of the helicopter's roof and went into the tail rotor drive shaft. The actuator acted like a lathe and cut the shaft in two, resulting in total loss of tail rotor thrust. Without the tail rotor to counteract the torque created by the main rotor in a hover, the aircraft went into a violent flat spin in the opposite direction of the turning main rotor.

If you are in forward flight and lose tail rotor thrust, the aircraft speed may keep the fuselage streamlined enough to allow the pilots to do a high-speed running landing like a fixed-wing normally does. In a hover, complete recovery from loss of tail rotor thrust is nearly impossible. You are quite probably going to crash. The only question is how. Will the pilot be able to maintain some control or is he just a passenger until impact? The only real option the pilot has to maintain at least minimal control is to remove the torque from the aircraft by shutting down the engines. One of the pilots did exactly that as the 53 began its violent spin. Even though the aircraft was spinning at a terrifying rate, one of the pilots managed to reach the engine controls and shut both engines off. As he did so, the spin stopped, but now they were falling straight down, straight down from 100 feet.

Had one of the pilots not shut down the engine, it is very unlikely that anyone would have survived. The CH-53D would have hit the ground out of control and the operating turbine engines would probably have ignited the fuel from the ruptured tanks, creating a giant fireball and leaving only shards of blackened, melted aluminum.

Both pilots survived the impact of the 100-foot fall, their seats absorbing some of the force. Both were unconscious and badly hurt, but alive, as were three of the men in the main cabin. The other four in the cabin were dead, some from the impact, some crushed by the transmission as it came down.

After medevac from Spain to Germany and treatment at the big hospital at Frankfort, both the pilots were well enough to return to duty several months later. The major and the aircraft commander moved on to another assignment.

*The first lieutenant copilot was promoted to captain and returned to the squadron in time for our next LF6F. One year after the crash in Spain he was in the front seat of the Cobra, taking an orientation flight, a "dollar ride," that soft Greek spring day. There was no surviving this one.*

*We were supposed to be in the back of that aircraft, but because I had been bored waiting for it, we were not. Luck and superstition?*

---

For the longest time, we sat there on the banks of that Greek river, engines burning and rotors turning, watching the small crowd of men in the river working with what was left of the Cobra. After a while, I saw some of them bring something to the shore and then return for another load. We were too far away to see exactly what it was, but that wasn't necessary. I knew. After wrapping the loads they carried ashore in ponchos or some similar material, they lifted both bundles onto waiting stretchers and started carrying them toward my helicopter.

"Corporal," I called over the ICS, but I didn't have to. He was watching and had already begun folding up some troop seats and stowing them against the side of the cabin so that we could put the stretchers inside. I watched him in the cockpit rear view mirror as he made the cabin ready for the remains of our squadron mates.

I continued watching in the mirror as the stretchers and their loads were carried up the ramp and strapped down. Everyone except the CO got back off the aircraft and stood just outside the rotor disk looking back at us. The CO climbed back in through the ramp but he strapped into one of troop seats in the back instead of coming up to the cockpit. The crew chief offered him a long cord to hookup to the ICS but he didn't take it. He just looked forward, toward the cockpit, and without really looking, sadly gave a thumbs up to signal that he was ready to go. "All set in back," the crew chief called over the ICS. The copilot and I completed the checklist, turned three on, and lifting directly into forward flight without a hover check, I climbed the aircraft up from the riverbank and turned toward the sea and our ship. Just before crossing the shore, we did our "feet wet" checklist, nose wheel and brakes locked, and headed to the ship, three miles out to sea.

"Center, 04, feet wet inbound, four souls onboard, one point oh to splash, two routine medevac," I called over the control center radio channel, "Purple" in ship speak.

"Roger 04," Center replied, "Cherubs three, your signal Charley. What assistance do you need? Say state of medevacs. How many corpsmen do you need?" all came out in a rush.

"Center, 04, two routine medevac. Require four stretcher bearers," I replied.

"04, Center. Say state of medevac," Center said again, more urgently this time.

In Vietnam what I was doing had been a normal course of events for those of us who flew the helicopters—men died every day and every day helicopters brought them into the hospital, but the peacetime Navy was not used to wartime radio calls, and for a moment I lost it.

"Center, 04. Both men are dead. This is a routine medevac. All I need are the stretcher bearers. Do you understand?" I shouted into the mic.

For a long moment there was silence. Then Center said, "Roger, 04. Switch tower when ready."

My copilot changed the radio frequency as I headed down the starboard side in a normal approach pattern. When I passed just ahead of the ship, I turned across the bow, maintaining my 300 feet, to roll out on the course opposite of the ship's course. When I called "abeam," Tower cleared us to land spot 4. I rolled smoothly into a bank, turning the helicopter to 45 degrees off the ship's course and reducing power to descend. As the helicopter crossed the deck edge, I saw the men that would carry the two body bags below, standing by the island in their white float vests with the red cross on them, waiting. I came in without stopping in a hover to position over the landing spot. Instead, I landed the helicopter immediately on spot 4, with the wheels exactly in the three boxes marking the proper position. I did it to the best of my ability, to give them, my squadron mates, their last ship landing as smoothly and as close to perfect as I could.

Once on deck, I waited while my copilot turned three off and the green-shirted deck handlers installed the chocks and chains. I looked back into the cabin through the rear view mirror and watched the men lift the two stretchers and move down the ramp. I did not watch them as they carried their loads to the starboard elevator to go below to the ship's hospital and on to the morgue. I gave the "drinking" hand signal for refueling to the yellow-shirted LSE. He signaled for the purple-shirted refuelers and my copilot and I sat without talking while they pumped the fuel into the tanks. When it was complete, I signaled for takeoff. At the yellow shirt's signal, the blue shirts ran under the rotor disk, pulled the chalks, and removed the three chains holding my 46 to the deck. They ran back out and held them for me to count so I would know all restraints were removed from the aircraft.

Chocks and chains off, the copilot turned three on, and after a "ready aft" from the crew chief, I lifted the helicopter into a hover at the LSE's signal. My copilot called "gauges good to go" and I slid left as I added power and lowered the nose, we crossed the deck edge climbing and gathering speed and we were on our way back to our base camp on the beach. The death of two comrades and the loss of an aircraft does not end your mission.

Every flight requires you go into a room in your mind where there is nothing but the mission you have been assigned, nothing but flying. When you enter, you must close the door to that room behind you, shutting out everything else and look at nothing but the flight in front of you. Fail to do so and you may join the lost aircrew in death.

I closed the door to the room they died in, stepped into the one for flying, and my mission continued. The mission must be done. Always.

## 20

# EXTERNALS

## CAMP LEJEUNE, NORTH CAROLINA ■ MAY 1980

*Very, very few people are natural pilots. Most people who become pilots learn slowly and while they are learning, they are very, very dangerous to everyone else because they are inept. But even more dangerous than normal slow learners, are the few that are "naturals," the ones born to fly. They are more dangerous because they sometimes come without the fear of death. They have to be taught that their abilities will not save them if they take the aircraft too far or think their skill will get them out of a situation that no one can resolve.*

MCAS New River, as are all Marine Corps Air Stations, is named for a local feature. Some are named for a town—MCAS Beaufort and MCAS Yuma come to mind. Some are named for geographic features, like MCAS Cherry Point named after a point of land on the Neuse River. MCAS New River is named for the New River, the brown, yellow, muddy feature that separates the base from Camp Lejeune. The New River is a bit unusual since it begins and ends in Onslow County, North Carolina, starting as a black water creek in a swamp that becomes an alligator swamp until it changes downstream into a wide, very shallow river that passes on the south side of the air field. The Marine Corps' East Coast Training Squadron for cargo helicopters, HMT-204, is located at MCAS New River.

HMT is Marine for "Helicopter Marine Training," as opposed to "HMM," Helicopter Marine Medium, the name of all tactical CH-46 squadrons. HMT-204 provided training for both the CH-46 and the CH-53D. The squadron's aircraft were all parked at the east end of New River's concrete ramp, arranged in neat rows by aircraft type, the more numerous CH-46's here and the CH-53's there. Flight Operations at HMT-204 normally consisted of two day launches, one in the morning and one in the afternoon during the week. There were three types of flights: student training flights, instructor training flights, and maintenance check flights. Night training flights went out two or three times a week. If the student through-put load was light, the squadron took the weekend off.

Instructors in HMT-204 were generally cruised-out captains finishing out their first Fleet Marine Corps tour, meaning they were assigned there from the deploying squadrons after completing two six-month LF6F deployments. They would be instructors for, at most, a year before they went off to Amphibious Warfare School or headquarters duty or some other non-Fleet assignment. Even now, Fleet tours are the only ones that are really important to a Marine. Why would you want to be a Marine if you weren't in the "Fleet," where real Marine things are done? My HMT-204 tour would be longer than most since I got there much faster than usual, and I completed the Marine Corps' aviation training program sooner than a typical pilot due to my prior aviation service with the Army. It doesn't take nearly as long to train a pilot who already knows how to fly, so I got to the Fleet as a second lieutenant and finished my two med cruises much sooner than typical.

I was a prime candidate for HMT-204. I was cruised out and had been on station at New River for less than three years. I was easy to train as a CH-46F instructor since my instructor career had started in wooden rotor-bladed OH-13Es in 1969. After that, I was the company senior instructor pilot in Chinooks in 1971 in Vietnam. There, I flew the first 25 hours with all newbies, gave copilot and aircraft commander check rides, and trained new instructor pilots (IPs). During the time I had been an instructor, I had seen about all types of pilots come through training. I flew with cocky ones, scared ones, marginally competent ones, all types except a truly natural pilot—someone who took to flying completely and so thoroughly that instruction seems superfluous. Oh, I had known a couple of natural pilots, men who did everything so effortlessly that you could not help but feel somehow inadequate, but I never had one as a student.

One day at HMT-204, I finally had one.

Natural pilots, on the surface, look like everyone else, unlike many athletes who seem designed for their sport. It's not that their eyes are better than other pilots since all military aviators start with at least 20/20 vision. Nor are they more physically fit, as all military pilots start out in excellent health and fitness. Ground school is not an indicator. It is very possible to ace every test they throw at you and still be a terrible pilot, and it's possible to squeak by on tests and fly like Eddie Rickenbacker (Medal of Honor recipient and WWI fighter ace). The only way to tell if someone is a natural is to take them flying, hence the aeronautical adaptability programs some services run. Take the prospect up in a light aircraft and see if they take to flying, thereby weeding out the weak ones early. After that it is up to the flight school instructors to complete the selection, to decide who makes it and who doesn't.

The brief that morning was normal in all respects. I had reviewed the student's training record and saw only the way-too-normal write-ups by lazy flight instructors, "good flight, no problems," which tells you absolutely nothing. Our flight today was to be the lieutenant's first external load mission. Like all naval aviators, he had done a few easy externals in flight school but at Pensacola, they used light weights, usually small concrete blocks that were well below the maximum weight limit for the Hueys he was flying.

---

*I had first learned how to handle externals using Huey's in Army flight school, but just like Navy flight training, the lesson was quick and the loads were light. When I got to Chinook transition, prior to Vietnam, the sling load training got serious; moving external loads was the aircraft's primary mission. The serious sling load training took place at Fort McClellan, up near Anniston, Alabama.*

*To save on manpower and more importantly, to teach us how hard a job the hookup man has, we students would do all the attaching of the loads. After a five-minute class, complete with a warning that if we did not properly ground the aircraft with the grounding wand, the static electricity the aircraft generated would knock you on your ass, if not kill you outright, we were considered trained. The instructor would land and drop us off in the field with the loads and a list of which ones we were to hookup and in what order, as the helicopter came in for pickup. We would go to the appointed load and climb up on top holding the "donut"—a heavy-duty ring of nylon cloth holding all the legs of the sling together—and the grounding wand.*

*The idea was to touch the cargo hook with the wand and then slide the donut on the hook with the wand still touching. The aircraft would land short of the load and hover forward. The 100-knot rotor wash would hit you as they came to a hover and build as they came over you. You were looking up at the flight engineer through the hellhole as he directed the student pilot to come left, right, back, forward, as required to position the cargo hook over the load. Once the student pilot got the aircraft close enough to the donut for you to reach it, the flight engineer would direct the student pilot to come down until at last you, the hookup man, could get the donut on the hook. Once the donut was secured to the hook, we would jump off the top of the load and run away from the rotor wash before they began to lift the load off the ground.*

*With the Chinooks, we had all types of loads: trucks, old helicopter fuselages, an old airplane or two, and of course, concrete blocks of various weights, right up to the maximum the aircraft could handle. The cement block practice loads were all labeled with their weight painted on the sides and top. The aircraft practice loads did not have their weights listed but were all light enough to be well within the limits of the aircraft. Even so, the aircraft were far more difficult to carry than the cement blocks; even with their wings removed, they presented a lot of surface area for a light weight to the air as you began forward flight. They would swing back and forth and twist around, unlike the cement blocks which generally just hung straight down. The blocks were small and heavy, nearly perfect loads, at least perfect loads for student pilots because you couldn't hurt them if you dragged them across the ground on landing or even dropped them before they touched down.*

*It was quite a sight, that huge helicopter wobbling a few feet above you as the student pilot tried to get the aircraft into position to hook up the load. You could tell instantly whether the student or the instructor was flying. The aircraft was steady and the hookup quick if the instructor was flying. If the aircraft wobbled and drifted up and down, right and left, backward and forward, it was the student. But of course the first hookup was always the instructor as he demonstrated the maneuver—all the rest would be the student.*

*Who was flying was particularly worrying on the last load of the training flight because they would not land to pick up the student pilot acting as hookup man. Instead, after the last load was securely on the donut, the pilot at the controls would lower the aircraft down to the point where the hookup man could climb onboard through the hellhole. To get that low, the student pilot would have to bring the Chinook down to where it was only a few feet above the concrete block. If he wobbled badly, he could easily crush the hookup man between the aircraft and the load. The instructors did it to show you how much you must appreciate the danger hookup men face on each and every load. The pilot must always respect the hookup man and be as smooth as possible during the procedure because his life is literally in your hands every time you pick up a load.*

*I remembered standing on the load and climbing up into the aircraft later when I was flying in Vietnam, watching the hookup men risk their lives on every load. While hovering forward to pick up a load of 105-howitzer ammo one day, I saw the legs of the sling were fouled, partially stuck under the ammo, preventing the hookup man from lifting the donut above his head. Instead, he was lying on his back on top of the load, holding the donut about a foot above his chest. To hook the load up, I would have to get the hook one foot above him. The slightest twitch on my part and he would be dead. What trust he had in us pilots, or was it just that he was 19 and nothing could hurt him?*

*Another time, we were extracting a mountaintop firebase while it was under attack. Mortars were exploding all over the hill as we came roaring up the mountain side in a cyclic climb, trading airspeed for altitude while keeping the aircraft as close to the trees as possible to stay out of the enemy machine gunner's sights. We needed to hook up the 105s as quickly as possible and jerk them off the ground and over the hillside before the mortars got us. As we crossed the wire around the perimeter, the hookup man would jump up on top the gun and stand there with the donut held over his head while the explosions went off all around the hilltop, black flashes and shrapnel flying through the air. Time after time they stood there until all the guns were hooked up and gone. Doing it once and it could be that you were just pissed off at the enemy for shooting at you; doing it time after time and even though you know that death waits, requires a conscious decision. But then, hooking up loads is the mission for these men. The mission must be done.*

*Later I reflected on the fact that the NVA had about 15 seconds to get me when I came up on top of that hill, but those soldiers stood there for at least 30 seconds time after time. Like I said, do it once and maybe you were just not thinking about it, but do it over and over and you are brave. The hookup men were brave men, all of them*

But those days are gone, at least temporarily. Now safety comes first, so no climbing through hell holes and no student hookup men. Here in peacetime, our training would take place down the New River on a small peninsula that stuck out in the river on the Camp Lejeune side, close to where the AMTRAKs, the big amphibious assault vehicles Marines use to get from ship to the shore, are based. There will be no mortars exploding or shrapnel flying and with a real helicopter landing zone team doing the hook ups, not another student pilot. The advantage of this remote location is simply because there is nothing else there; if the student inadvertently drops a load, it is only going to hit the water, not someone. It happened often enough that we instructors joked among ourselves that the bottom of New River was paved with cement blocks students had dropped into the water.

As with every hop, I quizzed the student about what we were going to do on this flight. His knowledge was average at best, but he was qualified. Preflight, start, and taxi were normal. His taxi out to the active runway was as smooth as I had ever seen, unusual for a student only halfway through the syllabus. As I always do, I took control of the aircraft for the first takeoff, but as soon as we were safely established in a climb, I turned the 46 over to the student. He rolled out on the correct heading and stayed firmly on altitude and airspeed, again, a bit unusual for a student. I was impressed, always a problem. It should have been a warning sign, like the big, red master caution light on the dash of the helicopter.

The LZ control team was already on site when we arrived. I took the flight controls back from my student and landed the 46 close to them. The team leader came over to just outside the rotor disk and gave me a thumbs up, indicating that they were ready to go. I would do the first load and talk the student through what I was doing as I demonstrated the procedures.

The normal CH-46 "three on" and an "all set aft" later, I lifted the helicopter to a 20 foot hover. The crew chief announced that we were clear to the rear and I moved the helicopter backwards until I had a clear sight of the load with the hookup man standing on top of it. His assistant was next to him with the grounding pole. I hovered forward and with the crew chief's direction, quickly hooked up the load.

"Come straight up. Tension coming on. Up. Load's off, up 20. Load's off 20, cleared to go," the crew chief called.

We flew the traffic pattern with the load riding smoothly beneath us. I talked about what to do if the load starts to swing and the possible troubles if it did. Once in Vietnam, when I was still a copilot, I had a vivid demonstration of one of the worst-case scenarios, "settling with power." Settling with power is a condition that can rapidly turn fatal if you do the wrong thing or are at a low altitude when you get into it. When you get a helicopter slow at a high altitude, nearly to an "out of ground effect" hover, start a slight descent that takes you out of effective translational lift and try to stop it by adding power, the helicopter can start falling straight down in its own disturbed air. The natural reaction of the pilot is to add more power to break the fall, but that only increases the rate of descent. The more power you pull, the faster you fall. The only way out of settling with power is to get forward speed so that you get back in effective translational lift. Once you push the cyclic stick forward and get any air speed, the helicopter moves out of the disturbed air into clean air and the descent immediately becomes a climb.

---

*We had a crashed Huey hanging below our Chinook that day, a routine mission to take the wreckage to a depot for repair or stripping. The damage to the Huey kept it from hanging straight below us docilely like they usually do. Instead, it had a tendency to start swinging slightly, not a problem really, at least at first. We climbed to 6,000 feet to get out of range of any ground fire and to enjoy the cool air away from the tropical heat. We were holding the usual 90 knots airspeed as per company Standard Operating Procedure (SOP) when the Huey started to seriously swing, oscillating around to the point where it was becoming a threat to our Chinook. If it hit the bottom of our aircraft, it could possibly take us out of the sky.*

*To stop a load from swinging, the usual procedure is to slow down and make the load heavier by adding weight, i.e. add power to increase "G" on the load. The AC immediately started to slow down and add power. As we slowed, the swinging began to decrease when suddenly we were going straight down, aircraft level but falling so fast the vertical speed indicator was pegged on full down, meaning in less than one minute we would hit the jungle below.*

*"Pickle! Pickle!" the AC yelled over the intercom, meaning jettison the Huey. The Chinook has triple redundancy for getting rid of external loads: electrical, using the button on the bottom of the cyclic stick; mechanical, using a pedal between the rudder pedals on each side; and emergency, activating a red-covered switch that discharges an air bottle thereby blowing the hook to the open position. He was yelling for me to do it because, as per our SOP, we had turned off the electrical jettison system once we were safely in forward flight, to prevent an inadvertent release. Instead of using either the manual or emergency system, I was reaching for the electrical switch on the overhead panel when we looked across the cockpit at each other and simultaneously realized that we were in "settling with power."*

*The AC pushed the nose of the Chinook forward and we instantaneously went from a 6,000+ feet per minute descent to a 4,000+ feet per minute climb. He reduced the power as our airspeed came up to 90 knots. After a few seconds, the flight engineer called "Load's steady." About ten minutes later, we got our heart rates under control again. The Huey stayed where it was supposed to be without another swing for the rest of the flight. Give the crew due credit, none of them said a word about how close we had brought them to death—cool counts for them too.*

---

Later, in CH-46s, I tried to induce "settling with power" so that the student pilots could see and recognize it, but the 46 just would not go into it. The closest I could come was a zero airspeed autorotation, but the rate of descent was nothing like power settling—way too slow. When I tried it in the Sea King, I found out that not only would the aircraft readily enter "settling with power" after it entered, it would not fall straight down but would begin to oscillate violently. As soon as it started to oscillate, I would reduce power and lower the nose to fly the Sea King out of it. No point in scaring yourself any more than absolutely necessary.

But today there would be no "settling with power." Don't think we could have made that cement block swing if we wanted to; it was just too heavy and had a nice small surface area. It was a lot like the 8,000-pound loads of 105mm ammo that we carried into Laos in February, 1971. One major difference that I would not demonstrate to my student today was how we did our final approach and landed the load in 1971. Today it would just be a normal approach, coming to a high hover with the load 20 feet off the ground before moving it forward into position and setting it down. In 1971, we Chinook pilots used a procedure I've never seen before or since.

When the enemy has small arms or light machine guns around the landing zone where you are taking your external load, you want to keep your helicopter right over the secure zone and out of their range as much as possible. In a 46, you can do this flying directly over the LZ at 1,500 feet or more, then putting the helicopter into a tight spiral down, rolling into a 45–60 degree angle of bank, while dropping the power all the way down to enter autorotation as you auger down. This keeps your aircraft right over the LZ and out of enemy range, at least a little.

That was the theory anyway . . .

At some point, you roll your 46 wings level and transition back to a normal approach. You can't do this in a Chinook because the aircraft is limited to 30 degrees of bank, making your turns really big, thus very much limiting your ability to stay over the landing zone and out of enemy range.

---

*In Laos, we would fly our Chinooks directly into the wind, toward the landing zone at 3,000 feet or more, and above the ground to stay out of AK-47 and 12.7mm machine gun range. We would slow our airspeed as we got close, until at last, we were just about stopped. Power settling was not an issue because we kept the aircraft pointed into the wind. Instead of adding power to maintain altitude, when we could see the landing point between the rudder pedals, we would put the thrust all the way down to enter autorotation. With zero forward airspeed, the Chinook would be moving backwards through the air at whatever speed the wind was blowing. Since we did not have a radar altimeter at what we estimated to be 500 feet above the ground, we would lower the nose to regain airspeed and at around 200 feet we would pull back stick to flare the aircraft while adding power to break our rate of descent and ideally, transition to a normal approach. If you worked it just right, you could drop the load where they wanted it and be back in a very rapid climb within seconds.*

---

But we wouldn't do that today. We would just fly the pattern and land the load. Lift the load to about 20 feet off the ground, add power, lower the nose, climb to 300 feet, fly the pattern at 300 feet, call abeam, roll into the turn to final, bring the aircraft to a hover with the load 20 feet off the ground, and finally drop it where the LZ control team wanted it. After that, we would hover the helicopter backwards until we could see the load again and then repeat the process. We would do that for about an hour so that the student could get as many practice external loads as possible before we had to return to the airfield and real life.

After I dropped the load and moved the aircraft backwards into position, I gave the flight controls to the student. He held a nice, steady hover and at the crew chief's direction, smoothly moved forward over the load.

"Forward 10, over the load, down 10, 5 hold, steady, steady, load hooked, hookup man clear. Come straight up. Tension coming on the load. Sling's tight, up, up, load's off. Up 20, 10, steady. All ready aft, clear to go," the crew chief called. It was as smooth a pickup as I've seen and I relaxed.

The student smoothly added power and lowered the nose. But then he didn't add enough power and he lowered the nose too far and in a second the concrete block load hit the ground and dug in, rotating the helicopter at the top of the sling directly toward the ground 40 feet away, nose first. We would hit the ground in less than five seconds; first would be the forward rotor blades and as they came off, the cockpit. We might or might not burn. The crashworthy fuel system worked sometimes and sometimes it did not. But we didn't crash.

When I am not at the flight controls, I always rest my right hand on my right leg, near the cyclic stick. When I saw the nose start to rotate forward my hand moved, without conscious thought, to the cyclic and the hook release button. Without a word, I pushed the button, the hook opened, the load fell away and the aircraft began to move forward, but no longer nose first toward the ground. My right hand closed around cyclic and my left, the collective as I said, "I've got it!" The student immediately released the controls and I stopped the helicopter in a stable hover. Moving over to a clear spot, I asked the crew chief, "Clear below?" We were and I sat the helicopter down.

My crew chief was an old hand and had realized, as I did, what was happening as it happened and was moving for his release. He would have released the load if I had not. He also knew to get back out of the way because when you release a load under tension, the cargo hook will swing up and can easily hit an unwary crewman directly in the face.

The student was not even slightly upset. Ah, the joy of ignorance when you do not know how close a call you just had. I calmly went through what just happened with him and explained why it happened. He nodded and said he understood. I gave the flight controls back to him and told him to try it again. He lifted smoothly into a 20-foot hover and at the crew chief's direction again, moved the aircraft backwards until the load was visible over the dash. The crew chief talked us into position over the load. The student had no problem getting the 46 directly over the load, lowering the aircraft down until the hookup man could get the donut on the hook.

He lifted us up until the load was 20 feet off the ground, and transitioned us to forward flight absolutely perfectly. There was no hint of his first time mistake. He did five more lifts, each time with a heavier load, and each, absolutely perfect from hookup to drop back in the LZ. Training hop complete, we flew back to New River with a GCA to a final landing, hit the fuel pits to top off the tanks and taxied back to the ramp. I gave him all "above average" marks for the flight on the write- up since he did all lifts as close to perfect as pilots get after almost killing us on the first try. Like I said in the beginning, he was a natural pilot.

Luck and superstition . . .

# 21

## THE RITUAL

### MARINE CORPS AIR STATION, NEW RIVER,
### NORTH CAROLINA ■ NOVEMBER 1985

*Most things change over a flying career. Flying uniforms change: I started flying in cotton fatigues, then two-piece nomex flight suits, and then one-piece nomex coveralls. Aircraft change: when you are in the Marine Corps, you start Navy helicopter training in the TH-57T and then move up to UH-1E/L model Hueys; then the Huey is gone and you are in the Fleet Marine Corps flying a CH-46F. Even military services change: first I flew in the Army and then the National Guard and then the Marine Corps. Clothes change, aircraft change, even services change for some of us, but what never changes is the ritual that leads to a flight. If anything, the ritual becomes stronger and more ingrained with time.*

As nearly always, my eyes came open about five minutes before the clock went off. Somewhere along the line, my internal clock took over from the teenage desire to sleep longer, and my eyes open before they have to. In the darkness, as my eyes opened, the same two feelings were always there. First, I had to piss and second, I needed some nicotine. Shutting off the alarm before it had a chance to ring, I climbed from bed, carefully trying not to wake my wife and headed for the bathroom. From there I went to the kitchen, turned on the light and plugged in the coffee peculator I had prepared the night before. Then, as it began its work, I went back to the living room and lit my pipe for the first time of the day.

It takes a long time to get a military flight into the air properly. The ground crews and the enlisted aircrew checked everything on the aircraft the night before but there are many more checks to do in the morning before the pilots arrive. The pilots themselves must sit through a briefing, then brief themselves, view the aircraft paperwork, preflight, and start it up. For the pilots, it takes an hour and a half, so you must be there at least 15 minutes before the brief to get ready for it. Typically, the process from wakeup to takeoff took me two and a half hours, but I always gave myself a little extra time.

I always plan on getting up at least 15 minutes before I have to so that I can have the coffee and the smoke before I have to move into more complicated activities. By the time the bowl of tobacco was gone, the coffee was ready, so I went to the kitchen and poured the first of many cups of coffee I would drink that day. After the coffee, I shaved, brushed my teeth, and showered before dressing in a semi-clean set of utilities and combat boots. Semi-clean because they had been worn once but had not wrinkled to the point that a new set was required. I brought a cup of coffee into the bedroom and set it next to my sleeping wife while I gave her a small kiss before leaving for work. As I left the bedroom, I heard a sleepy, "be careful" from behind me. My second cup of coffee went with me in the car in a red glass cup, like those my parents used to use.

Driving down the stretch of Highway 17 in the dark toward the Air Station, I faced a steady stream of cars going the other direction, even though it was only 0500 hours. The men in the cars were Marines on their way to the rifle range: go about two miles past my house and take a left turn at the blinking light by Dixon school, and then go another three miles before you turn off to the left. The rifle range always started at dawn, no matter the time of year. That meant the shooters could finish up early enough to get back to the base and clean their weapons by early afternoon, so the staff could do all the other things that go with being a Marine, like PT and paperwork. Six, sometimes seven days a week, you could hear the gunfire in the distance from my front yard. Sometimes further away, you could hear machine guns too, maybe even mortars over on Camp Lejeune.

Drinking coffee and listening to AM country music, I drove more or less without thought, until I turned the headlights off and parking lights on to keep from blinding the sentry, before going through the gate to the Air Station. The sentry waved me through without a glance, even though it was too early for the "proceed" sign to be out and all the cars that made up the morning rush hour to pass through unimpeded.

There were lots of parking places in the narrow lot in front of my squadron's hanger as I arrived. Later there would be none and some of the squadron would have to park illegally in the commissary parking lot and hope they would not get a ticket. But at 0520 hours no one was there except those who had to get the aircraft ready or fly in the early launch.

The cars of the young enlisted men, those with the red base stickers, were generally older models, covered with the emblems of various rock groups and semi-obscene bumper stickers—"All I want is a nice sweet girl who doesn't mind cleaning vomit off the dash." The staff NCOs tended toward bigger, American cars, while the unmarried junior officers had the sporty, import models. The older officers drove the typical second cars, usually economy models, with a year or two left in them. Given that the older officers were usually in their thirties, their other vehicle, the newer one, was likely to be a van, used to carry groceries and to haul the kids to soccer matches and little league.

Leaving the empty coffee cup in the car, I walked toward the gray steel door with my squadron's patch painted on it that led to the second deck and the squadron ready room. It seemed like I had taken this walk a million times, past the sign with the CO, XO, and sergeant major's names on it, below the plywood sign in the shape of the squadron patch. The dingy ladderwell to the second deck had one bulb out and needed sweeping but I was not the buildings and grounds officer or the XO, so I didn't even really think about reporting it to anyone. The once painted but now nearly bare metal rail left rust on my hand as I climbed the stairs.

Turning left at the top, down the passageway and through the empty ready room and into the locker room, I saw and heard no one else. The operations duty officer (ODO) board, a plastic sheet divided into rows and columns with names, times, and aircraft numbers, was filled out, so at least the ODO was here, just not at the duty desk. A noise from the toilet confirmed his location.

As I turned on the locker room light, a figure in the bottom rack of the bunk bed by the door stirred. The squadron duty officer, the SDO, a new lieutenant who had just joined the squadron, eyed me, the captain, sleepily. The location of the duty rack, a pair of stacked gray-steel bunk beds, one for the SDO and one for his enlisted clerk, between the head and ready room, made it nearly impossible for anyone to sleep there after Flight Operations started for the day.

"Morning, Sir," said a voice from under the scratchy green wool issue blanket.

"Quiet night, Lieutenant?" I asked.

"Ab-so-fucking-lootly dead, Sir."

Not really feeling like further conversation, I worked the combination lock and opened my locker. I took out a gray-green flight suit on a wire hanger. A quick sniff convinced me it was time to change to a fresh one, so placing the hanger on one of the top vents of the locker door, I began to strip the old one. The Velcro holding the squadron patch on the left breast made a ripping sound as I pulled it off. Next came the name tag from above the left breast pocket and then the pen and grease pencil from the left shoulder pocket. From the knife pocket, inside the left thigh of the flight suit, I pulled out the white parachute cord that attached a Swiss Army knife to the grommet at the top of the pocket. After un-tying the string, I pulled the knife out and laid it on the shelf with the patches. From the left calf pocket of the flight suit, I pulled out the pocket checklist that all pilots carried. Taking the clean flight suit from the locker door, I placed all the items in their proper places and re-hung it on the locker door.

Lifting my old green nylon helmet bag from the bottom of the locker, I sat it on the bench that ran the length of the locker room. I could have requested a new helmet bag but this one had been with me for many, many flights starting back in Navy flight school, so why change? Reaching into the dark locker, I found my steel-toed black flight boots and put them next to the helmet bag. Sitting down on the narrow bench that ran the length of the locker room, I unlaced my combat boots and tossed them into the locker with the dirty flight suit, producing a minor crash somewhat muffled by the dirty flight suit. Hanging my utilities on a spare hanger, I put the fresh flight suit on, reached into the top shelf of the locker for the shaving kit full of shoeshine things, and sat back down.

After polishing the flight boots, I laced them over the green British aircrew socks left over from my exchange tour—they stayed up better on my skinny legs—and stood up. I reached back into the locker and removed the survival vest from the heavy steel hanger from the flight equipment section. Slinging the vest over my shoulder, I took the old leather flight jacket off its hanger, picked up my helmet bag, and went out into the ready room to prepare for the brief and the day's mission.

Ignoring the sleepy SDO as I went by, I sat down in the front row of seats. I put my vest onto an empty chair in the second row. Setting the helmet bag on the floor next to my chair, I took out my battered black aluminum kneeboard and tore off the top sheet of paper so I would have a clean space to work on. Taking the black ink issue SkillCraft pen, made by the blind, from its storage tube on the right of the knee board, I clicked it open and began marking off spaces on the blank sheet of paper.

In the upper left hand corner of the paper, I drew a rectangular box. Below that, I drew several lines. One I labeled "Squadron Common," the next three I left blank. After labeling the appropriate spaces, I copied the numbers for the UHF and FM radio frequencies, the weather, including the barometric pressure and temperature, and the wind direction here at the airfield off the ODO board.

At 0528, the ODO came in and moved a stack of papers from the duty desk to the lectern.

"Seen my copilot?," I asked from my front row seat.

"Yes, Sir.," the ODO replied. "He went down to his car to get something; said he would be back in a couple of minutes."

As the last words were out of his mouth, another lieutenant, my copilot, walked through the ready room door from the hallway and took a seat next to me. He had his kneeboard in his hand with a folded piece of paper on it. It was 0533 hours.

"Any particular reason you're late for the brief?" I asked, trying to sound as bored as possible.

The lieutenant flushed, "Sorry, Sir, I just wanted to get my thermos out of the car, I didn't realize that it was so late."

I just looked at him and said nothing. After a moment I looked up at the ODO and said, "Shall we get started?"

The ODO had been silent until now. Usually I was the first one with a joke and I love war stories more than anything, but the ODO had flown with me enough to know that I had two personalities, one for flying and one for the rest of the time. The "flying me" still had the sense of humor but tolerated no lack of professionalism, especially in the brief. The mental door marked "flying" had closed and there was room for nothing else.

"Time hack (a military term for marking the exact time) in 30 seconds. Time at the mark will be 0535 hours," the ODO said.

"Hack in 5 seconds."

"Hack. Time is 0535 hours. All crews scheduled for the 0700 launch are present (a rather useless comment since the lieutenant and I made up the entire early launch, but he had to say it). Weather is 1500 scattered, viz 6 miles in haze; temperature is 16 degrees C; sunrise at 0658; PA and DA (PA is pressure altitude and DA is density altitude. They are used to calculate aircraft performance) are as posted; wind is 040 at 7 knots; forecast is for VFR all day. Missions are as assigned on the flight schedule. You are scheduled for the frag (fragment of a full mission order, contains only the portions of the order necessary to define a particular mission) supporting 2/8. You've got the frag sheet, Sir. Aircraft assignments will be posted when Maintenance calls them up. Hot ranges are posted on the board. No quiet hours today at New River or Cherry Point. The maintenance officer says all chock times (the time when the aircraft must be parked back on the ramp) are hard. He also said, "If you are late I will have your ass." Check in on Squadron common fox mike in and out bound. Any questions, sir?"

The ODO's words sounded like he was reading a script, which he in fact was. The words were spelled out clearly in the notebook he had open in front of him on the lectern. Under the tattered, plastic cover, the sheets themselves were wrinkled and smeared with illegible words scribbled next to and sometimes over the text. The ODO knew that I knew the words by heart and would remind him if he forgot something, even though all three of us could probably say them without even looking at the notebook. It is a religious exercise in all senses.

Turning from the ODO, I reached into my lower right flight suit ankle pocket and pulled out my copy of the checklist. With the words, "Our aircraft will be as assigned by Maintenance," the next part of the ritual, the briefing, began.

Five hours later and sitting in the chocks, our CH-46E went quiet as the auxiliary power unit (APU) died. It had been a long morning, and the quiet felt nice after the noise of the engines and transmissions and radios.

I took my helmet off, looked over at the lieutenant on my right and said, "Cheated death again, didn't we? Luck and superstition, that's all it is." After a quick post-flight inspection, we left the aircraft and walked across the ramp back to the ready room and the rest of our day.

We had exited the room marked "flying" and returned to normal life with all the rooms we go through every day.

# 22

# SPECIAL OPERATIONS CAPABLE

## USS *GUAM* ■ MARCH 1987

---

*The military loves acronyms. To be an acronym the letters must make up a word you can actually say, not just be a collection of letters. Neither FBI nor CIA, for two examples, is an acronym, because no one says "fib ah" or "cee ah," they just say the letters, but NATO, being a military organization, is an acronym. No one says "N-A-T-O," they say the word" NATO." Of the US Armed Forces, the Naval Forces are probably the worst. In this case I mean "MEU-SOC" (pronounced "Mew-Sock"), Marine-speak for "Marine Expeditionary Unit—Special Operations Capable."*

---

In the 1980s everyone had "Special Operations" forces, everyone except the Marine Corps. The Army had the Green Berets, Delta Force, 160th Special Operations Aviation Regiment, and others. The Navy, the SEALs, and even the Air Force had Special Operators, but the Marines only had "Recon" as "elite" forces. Recon has a very specific mission not usually involved with the things the other services' "special operators" do. Of course, the Marine Corps, quite rightly, considered every single Marine elite, but needed some designation to show that the units they were deploying were more than just your run-of-the-mill units, hence the need for "Special Operations Capable" units. Note that they are "capable" of Special Operations, not full time Special Operations units like the SEALs and Green Berets. Perhaps it is best to think in terms SEALs and Green Berets being sent out as precision instruments, a scalpel perhaps. A MEU-SOC can do similar things, but is more of a meat ax than a scalpel. The cutting gets done, but perhaps not as smoothly, and certainly messier.

A MEU is the smallest Marine Corps unit capable of independent operations. While it is rare for them to be identical in composition from one deployment to another, a MEU usually consists of a re-enforced infantry battalion, a re-enforced squadron (typically 12 CH-46s, 4 CH-53s, 4 Cobras, 2 Hueys, 4 Harriers, and when needed, 2 C-130s that would deploy from the states to the nearest shore base), and a re-enforced logistics unit. All three elements are commanded by lieutenant colonels under a full colonel, the MEU commander.

To gain the MEU-SOC designation, the MEU would undergo additional training on their build-up to deploying as the Landing Force 6th Fleet (LF6F) and take a complex final exam: a Special Operations Capable Examination, a "SOCEX," before receiving the designation. The SOCEX would be undertaken from shipboard and would involve a detailed series of scenarios covering many of the events that the MEU-SOC might be called upon to execute. Evaluators, the top Marine Corps experts in all areas to be examined, would come in from all over the world to observe and report on how well the MEU performed.

The SOCEX missions include such things as a "NEO"—Nationals Evacuation Operation (i.e. removal of US and allied civilians from a war zone) and "TRAP" (Tactical Recovery of Aircraft and Personnel—an expanded version of a traditional search and rescue). As an aside, I was there when the mission was first discussed for inclusion in the Marine Corps SOP. I told the leaders that "Tactical" was not the right word for the name since the mission would only be done under hostile conditions, so perhaps the word "Combat" should be substituted. I almost got away with it until someone deciphered the acronym—it would have been a "CRAP" mission. They stuck with "Tactical." The missions were usually done at night and using NVG (Night Vision Goggles). All missions were covered by an extensive checklist that listed all things that should be done to plan and execute the missions, which the evaluators filled out as they went along. It was not a "gentleman's evaluation"; squadrons could and did fail. For this particular evaluation, we were joined by our "real" Army Special Ops colleagues from Fort Campbell and Fort Bragg. They saw a chance to get some shipboard operations in and to see how they worked with us "regulars."

The mission was complex, but not for us Marines. We would take a flight of eight Frogs loaded with infantry to the outlying airfield where the "hostages" were being held, and land them at the north end as a blocking force so that the bad guys could not be re-enforced. Simultaneous with our landing, the Special Ops guys would swoop in onboard their Special Ops aircraft and storm the bad guys. To make sure everything was coordinated between the Marines and the Special Ops aircrews, one of our pilots would deploy with their Command and Control element in an unmarked "biz" jet that was outfitted with the latest in communications equipment that would be overhead during the mission. The Marine lead would be in touch with the Special Ops C&C aircraft by secure radio at all times so any changes could be made with no difficulties.

The CO liked to be in the lead aircraft on missions like this one, so he had the Ops O put me down as his copilot. In effect, that meant that I would do all the planning and heavy lifting, which is as it should be since I was the Weapons and Tactics Instructor (WTI) and an old combat pilot. He was the CO and also an old combat pilot, but did more paperwork than flying now, also as it should be. I was looking forward to the mission because I felt some of the Army Special Ops guys looked down on us regular, Marine Corps "Special Ops Capable" aircrews. Maybe I was more sensitive to it than I should have been because not only had I been an Army aviator for seven years, I thought I knew one of them from my long ago Army days.

---

*The Special Ops maintenance officer was a very old CW4. He was standing in the back of the ready room talking to our maintenance officer when I first saw him. Something about him was so familiar I could not help but introduce myself and tell him that I had once been an Army warrant officer myself. He laughed and asked me what Warrant Officer Candidate Company (WOC) I was in at Fort Wolters and I told him, "9th WOC, Dec 68—Jun 69." He laughed again and told me that he was the senior TAC officer (short for tactical officer, the main harasser of officer candidates) for the 9th WOC during that time. He, of course, did not remember me in particular since he saw so many of us go through, but he certainly remembered my platoon TAC officer and told me that we were right, the guy was crazy. Even the other TAC officers considered him crazy. It seems my TAC officer never completely recovered from being shot down in a Cobra and nearly being burned to death. His experiences let out a sadistic streak that went way beyond "normal" Officer Candidate School (OCS) harassment. Once I watched him swing a swagger stick, made* from a piece of stainless steel from a tail rotor drive shaft, at the head of a candidate he had braced up against a wall. He missed by a couple of inches and hit the wall so hard it bent the steel. Had he misjudged, he would have probably killed the man.

I asked the CW4 why some people "washed out," were eliminated from flight training, when there were others that we knew were not as good in the cockpit who were not eliminated. He laughed for the third time and confirmed what I always thought—it was quite often purely arbitrary. Higher HQ would take a look at the losses in Vietnam and the number of pilots staying in the Army verses the numbers getting out. From this they would determine how many they needed in the pipeline as replacements. Since there were so many of us going through training, word would come down to the senior TAC officer to "eliminate four." Based on flight and ground school grades, military bearing, and sometimes just because it wasn't your day, you would be told to pack your stuff. Flight school was over for you. You still went to Vietnam but instead of being a pilot, you were shipped out as a grunt or clerk or whatever. In retrospect, it may have saved some lives since casualties ran very high among the warrant officer pilots in those days. But that's not how it seemed to us in 1969— it was another arbitrary roll of the dice, like your draft number coming up.

We left Fort Polk, Louisiana in a convoy of buses immediately after our basic training graduation parade. We pulled into Fort Wolters late in the evening after a long day of excitement from graduation and the bus ride from Leesville, Louisiana, to Mineral Wells, Texas. Graduation meant the end of basic and the beginning of flight school, the end of "90 days between you and the sky." We all knew there would be harassment, but none of us were prepared for the scale of it. The TAC officers were waiting as the buses pulled in and as the doors opened, they came running in, screaming for us to get off the bus and into formation. Yelling and screaming far more than the drill instructors at Polk, more than we had ever heard. All around, men were on the ground doing pushups, jumping jacks—the weeding out process started right then.

As the Army always does when you arrive at new post, they immediately marched us off to eat dinner, even though it was 2300 hours and we had already stopped at a cafeteria for dinner three hours before. I was assigned to be equipment guard while everyone else went into the mess hall. I stood at attention over our duffle bags for three hours, forgotten in the excitement of fresh *meat arriving. Finally, one of the company NCOs saw me and sent me over to the barracks where the chaos was expanding as everyone tried to get "squared away" to the TAC officer's satisfaction, an impossible task.*

*That first night, my platoon filled both floors of the old WWII barracks. Six months later when we graduated from the first half of flight school, there were not enough of us left to fill even the lower floor. Between the TAC officer's arbitrary washouts, and the lack of flying adaptability, attrition over the entire class was about 60%, normal for late 1960's Army flight school.*

*Seven years later on the first night of Marine OCS at Quantico, I thought back to that first night at Fort Wolters. The yelling was the same, but this time all the fear was gone, for me at least. I knew exactly what was coming and that they would not kill us. I also knew that unlike Fort Wolters, if you washed out for any reason you just went home. At Fort Wolters you owed the Army two years and if you washed out, the next stop was Vietnam.*

---

But that was a long time ago and we both had our missions, so after a few minutes conversation the CW4 went back to his tasks and I to mine.

It was a good night for NVG operations, clear March skies and nearly a full moon. Our flight loaded up with troops and took off from the deck of the *Guam* in two waves of four. I made the takeoff into the night while the CO took the map to navigate. The high level of moonlight made the world very clear through the green lenses of the NVG. We arrived at our hold point on time and did a slow orbit in tactical cruise while the second flight of four took off to join us.

While we waited, our liaison officer had flown to Washington, DC, in one of their unmarked biz jets with the Special Ops command team. He put on a business suit instead of a flight suit and carrying a briefcase, went out with them to an unmarked Gulfstream IV (G-IV) parked in the general aviation portion of Reagan National Airport. To the casual observer they were just another group of "businessmen" off to carry out some corporate business. The G-IV was not a corporate aircraft but rather a flying command post, full of secure communications gear. Hooked into the Special Ops command center, it could control operations anywhere in the world.

That was the theory anyway . . .

In our orbit, we were maintaining complete radio silence. In my wide turn, I could see the remaining aircraft join us. When our flight of eight was complete, I called the G-IV on our secure UHF radio to tell them we were in position. No reply. I tried twice more but still had nothing in return. The plan, at that point, was to switch to a back-up frequency, so the CO changed the radio to the new channel and I called again. Still nothing. At that point the CO was contemplating aborting the mission. If the mission was compromised, the bad guys would know we were coming and be waiting for us. We would be taking eight CH-46 loads of Marines right into an ambush. Just then, we heard a call over UHF guard, the emergency frequency that everyone monitors. It was our liaison officer doing something that would never, ever have been done in combat, calling us to tell us to proceed with the mission. It seems they could not get the radios on the Command and Control G-IV to transmit in a secure mode so instead of aborting the mission, they gave up and called us in the clear—On Guard. Had the mission been real, the bad guys would have known for sure we were coming now.

Pushing the start button on the eight-day clock mounted in the helicopter's dash, I began the countdown to "push," the time we would leave our hold point and start on our route to the airfield where the blocking force was to go in. As I had been since takeoff, I was flying the aircraft and the CO was "navigating." I put it in quotes because we were flying in our local area and I had flown in and out of the target airfield many, many times as a flight instructor in MHT-204. I could find it day or night by following a big set of power lines until they made a sharp left turn. At that point the airfield was 30 seconds straight ahead at 90 knots ground speed. Even so, we had planned the mission exactly like we would have, had we never seen the area before. The maps were marked just so, the timing of each leg planned exactly, all the things that must be done for a successful mission.

Had it been a real mission, we would have been flying with our lights out; but it was not real and we were in the middle of North Carolina, not some far away war zone. That said, the Special Ops aircraft were flying lights out and right down on the trees in near nap-of-the-earth flight (50 feet or less). Us regular Marines had to follow normal stateside rules, but not them. They were "Special" while we were just "Special Operations Capable." We would go no lower than 200 feet on the NVG until we were on short final to the target airfield.

Our timing was working out just about right. I had been holding the airspeed close to what I had planned but we must have had more of a tailwind than forecast because we were approaching our final checkpoint 30 seconds ahead of plan. Our landing had to be exact to prevent the noise of our aircraft giving away the mission too soon. Just as I started to slow the 46, the CO said, "OK, I've got the aircraft. You take over navigation." I was floored as he handed me the map and took the controls. As he took over, he did a slight turn that took us a little off course and at the same time he descended below 200 feet, greatly shortening how far ahead we could see. No problem, while I might be slightly disoriented from the abrupt change from pilot to navigator, I had done this run many times. There went the power line on its turn so we should just continue straight ahead and we would be there in a few seconds. Then the right hand door gunner called, "Airfield at 3 o'clock."

It couldn't be. The airfield should be directly ahead. But maybe in the handoff of the flight controls, we got further off our course than I thought we did. "Turn right," I called to the CO over the ICS. He started the turn and as he did, I saw through the NVG that the gunner had mistaken a private grass airstrip for the target field. Behind us the other aircraft were handling the turn with no problems in the tactical cruise formation.

"Roll out and turn left to 020, Sir," I told the CO. As he steadied out on the new course, the target airfield came into sight. As we planned, we landed at the north end, leaving space for the other seven CH-46s behind us. As we stopped, the ramp was down and the Marines in the back were out and running to their blocking positions. I looked at the clock as our wheels touched. We were exactly on time, not early or late—exactly on time. Twenty seconds after touchdown the ramp was coming up and we were airborne again, climbing out rapidly to our holding point. Ten minutes later, we were coming back in to pick up the grunts. Their blocking mission was complete and we just had to fly them back to the ship.

The flight back was uneventful. We climbed to 500 feet and one at a time, took off the NVG and transitioned back to normal visual night flight.

Crossing the beach inbound to the ship, we made the normal radio calls. Emcon (emissions control, meaning no radio transmissions) was over now that the mission was complete. The first four aircraft landed in order and we barely got the blades folded after shutdown before they were towing us to the boneyard to make space for the second four Frogs. The entire mission had taken two hours, one and a half of it on NVG. Thirty minutes after the last aircraft landed, we all gathered in the ready room for the de-brief. Nearly all the pilots were there, even the ones that did not fly on the mission wanted to know how it went.

After the Marine infantry mission commander and his platoon leaders joined us, the CO, as flight lead, did the honors of beginning the de-brief. He was all smiles since our part went exactly as planned. The XO had been leading the second division of four. He complemented the CO on the "S" turn on the final leg to burn off the few seconds that would have made us early. The CO did not mention the turn was made because our crewman called of the wrong airfield. The aircraft commander of the last 46 reported the tactical cruise worked as advertised. All the other ACs agreed in turn that it had gone very well indeed, as did the grunt commander. We put them exactly where they wanted to go exactly on time. The projected re-enforcing bad guys did not show up, so no shots were fired and no casualties were suffered. Pickup and the return flight were uneventful from their viewpoint, just about as perfect a mission as you could get.

Our squadron debrief complete, the CO, XO, and I went down to the Ward Room for the overall mission debrief by the Special Ops major general. Because of how the mission had been conducted, we had no idea how it went overall, we just knew our portion was as planned. We had passed our "final exam" for the MEU-SOC designation.

The Special Ops guys were already there when we came into the back of the Ward Room. They were all very quiet, none of the earlier cockiness in evidence. The MEU commander (a Marine colonel) and the LF6F commodore (a Navy captain) were seated at the front table, but it seemed that we were waiting for someone. Then an Army two-star in camouflage uniform stomped, literally stomped, into the room. His face was red and it was readily apparent that he was very, very angry. He was the Special Operations overall commander and his Special Operations had not worked well, had not worked well at all. He started off strong and got louder and stronger as he talked.

The problems started when the Special Ops assault troops, the ones that would be taking out the bad guys and rescuing the hostages, elected not to fly down to Camp Lejeune with the helicopter unit. Instead, they would drive down. To do this they used three unmarked rental vans, the kind that tradesmen use. They would travel in "civies" so that the locals would not get too curious about all the military people passing through.

In a small North Carolina town not too far from the target area, they stopped to buy gas and several of them got out to use the men's room. One of the Special Operators left the door to the back of the van open just a crack. Of course three van loads of muscular young men did get the locals curious. One of the gas station workers casually walked past the open van door and saw a machine gun. Keeping as calm as he could, he went back inside and called the local sheriff, "Sheriff, we got a bunch of what looks like to me to be terrorists here at my station! They got machine guns and who knows what!"

The Sheriff had spent a lot of money equipping a SWAT team and now it looked like they would be needed. He hit the panic button, and in short order they were descending on the gas station. Faced with real armed men, the Special Ops guys tried to explain but would not tell the Sheriff what they were doing in his territory. Try as they might, they could not talk him into letting them go. In fact, they right pissed him off by being evasive about what they were up to. No one had told him about any military exercises in his county. Finally the Sheriff agreed to call their commander at Fort Bragg. When he talked to the general, he told him he would let them go if and when the general himself came down and signed for them.

The general had no power over the Sheriff, and if he wanted the mission done on time, he really had no choice. He called for one of the Shorts Skyvan Special Ops fixed-wing aircraft to take him down immediately. To try to maintain some sort of tactical posture, and to land as close as possible to the gas station where the Sheriff was holding his men, the aircraft would land on a logging road a half-mile away instead of going to the nearest airport, ten miles away. Unfortunately, upon landing the pilot lost control of the Skyvan and it went into a ditch. No real damage to the plane and no one hurt, but the aircraft would need a maintenance crew from Fort Bragg to get it out. When he finally got to the gas station the general signed and the sheriff released his very sheepish men to him.

Meanwhile, the Special Command and Control G-IV flying from Washington was overhead with all its communications electronics out of communication, meaning no contact with the assault force and/or blocking force. None of its secure radios and links were working like they were supposed to. Our liaison officer knew we would abort the mission at push time if we had not been given the "go ahead" to execute, so in desperation, he came up On Guard so give the order to execute. He had to use his personal call sign and the CO's personal call sign to let us know it was real. Everyone involved with the mission knew that if that happened in reality, the mission would have been compromised and would have been aborted, but this was an exercise so we went ahead.

Now, instead of flying into the target airfield, the Special Ops men would simulate that they had been inserted by helicopter some distance away and would assault the bad guy's hideout on foot. The hostages would be freed and Special Ops' "Little Bird" helicopter gunships would provide air support, if needed, and their Blackhawks would fly the hostages out after they were freed.

The Special Ops forces moved into position for the assault as planned, but bad guys had set up trip wires on the likely approaches to their hideout—nothing fancy, just some wires tied to tin cans that would rattle when they were moved. At the same moment the Special Ops men began to move forward, the airborne "little birds" were a bit off on their navigation and got too close to the hideout, close enough that the bad guys heard them at the same time they heard their trip wires being tripped. The bad guys then "executed" all the hostages and disappeared into the night, leaving only "dead" hostages for the Special Ops guys to find. The general saw and heard it all from his concealed position near the hideout.

The general finally ran out of steam. In the silence that followed, the Special Ops grunts and aircrews looked straight ahead. It was all the three of us regular "Special Operations Capable" pilots could do to keep from laughing. Sometimes "Special Operations Capable" supporting cast gets it right and sometime "Special Operations" superstars do not. Had we actually laughed, I think the general would have had us executed, or at least contemplated it. Instead, he addressed the commodore and the MEU commander directly and told them that the only part of this debacle that had gone right was the performance of the Marines in setting up the blocking force. They were in place on time and ready to meet the threat. With that, he thanked the commodore and the MEU commander for their cooperation and left the room followed shortly by the Special Operators.

The commodore and MEU commander remained behind. The commodore motioned for us to come over. All he said, after we gathered around him, was "Well done," the highest possible praise in the Navy and Marine Corps vocabulary.

We were now a MEU (SOC) and ready for our six-month deployment as LF6F.

# 23

# BROKEN ON A MOROCCAN BEACH
## EAST OF TANGIER ■ JANUARY 1988

---

*One thing about being a Marine is that you can never let some-
one else be in charge if you are senior. Officers never ever stop
being who they are no matter what role they may be in at any
given moment, and Marine officers like it that way because it
makes things black and white, no ambiguity. So while for training purposes we pretend, otherwise, pretension stops when reality
intrudes. This is not a bad thing; it is just the way it must be.*

---

W hen our helicopter had an engine that wouldn't start, I could not
just sit back to see what the helicopter aircraft commander, the
"HAC," would do. I was the major and he was the lieutenant and with the
engine problem, the section leader's evaluation I was giving him on this
mission was now over. So, there we were, stuck on a beach on the Mediterranean coast of Morocco with one engine that wouldn't start, 70 miles away
from our ship, as it got dark.

I arrived in Morocco via Lisbon. As the senior WTI and director of
safety, standardization, and NATOPS (DSSN), another officer and I were
sent ahead of our ship, the USS *Nassau,* via Marine Corps C-12 (a
Beechcraft King Air) from NAS Sigonella, Sicily, to Lisbon, Portugal, to
liaise with the Portuguese Marine Corps for an upcoming NATO exercise
we were going to execute down south of Lisbon. It was to be our final exercise of this six month deployment and we wanted it to be as nearly perfect
as possible, a sort of graduation exercise. When we arrived at Lisbon's International Airport, there was a brand new Mercedes SUV with a Portuguese Marine officer and driver there to meet us.

---

*As life sometimes works out, I was, unknown to me, a friend of the comman-
dant of the Portuguese Marine Corps. A few years before, I had been deployed
with my British Royal Navy (RN) squadron onboard HMS* Illustrious *for a*

*small bi-lateral exercise between the RN and Portuguese Navy. Two Portuguese Marine Corps (PMC) officers were also onboard, but for some reason, perhaps because they were Marines and not Navy, the RN officers were ignoring them. Seeing this and being a Marine myself, I introduced myself to them and in short order, we were the best of comrades, swapping stories about wars lost: theirs—Angola, and mine—Vietnam. We exchanged names and addresses and as men often do, never communicated afterwards; however, the senior officer remembered my name when he saw it on the list of inbound officers. It was golden.*

The Mercedes took me to the four-star hotel my friend had booked me into, at the "military rate" of $10 (US) a day. The PMC driver/body guard was stationed outside my door anytime I was in residence. When I came out the door he came to attention and drove me wherever I wanted to go. The first place was to HQPMC to discuss the mission and to thank my friend for his hospitality. Over the next three days, we completed the liaison, driving to the south coast to pick out the site for our squadron base camp and doing reconnaissance on the LZs we would use in the exercise. When we were finished with our work in Portugal, another C-12 flown by two Marine officers from Rota Spain flew into Lisbon to pick us up and take us to Tangier, Morocco, to meet the USS *Nassau*. In Morocco, we would complete a minor bi-lateral exercise a few miles down the coast from Tangiers with their military before moving to Portugal for the last exercise of this six-month LF6F.

The C-12 dropped us at Tangier's airport, about 20 miles south of the city, where US embassy people were supposed to meet us, take us through customs and get us to Tangier's harbor where our ship was to anchor. No embassy folks were there when we climbed out of the C-12. There was not a sign of a Moroccan Customs and Immigration Station either, so we went into the terminal building to wait. While the terminal building was full of exotic people coming and going, after an hour and two coffees, we were tired of waiting. We went out to the taxi rank in front of terminal and climbed into the old Mercedes that was first in line.

We were expecting to get ripped off as often happens in out-of-the-way airports but instead, found the driver reasonable in his rates, friendly in his fluent English conversation, and a willing tour guide as he took us into the city. As we headed toward the city at a leisurely pace, he pointed out objects of interest along the road, ruins, colonial buildings, etc. We told him we were waiting on a ship but did not know exactly when it would arrive. He told us he knew just the place for us to wait and dropped us at a slightly seedy but lovely bar overlooking the harbor. An hour later we were on our second beer when we heard the "whop-whop-whop" of a UH-1N out over the water. As the Huey headed further on down the coast, the bow of the *Nassau* appeared around the headland as the ship headed for its anchorage. An hour later, we were at the dock waiting for the first ship's launch to arrive. The Moroccans were more than a bit surprised that we had not cleared customs at the airport, but after a few signatures and stamps on our orders, things were cleared up and we were on the launch headed toward the ship.

Five days later I was on a mission in support of our Moroccan hosts, joint training with our SEALs and the Moroccan Special Operations troops, at a beach about 40 miles to the east, down the coast from Tangier and the *Nassau*. The mission required a flight of two CH-46E (a "section" in Marine Corps aviation terms), with my aircraft in the lead. Using the mission as a target of opportunity for training the junior pilots, I was acting as copilot while giving the real copilot a section leader check that would let him command a flight of two helicopters. The aviator taking the section lead evaluation was doing fine. He had hit all marks from the start of the brief to the navigation to the LZ and leading the second helicopter. Our flying was fun, too, just the two helicopters headed out east, down the Moroccan coast on a beautiful North African January day.

The SEALs we were supporting were already there when we arrived at the training site on the coast, having driven down with the Moroccans a few days before. After a short briefing, they had us doing interesting flying instead of just the usual landing and taking off, ferrying them from one LZ to another. Instead, we were flying low and slow over the water while they jumped off the ramp into the blue sea. Sometimes we would fly low over the water and they would put inflatable boats out the back and then jump into the sea after them. It was all supposed to be training for the Moroccans for their Moroccan counterparts, but the US SEALs were enjoying it greatly, too, after the routine of deployed LF6F life.

At the end of the day, both aircraft shut down on the beach above the high tide line for a final debrief before we flew back to the ship. Everyone was well pleased with the day's work. Brief complete, the SEALs and Moroccan commandos left by truck to continue their training at other locations. We too were finished for the day and had only to return to Tangier and rejoin the *Nassau* after a very satisfying day of flying. We expected to be back before dinner time and certainly before the movie in the ward room. The mission had been fun and the section leader check went very well indeed, but when we tried to fire up our 46, the Number 2 Engine would not start.

The engine motored over like it should. Through the helmets you could hear the turbines spinning up and the igniters firing like they should, but it would not light. The crew chief tried various things, magic things, routine things. The crew chief from our wingman came over and he too tried various things, all the magic they knew between them. Nothing.

The helicopter was on the beach, but close to a Moroccan village that was not far removed from stone-age construction, at least to our eyes. There were no power lines or telephone wires going in or out, meaning, of course, no electricity, and in the pre-cell phone days, no telephone communications. We were well beyond UHF radio range with the *Nassau* and so had no way to tell them we were broken. It was getting dark on this January evening and we were soon to be overdue for our return. Rather than have the ship launch a search for us when we did not return before dark, I told our wingman to fly back to Tangier and tell the squadron our problem. We would spend the night in the bird and they could come fix us in the daylight tomorrow, rather than go through the whole complicated dance of flying a maintenance crew down in the dark and quite possibly working all night.

I watched my wingman disappear off up the coast to the west. Before long, he would have to turn north to continue to follow the coast to Tangier. It is always easier to follow a coast, a road, railroad, than just cut cross country, at least it was before GPS.

*As I watched him fly away, I contemplated how many times I had broken down in helicopters and how it was usually in some very inconvenient place. Bermuda was one, not usually a bad place to get stuck, but the timing was off. We were on our way back from a six-month deployment, not on our way over to the Mediterranean. The ship's captain was very angry with me because he had to turn his ship around and come back so that maintenance people could come ashore and fix my aircraft. Istanbul was another, an exotic place that would have been worth exploring except we had to stay with our aircraft until maintenance could get to us. Farmer's fields from Alabama to Kentucky, very nice places I'm sure, but why did they always have dogs that came charging at you as soon as you stepped foot out of the helicopter? Now I could add Morocco to my list.*

In the fading light, I thought about how it was going to be a cold night. Because we had not planned on spending the night on a beach 40 miles from our ship, we had no sleeping bags, nothing beyond our normal flight equipment. It would be another cold night in the "Boeing Hilton," not an unusual event given the normal rate at which helicopters break down. One good point was that at least the Mediterranean has a very small tidal range here so I did not have to worry about trying to move the aircraft, on one engine, up higher on the beach and away from an advancing tide.

As I stood there smoking my pipe and looking out across the darkening Moroccan semi-desert, I noticed two men in uniform walking down the dirt track from the village, headed toward my aircraft. As they got closer, I could see that they were Moroccan policemen, the local beat cops. I wondered if they were from here or sent here as a form of punishment. The older one greeted me in Arabic but of course, I do not speak Arabic except the phrase phonetically rendered, "tatti tacalum swayee swayee, min fud-luck"—please speak slowly. Not helpful if you don't speak Arabic at all, since incomprehensible words are just as incomprehensible when spoken at any speed. I tried English, but neither of them spoke English. As a last resort, I tried my French, picked up from a "NATO French for Officers Assigned to Brussels" tape set I studied for a while on my last Med cruise. Bingo.

In my terrible French, "Le Helicopter et on pain. Nuh marsh pas." The helicopter is broken. It will not run.

"Merde," they replied.

Between us we established the fact that we were not going anywhere tonight and that my comrades would come in the morning and fix the aircraft. The senior policeman communicated that we should "dormay" and they would stand guard; given the circumstances not necessarily a re-assuring thought, but one that we had to accept given that we were on a beach in nowhere Morocco and they were the local authorities.

No sleeping bags, no blankets, January on a Mediterranean beach in Morocco and trying to sleep on an aircraft bench seat—it cannot be done, at least for more than a few minutes at a time. The red nylon seats nor-mally seat three passengers in each section. They have two metal bars that connect from the back of the seat to the front longitudinal bar to support the passenger's weight. Whenever you try to lie down on one of the seats, the nylon sags just enough that the bars dig into your back. Think of it as a very cheap pullout couch, only worse, since there is no way ever to get comfortable.

The crew chief, being a good Marine and knowing what could hap-pen, had a stretcher stashed in the back underneath some of the troop seats. When we did external loads, he would lie on it when looking down through the hell hole, instead of lying directly on the metal deck as di-rected. Sometimes he slept in his aircraft on the flight deck, so that he would not have to put up with the constant noise and motion of the troop berthing area below decks on the ship. He would be comfortable, if not warm, tonight.

After a few hours of fitful sleep, I gave up trying to sleep on the troop seats while staying warm with only my leather flight jacket, and climbed into the cockpit and tried to sleep in the pilot's seat. That didn't work very well either, so just before sunrise, I gave up altogether. I climbed out of the aircraft, walked 50 feet or so, and lit my pipe. I was jumping up and down doing a modified jumping jack in the wind, trying to warm up, when I saw the two policemen returning down the rocky trail from the village. As they got closer I could see one policeman held a large metal kettle in his hand, the other policeman had something wrapped up in towels held out before him.

The kettle held hot, sweet tea and the towels held local cornbread straight from the village's ovens and still hot. The policemen also had a small container of butter and another with some homemade jam. Their hospitality took me back to the Kentucky of my childhood and the way the mountain people, my relatives, always greeted strangers with food and drink. I don't think I ever had a better breakfast than that one, that morning on the beach in Morocco. We sat in the back of the 46 out of the wind and ate the cornbread and drank the hot tea with our new friends. We took all the MREs we had and after removing all the pork items that are forbidden to Muslims, gave them to the two policemen to thank them.

Later the villagers came over to see the helicopter stuck on their beach. We greeted them and gave them tours of the aircraft. Some of the less shy children loved sitting in the cockpit and pretending to fly. In due course, the repair aircraft arrived and the mechanics fixed the problem. As I took the aircraft off, I kept it away from the small watching crowd but then circled back, and descending to 200 feet, waggled the rotors as I went past to their excited waves.

An hour later we were back onboard the *Nassau*.

# FLYING LIFE FOUR

---

## THE BRITISH ROYAL NAVY
## 1983–1985

*The Sea King Mk IV "Commando" is a British-built version of the Sikorsky H-3. The Royal Navy uses the aircraft as their primary utility/medium lift aircraft to support the Royal Marines. The Brits often fly them single pilot, unlike US military helicopters which almost always have two pilots. The Royal Navy helicopter squadrons that support the Royal Marines are known as the "Junglies," a nickname given them by the British Army in the early 1960's. The locals in Borneo were in insurrection and the Navy flew their Westland Whirlwind helicopters (British-built version of the Sikorsky H-19) in support, giving the British infantry the mobility they needed to defeat them. A ten-minute helicopter flight took the soldiers farther than they could march through the jungle in an entire day—in other words, the same thing the US did on a much more massive scale in Vietnam a few years later. But in addition to jungle work, the "Junglies" must be prepared to fight anywhere, including the Arctic and the desert.*

## 24

# SAND

## EAST OF ALEXANDRIA, EGYPT ■ NOVEMBER 1983

---

A s soon as the Mark IV Sea King was turned up, engines running fine and blades spinning at full RPM, the wind through the small window had begun cooling off its interior. Even though it was January, the sun heated up the Egyptian air quickly in the morning. The gritty sand blew in both sides of the aircraft. My helmet visor and my squinting to keep it out of my eyes did not stop the overall dirty feeling I had from the last two days of sleeping in a tent beside a desert road, just below where the squadron's aircraft were parked, about ten miles west of Alexandria. The day before, we had flown in from the HMS *Hermes* after she had anchored in Alexandria Harbor.

This morning's mission was simple, to give a familiarization flight, a "dollar ride," to the two companies of Egyptian commandos that waited on the other side of our small camp. We would take them up one squad at a time for a quick flight around the area of the camp so they could get the feel of helicopter flying. After their morning familiarization flight, our five-helo assault flight would take them across 25 kilometers of desert to a landing zone for an exercise assault on a hypothetical enemy in the early afternoon.

Earlier, with the help of an interpreter, they had been trained in how to approach the aircraft, how to board and strap in, and how to exit ready for combat. Watching the training and observing how they handled their weapons made me glad they did not have live ammo. In American assault helicopters, the combat troops always point their rifle down toward the floor so that if there is an accidental discharge, the bullet will go through the aircraft floor and not up into the transmission or rotors. It doesn't help to point them at the floor of a Sea King MK IV because that's where the fuel tanks are, so at a minimum, should someone shoot down through floor, you will lose fuel. Worst case, you'll burn.

As I finished up my run-up checklist, I noticed the first commando platoon to ride was standing just outside the rotor disk waiting for the signal from the crew to board the aircraft. Satisfied that all was ready, the aircrewman waved them over, and led by their lieutenant, they ran in single file to the aircraft. Because they were unfamiliar with helicopters they were slow to settle down, strap in, and be ready to go. By the look on their faces I would guess that this would be their first helicopter flight.

The crewman finally tapped me on the shoulder and gave thumbs up.

"How many," I asked my Royal Marine corporal aircrewman.

"Eighteen, light marching gear," was the reply.

"All set?" I continued.

"Ready in the back," he replied.

Two Marines, one American and one British, flying Egyptian Army Commandos in a Navy helicopter, it was normal, just normal missions.

Eighteen lightly loaded troopers was well within the load limits of the Commando Sea King, given the fuel load, the early November temperature in the Egyptian desert, and all the other factors the pilot must consider. A final scan of the instruments showed all systems within normal limits. As I pulled up the collective, the sand started to blow around the rotor disk and pour through the window, so I lowered the collective, grabbed the stick with my left hand, shifted my right hand to the window and pulled it closed in nearly one continuous motion. Shifting my hands back, I reversed the process and began the lift off again, this time without the irritant of sand in the face.

As the helo rose into a ten-foot hover, the sand cloud continued to build. Bad, but not unanticipated, the sand began to obscure the surrounding world normally visible through the cockpit windows. My hover check, a look at the power it was taking to get the aircraft this high, was shorter than normal and as the power continued to come in, the bird began to move forward, out of the dust and into clean air. At about 20 knots airspeed the Sea King came out of the cloud, holding the 20 feet of altitude and gaining speed. As the aircraft passed through transitional lift, it shuddered as normal and then began to climb. I immediately opened the window to get some breeze through the cockpit. Ahead was a small sand hill and I turned right to avoid it.

As I turned, I heard over the normal helicopter noise a rhythmic shout in Arabic from the back of the aircraft. The shout was answered by three short yells, and a loud three bangs. Glancing left over my shoulder, I could see the Egyptian lieutenant grinning ear to ear and repeating the shout. His troops were fired up and again gave the correct response, again with the same stamping in unison on the cabin floor, all their faces alight.

I grinned to myself, and as the aircraft gained altitude, I banked to the left, a little harder than necessary this time. Again from the back came the shouts and stamping. I circled the camp twice, once in each direction so that every one of them had a view, and then came back for an approach to the spot I lifted from. Before I began the final approach I pulled the window closed to avoid the blowing sand. I made the approach straight to the ground so that I did not have to hover in the dust and make the landing any more difficult than necessary. As the lieutenant led his troops from the aircraft out the cabin door, he turned and gave a smiling wave to the cockpit. His troops looked happy and confident as they cleared the disk and headed toward their camp.

As soon as the first bunch of troops was clear, the crewman signaled for the next squad.

"Same numbers as the last lot, ready to lift," he called.

"Lifting," I relied.

This trip was a repeat of the first. I made the same small turn and the officer would shout and the troops would answer with three shouts and a stamping on the cabin floor. Because I understood what they wanted now, I moved the aircraft more crisply than before and with each turn or pitch of the helo, again they would shout. Grins and waves as they debarked.

The third and final load climbed aboard and strapped in, and I began by making a more abrupt takeoff than the first two and turning immediately to avoid the hill. This time there was no shouting from the back. Looking over my shoulder at the officer, I saw the lieutenant's face express pure fear, not the joy of the first two officers. The fear in their officer was immediately passed to the troops and they, too, were afraid. I immediately leveled the aircraft and kept the rest of the flight as smooth as possible. No point in scaring people any more than absolutely necessary.

After the final group de-planed, I made the short flight back to our

Operations area, shut the bird down, and walked over to the group of air-crews standing with their ground officer counterparts near one of the tents. The senior officer, a lieutenant commander, "Two and a half" as the Brits call them because of the two broad and one narrow gold strips that they wear to delineate rank, was standing over a map spread on a field table waiting for me to get there so he could start the mission briefing.

As usual with the Brits, the brief was more or less, "Right, chaps! We are here. We are going there. Any questions at all? Anyone?" There were none and we walked back to our individual aircraft and started them up. Our aircraft parking area was more hard surface than loose sand, so we did a normal formation takeoff instead of a "no hover," like I was using with the familiarization rides. Aircraft back in the formation always lift off before the aircraft in front of them so that they do not get the rotor wash from the aircraft in front. The lead does not hover around but adds power and goes straight from the ground so that everyone gets airborne as soon as possible.

We picked up our Egyptian troops at about the same spot where I had done the familiarization lifts and headed across the desert to the LZ. After picking them up and taking off again, we flew a tactical cruise, meaning that instead of holding a constant position relative to the aircraft in front, we weaved about, changing from the right side of the aircraft in front to the left and back again, so that gunners on the ground would have a more difficult targeting solution.

That's the theory anyway . . .

Tactical cruise does make it more difficult for an attacking fighter to shoot down more than one aircraft at a time. During the Weapons Tactics Instructor Course a few years before, the Marines told us that the Egyptians themselves learned this the hard way in October 1973, when Israeli F-4s killed five of six Egyptian MI-8 helicopters flying in a tight formation, instead of a loose, shifting one like tactical cruise. But then tactical cruise probably would not have done any good today because we were still slow, large helicopters, flying over open desert and visible for miles from above or below, but the theory made us feel better.

As we flew across the desert, the flight lead dropped his Sea King down to between 50 and 100 feet above the ground, more low level than contour flight—there are no wires out here and no one to complain about the noise, so "flat hatting" was not a problem. Then, ahead of us, traveling in the same direction as we were going, I saw a car, or rather I first saw the dust rising from behind it. Lead saw it at the same time because he went down even lower and turned to put himself directly behind the car. The next two helicopters closed in tighter to lead so that seconds after lead flew directly over the car, not more than ten feet above its roof, they flashed by it on both sides. I could see the driver swerve, startled by helicopters that appeared from nowhere. No danger of him losing control and hitting something. There was no road, only empty sand, and nothing to hit.

After about 15 minutes, lead climbed to around 200 feet and decided the patch of desert directly in front of us, looking no different from any other patch of local desert, was the LZ and started down to land. We closed up to a tighter formation so that the troops would be closer to each other when they exited the aircraft. As we started to land, it became apparent that the surface of the landing zone was pure soft sand, finer than that at our departure point, when it started to billow up in a worse than usual blinding brown cloud.

If you know when a whiteout in snow, or brownout in dust, is coming as you are landing, you don't even try to hover your helicopter. You must keep it moving forward and go directly to the ground, lest the cloud envelop you and remove all visibility and with it any idea which way is up or down. Ideally, if you think whiteout or brownout is going to happen, you pick out an object, a rock, a tree, or worst case, a person, as a visual reference. You land with the object at your 2 o'clock position just outside your rotor disk so that you have some reference to know if you are level. In this case, there was nothing to pick for a reference, no trees, no rocks, no people, only sand and more sand.

One of the aircraft in front of me apparently came to a hover because the sand cloud blocked all visibility. I could not see and so could not land. I immediately pulled all the power the Sea King had, lowered the nose to gain airspeed, and while sucking the seat cushion into my rear end, I waited for the mid-air collision with one of the other four helicopters that were quite probably doing the exact same thing I was doing.

Even though we were all flying blind, the mid-air didn't happen and suddenly I was clear of the dust cloud. I watched as the other four Sea Kings all headed out in somewhat of an air burst away from each other, like they do at air shows. Somehow we had all missed each other. We joined back up and went in for a second approach to the same area. This time we all did it right. The aircraft in the back landed sooner than the ones in front of them and everyone continued straight to the ground instead of stopping in a hover. The Egyptian infantry leaped out of the cabin of the helicopter into the sand and we took off again, sand swirling around us, and headed back to our base. We waited there on the ground before we took off to pick up the troops and bring them back. Total flight time for the day was one hour.

We did it again the next day, two hours in the air that time. It must have been a perfect flight that second time, because I do not remember it.

Cheated death again. Luck and superstition, that's all it is . . .

# 25

# INTRODUCING THE ARCTIC
# TO CAPTAIN CURTIS
### NORWAY ■ JANUARY 1984

---

*Norway, in winter, is an incredibly beautiful place. Not as cold as you think it will be either, usually only around –15 degrees centigrade in the valleys by the fjords, not bad for 200 or so miles north of the Arctic Circle. The Canadians, working with the Brits in the annual exercises, usually whine about how they brought their cold weather gear to this "warm" place. To me though, it was more than cold enough.*

---

As a US Marine captain on exchange duty with the Royal Navy, flying in support of the Royal Marines, I did whatever they did, and what they did in winter was go to Norway to provide the UK's portion of the NATO defense of the Northern Flank. The Brit's did not take Norway lightly. Too many cold winters, and sometimes bitter experience in the north of their own cold island, not to mention their World War II battles around Narvick, had taught them to take the cold very seriously indeed.

The first event for any first-timer in Norway is Clockwork, the Royal Navy Arctic Flying Course. I was scheduled for the first class of the New Year and was to fly a Sea King over from Scotland on the 4th of January to begin training the next week. Because it was the first class of the winter season, another pilot and I were to fly two of the aircraft to be used in the entire winter's training from our base in Somerset to Bardufoss, the main base for British helicopter operations in Norway. Bardufoss is over 1,200 miles north from Oslo. So we had to fly first from the mildness of the Somerset winter to colder Scotland, then 340 miles across the North Sea to colder still Bergen, and finally up the Norwegian coast to our base roughly 200 miles above the Arctic Circle. Never mind the winter cold, I had never done an over-water flight that long so it would all be an adventure, starting with the leg between Scotland and Norway.

We figured our fuel carefully for the leg of the trip across the North Sea. Even though the Sea King can carry enough fuel for about a 500-mile no-wind trip and this one was only 350 or so, you cannot take excess chances crossing the North Sea in winter. A light head wind can make it tricky and a strong head wind can make it impossible. The flight is even more of a challenge when it is dark and January, and in Scotland it is dark a lot: 20 hours or more a day at that latitude.

For the ferry flight east across the North Sea and then on to our training area 200 or so miles north of the Arctic Circle, a Royal Navy lieutenant from my squadron would fly one Sea King and I would fly the other. The Brit's fly their aircraft single pilot, something I had not done since I was flying OH-58s in the National Guard seven years before, but we would each have another pilot in the left seat. Two of the Clockwork instructor pilots needed a ride to Bardufoss and we were the quickest way there outside of expensive SAS commercial flights. We thought it was a good idea because neither the other pilot nor I had done Arctic flying, and we would certainly encounter the Norwegian winter on our way north. The instructors worked with us planning the flight. If the weather was good, we could make it in two days, about twelve hours flying time.

The flight from Yeovilton, England, to Scotland was routine, even scenic at some points. Although I was a little tense, the entire trip from Scotland to Bergen, Norway, was uneventful, too—"good hop, no problems" as the saying goes. Completely loaded with fuel, passengers, and cargo we did rolling takeoffs on the RAF runway instead of hovering to minimize the stress on the aircraft. We were either over maximum allowable gross weight or very near to it, so hovering, and almost certainly single engine flight, was out of the question.

Our flight began just before sunrise on 2 January and 5.8 flight hours later, we landed in Bergen just before it became completely dark. The sea had been relatively flat and the winds slightly on our tail, as routine as the trip up from Yeovilton had been. The only sights to be seen on the flight were the occasional fishing boats and oil rigs scattered here and there, gas flares burning in the sky.

After parking the helicopters at Bergen's airport, we took a bus to a downtown hotel. As we rode in from the airfield in the dark, I could see that there was some snow on the ground, but not enough to comment on. Passing through residential areas on our way to the hotel, my impression was that most people still had their Christmas lights up; not unreasonable since it was not yet "little Christmas" (6 January). Later I found out that what I saw were not Christmas lights—Norwegians just like numerous small lights in their houses instead of the bright lights Brit's and American's usually have. Also, as I found out to my pleasure, the hotel had heated floors in the bathroom, something I filed away for future use.

Early the next morning we started north to Bardufoss with another rolling take-off, since we were just as heavy as we had been when we started the flight across the North Sea. As it always is that far north in January, it was semi-dark when we took off and headed up the coast along the fjords. Our Sea Kings were equipped to handle some heavy winter weather, something I had never experienced in my mostly southern US, Mediterranean, and Southeast Asia flying career. Although I had flown many different types of helicopters, none had been equipped to handle icing.

My most recent aircraft, the CH-46E, could not take any ice at all. The wire mesh screens over the engines were intended to prevent foreign objects like rocks from being sucked into the intake, but in icing conditions the screens quickly, in seconds actually, completely iced over, shutting off the air into the engine. Within moments the engines would stop and you would have an opportunity to find out if all your training in autorotations had been worthwhile. Having had two engine failures in single engine helicopters early in my flying, and successfully landing the aircraft without damage, I did not want to have a third try in the much, much larger Sea King. The Sea King did not have a screen over the intakes but instead had a shield in front of them and anti-icing fluid that the pilot could activate to prevent the ice from forming.

Mostly though, in January, in Norway, anti-icing equipment is moot because it is too cold for icing. The moisture is snow and falling snow is mostly harmless to an aircraft. If it falls hard enough it can and does reduce visibility to nothing, a very serious situation when you are flying below the mountaintops, but it will not shut your engines down.

On my second day in Norway, as we flew north from Bergen, the snow became too much for me. We had been fighting our way through heavy snowstorms with their attendant greatly reduced visibility in unfamiliar terrain, with high mountains and unknown power lines, until we arrived at Bodo to refuel and check the weather before proceeding north. Adding to the non-existent visibility, it was now dark, very dark with clouds and snow obscuring everything. After landing on the runway at Bodo's airfield, the mere taxi from the runway to the parking ramp in front of the Operations building had been a white knuckle exercise, with intermittent whiteout in blowing snow on the taxi way. I was the AC, but my copilot was one of the Clockwork instructors and he was very keen to make it to Bardufoss in only two days after leaving Somerset, sort of like the ocean liners racing across the Atlantic to take the Blue Riband—the instructors wanted it to be the shortest time it had ever been done in a helicopter. Both the instructor copilots left their aircraft leaping out to check weather while the two ACs stayed with their aircraft during refueling.

As soon as they left, I called the other AC on the fox mike and told him, "I'm done. Shutting down now." He agreed without further comment and also shut his aircraft down too. Together we walked into the Operations building to be greeted by incredulous looks from our copilots, the Clockwork instructors. I learned very early that taking excessive chances, particularly with bad weather, was often fatal—five friends and their 29 passengers died when they flew a Chinook directly into a mountain in bad weather in Vietnam 12 years before. They didn't even find the wreckage for two weeks. I was not going to join them if I could help it, particularly for a mythical Blue Riband.

"Why are you in here?" the Clockwork instructors/copilots asked. "You should be back in the aircraft ready to takeoff just as soon as we get the latest weather at Bardufoss."

I told them that since I had signed for the aircraft, it was my decision, not theirs, as to what we do or do not do, and that I was through flying for the day. Tomorrow, in what little daylight Norway had in January, we would complete the flight north; or not, if the weather was still terrible. They were not happy, not happy at all, but whether or not they objected, their input was moot. The aircraft was mine, not theirs, and so was the final decision. We made the RON call to our squadron back at Yeovilton and went to another hotel. Love those heated bathroom floors.

The next day dawned clear and without falling snow from the blue sky. The Norwegian snowplows had done their work on the runway and the taxi out to takeoff position was not a repeat of the previous evening's white out. Our flight into Bardufoss was a routine 2.0 hours in the air, beautiful as we flew up the fjords, with no high-tension moments at all. I enjoyed seeing the mountains and the snow-covered landscape as we flew north and east, instead of wondering if I was about to fly into something in the dark. Even though the snow showers, like those of the day before, are often a problem that far north, none bothered us that day as we flew in the postcard perfect sky.

Flying up one of the fjords, I saw a house on the edge of a small beach beneath a towering cliff. What a lovely summer place, I thought, only to see a light on the front porch and a person run out the door to wave as we flew past. The sound of helicopters coming up from the south must have been a real change from the silence of the fjord in winter. How lovely it was there. How lonely it must have been there.

Day and night arctic flying training was completed in due course and I took my turn flying the assigned missions. A month or so after completing training I was flying a mission, its purpose long since forgotten, when snow started coming down too hard to continue flying safely. Spotting an open area near some Norwegian houses, I plopped my Sea King down in the snow and settled in to wait for the weather to clear. After shutting the aircraft down I noticed my aircrewman was missing. Following the footprints, I saw him knocking on the door of one of the houses and overheard him say (in his best Russian accent), "Dis Norway? You see cruise missile?" The Norwegian householders froze and then slammed the door as I yelled, "It's a joke! It's joke! We're British! We're British!" which of course I wasn't, but never mind. Shortly thereafter a five- or six-year-old boy came running bright-eyed through snow to see the helicopter. I hauled him up inside and let him into the cockpit.

We had all learned a few phrases in Norwegian, but the most popular was, "min flyr båten er full av ål," or, roughly, "My flying boat is full of eels." We tried it on the little boy and he immediately began looking under all the seats. When he didn't find any he turned to me indignantly, and said "NO." When the snow storm cleared and it came time for us to start the aircraft he said good-bye and then stood in the door of the helicopter before falling out backwards into the four feet of snow on the ground. Sinking down while making a snow angel, he wished us safely on our way.

Like I said, I don't remember what the mission was that day or anything else about that flight, but I remember that little boy.

# 26

# ROYAL NAVY NIGHT FLIGHT—
# THE DIFFICULT VALLEY
## NEAR BARDUFOSS, NORWAY ■ JANUARY 1984

*Flying in Norway in winter presents constant challenges; night flying in mountains and the occasional heavy snow are two of the obvious ones. Because night in northern Norway lasts a really long time, all "day" in fact, in winter the pilot must learn to deal with it and be able to always operate normally. One of the skills to do so requires that he know "difficult valley" flying techniques. Like the early days of NVG flying, night difficult valley flying is particularly difficult, in some ways even more so than the night flight described in earlier chapters.*

The "difficult valley" Clockwork uses for training is aptly named. The first difficulty in all flying is finding where you are supposed to go, but in this case that was not the difficult part since finding this particular valley at night is easy enough. Fly down a fjord northeast of Bardufoss until the fjord turns east and look for a tall, lighted smoke stack along the shore. Turn east to climb up the hillside to the north of the stack. If you can't see it from a distance, start looking in earnest for the valley entrance as you clear the tree line. At that point it's not hard to find because the valley itself is a glaciated "U" that is located above the tree line, at about two thousand feet where you enter and climbs to about 3,000 feet above sea level at the highest point of the valley floor.

As the altitude increases, the valley narrows until you can't do a coordinated turn at 90 knots out of it. It envds in a "T" with another glaciated "U" valley that runs north to south. This valley has sheer rock walls on both sides reaching up about 1,000 feet higher than the floor, high enough that you cannot "cyclic climb" out of it, meaning trading airspeed for altitude by bringing the helicopter's nose up. Helicopters just don't have that much energy to trade; if you try it you will shortly find yourself out of airspeed, altitude, and ideas all at the same time. Once you are above the tree line, there is really nothing to look at except the rock wall and featureless snow, particularly featureless in the dark Norwegian night.

Syllabus flight or no, I would never have gone into that valley on a moonless night except that my instructor, fresh from the Falkland's War, was acting bored and said, "Oh, if you think it's too hard we can go around it," which got my Irish (American?) up to the point where we were going up it even if it meant becoming a greasy black spot on the valley wall.

As I was expecting, once we cleared the tree line there was nothing left to see, with the sky, valley floor, and walls a more or less uniform black. Out to the starboard side of the aircraft, my side, parts of the blackness were blacker than other parts—rocks sticking out the side of the cliff, I think, but all was just black on all sides with a black rock wall in front of us.

After we cleared the tree line and were into the valley proper, my air-crewman, who had navigated us blind to this point, began counting down, "Three, two, one, turn right to 180 degrees NOW."

Looking to the right to where I was to turn, all I saw was just more blackness. Turn early into a rock wall or turn late and fly straight ahead into another one? I trusted my aircrewman and his work was perfect, as you have probably surmised since I'm writing this many years after the fact. About 30 seconds after I steadied on the new heading he had given me, we started to see lights of a village down on the fjord. It took half an hour to get that seat cushion out of my rear end when we finally landed.

Talking to my fellow "students" over beer a few days later I found out I had been the only one that night to fly through the "difficult valley." All the rest had flown around it and were of the considered opinion that I was insane. In retrospect, I agree.

Luck and superstition indeed . . .

# 27

# TROOP LIFTING, WITH NIGHT AND HEAVY SNOW SHOWERS

## NORTHERN NORWAY ■ MARCH 1985

---

*Me: "Fearless Tower, Victor Hotel. Three miles east for landing."*

*After a pause—HMS* Fearless: *"Victor Hotel, why do you wish to land three miles to the east?"*

*After a pause—Me: "Fearless Tower, Victor Hotel. I do not wish to land three miles east. I wish to land onboard your ship."*

*HMS* Fearless: *"Ah, you wish to join."*

*Me: "No, I have already joined some years ago. Now I just wish to land."*

*(A typical example of American to English translation difficulties)*

---

I was dash two of a two Sea King mission to insert troops behind the "enemy" for a surprise attack. We would launch off HMS *Fearless*, a Royal Navy LSD (Landing Ship Dock—which meant it had two nice big helicopter landing spots aft and the capacity to carry a company or two of Royal Marines). The mission was straightforward—takeoff from *Fearless* at a certain time, drop the Marines in the selected landing zone at the appointed time and return to the ship—nothing fancy, like NVG flying or dodging missiles, real or simulated here, just out and back and done for the day. Or more accurately, for the night, since most missions in northern Norway in March were at night.

The flight out to *Fearless* from Bardufoss was routine, as was the landing onboard and final pre-mission briefing. *Fearless* was steaming slowly, keeping pretty much to the center of the fjord. My aircraft was an "all colonial" crew, as the Brits were fond of saying, with an American aircraft commander, an Australian copilot, and a Kenyan crewman. For this mission, I was dash two aircraft, the wingman, so all I had to do was keep up with lead and land somewhere behind his aircraft so as not to interfere with his landing. The Royal Marines would rapidly disembark and proceed to their attack point, and we would depart the area as soon as they cleared the aircraft. We did not have to come back and pick them up after the assault. As was usual with my squadron, radios were not to be used except in the case of an emergency.

The weather was forecast to be about perfect, a little moon and clear except for scattered snow showers, as nights normally are. When my Australian copilot and I went to strap into our aircraft, the scattered snow showers arrived, really, seriously arrived. Visibility went from clear—with both sides of the fjord that *Fearless* was cruising within sight—to not being able to see the rail of the ship about 20 feet away from the cockpit. Figuring the snow would pass since it was just a shower, we continued with the run-up in preparation for takeoff at the appointed time.

The problem arose when the appointed time arrived and the snow had not stopped—it just got worse or remained bad enough that visibility was near zero. I assumed that lead would hold the flight on deck until the visibility improved, and signaled the LSE to remove the chocks and chains so we would be ready when the shower passed. The deck crew pulled them off and LSE showed them to us so that we knew they were all removed. Then suddenly, with no warning whatsoever, or launch signal from the LSE, lead took off. He did not appear to do a hover check, but instead lifted directly into forward flight. The Sea King vanished from sight as soon as he cleared the flight deck rail.

My copilot and I looked at each other in dropped-chin amazement. You could see absolutely nothing beyond 20 feet from the cockpit, yet lead had departed into the snow shower. While the fjord that *Fearless* was sailing through had low lands for a short distance on each bank, the terrain soon rose steeply into cliffs, a real problem if you did not know where to look for them.

I knew that if I took off immediately, the risk of a mid-air collision was very real; we would be unable to see him and he us. Had I known he was going, I could have taken off nearly simultaneously and kept him in sight by staying very close, a high tension but normal procedure. Had he done a hover check, I would have known he was going and would have been airborne right after him. But he didn't do a hover check and that moment was gone, so I held on the deck, still waiting for the shower to pass. It did not pass. Fearing the worst, i.e., that he crashed into the water or into the ground just on-shore, I told my copilot that we were going too. I lifted to a hover for final checks and pushing the nose forward, we were off.

After we cleared the deck of the ship, I did not climb to a cruise altitude. Instead, I leveled off at about 100 feet on the radar altimeter and kept my airspeed slow, around 60 knots, enough to move forward and keep the helicopter out of danger but slow enough to stop or turn should an obstacle appear before us. My idea was to get over land, get oriented in where exactly we were, and then proceed. After a couple of minutes (but probably actually only 30 seconds), I could tell that we'd crossed the shoreline because I could see trees directly below us. I tried turning on the landing light for a better view, but the snow just blinded us, so I turned it back off.

"This is stupid," I said over the ICS, "I'm landing in the first clear area we see and waiting out this shower." Returning to the ship was impossible because trying to find it while flying blind might well result in us hitting it instead of landing on it.

My copilot agreed that it was stupid and as I started down the last 100 feet to land in an open field, we came out of the snow shower into a beautiful, clear Norwegian night. There in the middle of the fjord was *Fearless*. Nothing of the other helicopter could be seen.

For a moment, I debated in my head returning the troops to ship and then beginning a search for the other aircraft but decided that it would be quicker to just drop them in the LZ and then start a search. Besides, if we came across wreckage and they were still onboard, they could help with security and the recovery. I turned the Sea King to the east and flew toward the landing zone. As I crossed the shoreline, another Sea King flew by on my port side. It had to be flight lead since no one else was flying that night, so I joined up on them and we proceeded as a flight of two to the LZ, dropped the troops and then returned to *Fearless*.

After I shut the aircraft down and it was secured, we joined the other crew in *Fearless'* ready room for the debrief. Both pilots from the lead aircraft were pale and somewhat shaky. Me? I was just mad at their stupidity, but I didn't say a word as the flight leader began his tale. He did not explain his sudden takeoff into the near zero-visibility shower but instead launched into what happened next after he cleared the ship's rail and headed for land.

The fjord we were in runs east and west from the location where we took off. *Fearless* was headed east, and since we were headed across the deck from the two helicopter landing spots, we were to takeoff to the south, fly straight ahead until we intercepted the southern shore, then turn left to the east and proceed up the fjord until we reached the checkpoint for the final turn and our run into the LZ. It couldn't have been easier.

That was the theory anyway . . .

When lead came off the deck, he immediately became disoriented and did a 180-degree turn, somehow blindly missing *Fearless'* superstructure, and now unknowingly, was headed north, not south. In a few seconds he intercepted the northern shore, and turning left as briefed, headed out west in exactly the wrong direction. Unfortunately for them, the snow squall was also headed that direction and their visibility remained near zero. Taking the helicopter as low as they could, they went slowly down the fjord nearly blind until, at last, it dawned on them that they had been going west. Instead of going south they had followed the shore of the fjord as it turned north.

The arm of the fjord they were following had narrowed considerably and they were able to reverse course while staying low and in sight of the surface, all the while engulfed in the heavy snow shower. They finally recognized a manmade object that allowed them to determine their exact position—old abandoned Nazi-built submarine pens left over from World War II. Continuing on, they finally flew out of the snow squall and saw my Sea King's lights up ahead of them. Putting on a burst of speed they passed us and took the lead on into the LZ and completed the mission.

The reasons they were still pale and a bit shaky were quite simple. First, they came within a hair of crashing into the water following their takeoff into the snow shower, and were subsequently disoriented with its 180-degree turn around the ship. Second, they could well have flown directly into *Fearless* since the snow would have prevented them from seeing her until the last possible second. Third, and probably the most serious, was that just north of the old sub pens there was a set of large power lines that came within 150 feet of the surface of the fjord. In the course of their mistaken route, they had flown underneath these power lines twice—once going north and again coming back south after they realized they were headed the wrong direction. They could not have missed the wires by more than 100 feet. They never saw them.

Luck and superstition yet again . . .

# LONG FLIGHT HOME
## VOSS, NORWAY TO YEOVILTON,
## ENGLAND ■ MARCH 1985

---

*There is a condition called "get homeitis" that strikes many aircrews with sometimes fatal results. This condition sets up in the pilot's mind the thought that no matter what, he must continue on so that he can get back to his home base RIGHT NOW, TODAY, never mind that there is usually no reason to risk life and aircraft if he is not at war. "Get homeitis" nearly always occurs on the way back from a deployment and almost never on the way to a deployment (there are exceptions—see the chapter on flying to Norway). There also comes a moment when you make a decision to live, a decision not to let someone else kill you through their bad decision or "get homeitis" infection. When you make that decision you must stick with it.*

---

From Stavanger, Norway, to Scotland is 340 miles. That's 340 miles over the North Sea and as described earlier, it is not an easy 340 miles. If the wind is wrong, a head wind instead of a tail wind, if the snow turns to freezing rain, if you lose an engine, if, if, if.

The weather was, at best, marginal. To be safe, we needed a tail wind, and the forecast was for it to be only a few points on the tail. If it shifted a few degrees around to the west and back to a head wind, we would be very low on fuel when we arrived in Scotland. If it shifted to a strong head wind and we had to abort back to Norway, depending on how far out we were, it might be close on fuel. Our navigation system would let us know how we were doing moment by moment, but still . . .

Before we went out to our aircraft, I went through my helmet bag and threw away all unnecessary things, old maps, expired approach plates, etc. Weight is weight, and I wanted my aircraft as light as possible. This was purely psychological, since the perhaps two pounds I was removing would make virtually no difference, but I went through the exercise anyway. Superstition?

We were a flight of five Sea Kings led by our squadron CO. I was aircraft commander of the third aircraft. Unlike the US Marines, the Royal Navy did not organize the flight into sections of two or more aircraft, with a section lead for each, but instead, just used a single flight. The plan was to fly to Scotland and, weather permitting, refuel and proceed back to our base in Somerset, clear at the bottom of the UK. It would be a long day even if everything went perfectly, probably six hours flight time.

The day was not promising—low clouds, intermittent rain, strong, gusty winds—a typical North Sea day, but the CO was adamant: we were going. As always on these long ferry flights, our aircraft were overloaded with personnel and their baggage, and various bits of maintenance equipment, personal gear, tents, mess gear, etc. So, as always on these ferry flights, we ground-taxied to the end of the runway for a rolling takeoff. By keeping the aircraft on the runway until we reached flying speed, we would avoid over stressing the aircraft by trying to hover it—in other words, a repeat of my first flight across the North Sea. We all lined up one after another on the runway and one after another, added power and began to roll forward. At about 20 knots, I added more power, lifted off and followed number two into the rain.

As we flew over the North Sea, we all knew that an engine failure meant that the aircraft would quite probably go into the water. Oh, we could jettison enough fuel to stay in the air. After all, the Sea King Mk 4 has powered fuel jettison pumps instead of the gravity system used on the CH-46E, so great quantities of fuel can be pumped out of the tanks very quickly. And though we could stay in the air, we would probably not have enough fuel to make land and so would have to ditch anyway.

The sea state was high: huge confused waves crashing about, again a normal North Sea day, so that the odds of keeping the aircraft stable long enough for everyone to get out in a controlled manner after a water landing was problematic. An additional factor was that only the aircrew had dry suits, so if the passengers did get out and inflated their life jackets, they could look forward to freezing to death in short order, around 15 minutes tops. They would be unconscious in ten minutes or less. Once I had a live demonstration of how quickly you deteriorate in cold water when I saw a man fall off the deck of a ship into the North Sea off Norway. A crewman of one of our helicopters in the air also saw him fall. The aircrew was trained for water pickups and immediately flew down to rescue him. He was in the water less than five minutes, but when the helicopter landed on my ship, he was barely conscious and had to be carried below to sick bay in a stretcher.

Because our passengers did not have the dry suits, we aircrew did not wear them either. One might say it was extra incentive for the aircrew not to ditch the aircraft.

As we flew to the west the wind stayed with us, not by much, but enough that it was soon apparent that we would have no difficulty making the flight with fuel to spare. But of course, even though the wind was with us, the overall weather was decidedly not. The air temperature was such that going into the clouds would have instantly resulted in icing, an ice buildup on the rotors and fuselage, and while the Sea King Mk IV can take some ice, it cannot take much. Even with the ability to fly in icing, the added weight would greatly reduce range and might even force the aircraft to a lower altitude. To keep from going into the clouds, we continued to descend closer and closer to the sea the nearer we got to Scotland. By the time we made radio contact with the tower at the RAF base, we were all skimming the waves at 100 feet and not too happy about it. But on the bright side, our navigator's skill was spot on and when the runway lights finally appeared through the rain, they were exactly on our nose. We all did running landings again to avoid hovering, and one by one taxied to the ramp where we shut down to await customs clearance.

Customs clearance was always required whenever we returned to the UK from any foreign location because the lads, being lads, bought the maximum (and sometimes then some) duty free allowance of booze whenever they could. At the end of each deployment, one or more of them would become my "best friend" because as an American in the UK, I already had a duty free allowance from the US forces that was far bigger than anything I could use, so my British allowance was always available to someone else. The customs officer slogged from aircraft to aircraft through the rain and wind. While we were slightly giddy at having made it across the

North Sea in the face of the low clouds, wind, and rain, he was not happy to be here on such a foul day.

"Customs forms, please gentlemen," he said. He went through them wordlessly until near the last when he stopped and said, "Smith, you've made a mistake on this form. You meant to put down you had less than the duty free limit."

Smith, one of the young lads on is first deployment overseas, quite possibly his first trip ever out of the UK, replied, "Oh no, sir. I put the correct amount down."

The customs officer now grew quite red in the face and said, "I said, *YOU PUT THE WRONG AMOUNT DOWN. YOU HAVE ONLY THE DUTY FREE ALLOWANCE!*"

One of the other lads gave Smith a sharp elbow to indicate that the customs officer was not at all interested in preparing the extra paperwork that would be required to collect the small amount of extra money for one too many bottles. All he wanted to do was to get our paperwork and leave this cold, wet ramp and get back to his home and warm fireplace, or, more likely, the pub. Smith, twigging it at last said, "Oh, yes, sir, my mistake; let me fix it." Paperwork complete, we were now clear to head into the Operations building and see where we were going to spend the night before flying back to Yeovilton the next day.

When I asked the question: "BOQ or hotel" of the assembled officers, the CO replied, "Oh, no. We won't be staying here. We're going to fly on back to Yeovilton as soon as we are refueled."

I took a look at the weather briefing—rain, sleet, low cloud, filthy weather over the entire UK for the rest of the day. I knew there was no point in arguing, they were going and I was going with them. But I also knew that I was not going to let them kill me by flying into a Scottish mountainside or a set of power lines that I did not see until too late. I still remembered Greece and flying my dead squadron mates and friends back after they found that power line over the river. I was pretty sure that none of the Brits shared that experience. If things got too bad, I would simply land my aircraft and wait out the weather. They could do what they liked. We were not in a war and there was no urgent reason to risk death and killing your passengers just to get back a day earlier.

The CO outlined a route that, in good weather, would have been a pretty flight over the wild countryside. Once again, we fueled the aircraft completely up and loaded all passengers back onboard. Once again, we taxied to the end of the runway for an over-maximum-allowable-gross-weight takeoff. Once again, we in turn bounced down the runway until we got enough speed to lift off into forward flight without hovering. Once airborne, we joined in a loose trail formation, one aircraft following the other, but free to swing from side to side as desired. Like that long ago night flight in the National Guard Hueys, flying the "nuclear formation" with aircraft spread out so far apart that a single atomic weapon would not get them all. We were popping in and out of clouds at 200 feet as we cleared the airfield fence and started south. It took about 30 minutes to get into serious trouble.

Our crewmen were extremely well trained and proficient navigators. Our navigation equipment was excellent. Unfortunately, neither of these made much difference as we dodged in and out of clouds at altitudes below the legal limit for authorized low-level flight, where the aircrewmen could not see to navigate, and the navigation equipment could not receive a signal to tell us where we were. All this came to a head when the CO led the flight of five overloaded helicopters up a blind canyon that narrowed to the point where he could not make a coordinated turn without a risk of hitting dash two. All five Sea Kings slowed to a near hover while deciding what to do next.

I looked at the amount of power it was taking to hold this position and could see that because of the overweight condition of the aircraft, I was about to over-torque the aircraft (risk possible catastrophic damage to the main transmission). I was also squarely in the middle of the "deadman's curve," the point where a safe landing cannot be made in the event of an engine failure, because you don't have enough altitude to trade for airspeed to break your rate of descent before you land. From the first day at Fort Wolters, I had it beat into my head to never, never do either of these things and I wasn't about to start now.

Being number three, I had two helicopters behind me but also had more turn space without the risk of the narrow valley. I called over the squadron radio frequency, "Victor Hotel turning right and landing in the area to our rear to wait for better weather."

Instead of a negative comment from the CO, much to my surprise he instead called, "Roger, Victor Hotel. Victor flight, all aircraft return to base on your own."

As I turned to the left, I could see the two aircraft behind me had already made that decision on their own without waiting for the CO. They were both 180 degrees from the direction we had been heading and were already up to cruising speed. They were also very low, dodging clouds—scud running, it is sometimes called—something I just was not in the mood for right now. Spotting a nice, clear, level field near a farmhouse I set my aircraft up for an approach to land, and in about two minutes we were on the ground.

We were not even fully on the ground when the family from the house came running out to see the Sea King sitting in their field. My aircrewman motioned for them to stay back from the rotors while we shut down. As I climbed out of the aircraft and walked toward them, I could not help but ask, "Excuse me, where are we exactly?" I was only half kidding; I had been far more concerned about not hitting things, wires, antennas, other helicopters, etc., and had not done much navigating, nor had my aircrewman. The other half was that as soon as we could get a clear signal, our navigation system would tell us exactly where we were, but we still had to figure a way out that kept us clear of obstacles until we were out of Scotland and back into more level terrain.

After a few minutes, the clouds cleared enough for us to continue. After loading everyone back onto the helicopter and saying goodbye to the still very excited family, we took off, headed generally south. As we flew, the weather was up and down. At one point I again sat the aircraft down for a few minutes until it cleared, but we were slowly working our way south and back to Yeovilton. We were on the edge of possible icing but had been lucky and stayed just out of the temperature range where icing develops.

Just as I thought it would be, it had been a very long day. We had departed Norway before first light, crossed the North Sea, refueled in Scotland, blundered about in and out of clouds and scud, made a couple more precautionary landings to wait out weather, and consequently it was now getting dark. The good news was that we were getting within radio range of our base. I had not heard from any of the other aircraft since we went our separate ways, and because of the way British airspace is controlled, we had not spoken to any Air Traffic Control Facilities on our way south.

As we flew south, the temperature had actually dropped, but the clouds had risen so we were flying at 1,000 feet or so, normal VFR altitudes. When we were in radio range, I called squadron base and they were glad to hear from us. My Sea King and one of the other aircraft were the last to return, the other three having straggled in over the last hour. Finally, ten hours after we started from Norway, I shut the aircraft down on our own flight line.

One of the pilots was yelling something to me from outside the rotor disk, and I stuck my head out the window to hear him better, only to get de-icing fluid from the rotor shield dumped on my helmet. Somehow I had accidently activated the switch and the fluid was being pumped out, as advertised—to no effect since it was not snowing, but still it is always good when a system works as advertised. He yelled only to tell me that the deicing system was on. What a perfect ending to a very long and draining day.

Mine was not the last aircraft back. The final wandering helicopter came straggling in about an hour later. Each of us had our own story to tell, mine was not the strangest by any means. One of our aircraft took the real scenic route from Scotland to Somerset. He flew all the way around the western coast of Britain, at least until he got to Wales where the weather improved enough to fly inland and take the shorter route. He did what we called the "weather too bad for Visual Flight Rules or Instrument Flight Rules" flight plan.

But everyone was safe on the ground. Even with the drama and less than perfect planning, luck and superstition got us through—again.

# SEA FOG

## OFF THE SOUTH COAST OF
## ENGLAND ■ OCTOBER 1984

*The Royal Navy does not feel the same way the US Navy feels about flying out to sea. The RN sees it as no big deal if you fly far out to sea with no wingman, while the USN limited us to 25 miles to sea if you are a single aircraft. The RN fully expects a pilot to do everything possible to get aboard, even if he could wait ashore for the weather to improve.*

The mission was to fly onboard HMS *Illustrious* for a two-week deployment. The ship was headed to Portugal for a NATO exercise that was ship maneuvers only. The aircrew would not be hauling Royal Marines on assaults but instead be an administrative aircraft to do passenger transfers, pick up mail, look for submarines (visual only since the aircraft had no Anti-Submarine Warfare gear), etc.— what we called Ash and Trash in Vietnam—between the ship and shore bases in Lisbon and Gibraltar. *Illustrious* was steaming off the south coast, near Plymouth. I, as aircraft commander, would fly the aircraft, call sign Victor Hotel, from HMS *Heron* to join the ship at sea. My copilot was already onboard, having gone down before the ship sailed to act as liaison. The eight maintainers who would keep my Sea King flying were there too, all waiting for what promised to be a less-than-stressful deployment. The flight down was easy and smooth on a beautiful, clear day, but upon arrival at the coast, there was a wall of sea fog, solid as a mountain wall, right off shore. Somewhere in the sea fog was *Illustrious*.

The sea fog off southern England was something I had often heard about, but had never seen. My squadron mates used to describe the sea fog down the coast to the west in Cornwall as being so thick that you could not see across the road, even though the wind was blowing 40 knots. I wrote it off as pilot exaggeration but here it was: sea fog, solid, gray, and not moving. Perhaps the ship was in the clear and the fog was only right there on the coast? My first call to the ship dispelled that idea. The ship reported they were in near zero visibility.

"Tower, Victor Hotel, feet wet, two souls onboard, two point zero to splash (two hours fuel onboard the aircraft)," I called over UHF.

"Victor Hotel, Tower. Switch Center and they will give you a vector to us."

"Roger, Tower. Victor Hotel switching center."

After switching radio frequencies, I transmitted, "Center, Victor Hotel. Crossing the coastline five miles east of Plymouth, at angels one (1000 feet)."

"Victor Hotel, squawk ident"—meaning, activate the radar transponder that would highlight my aircraft on their scope. Moments later, "Victor Hotel, Center, we have you. Turn to 170 degrees and descend to 500 feet. You are five miles out. Report ship in sight."

At 500 feet I could see nothing but gray fog slightly below us, the tops of the fog ragged with small tuffs sticking up here and there.

"Center, Victor Hotel. Ship not in sight.

"Victor Hotel, Center, standby for vectors to CCA (Carrier Controlled Approach—radar control in both course and altitude. CCA will bring you down to around 125 feet lined up directly for landing). Turn heading one-seven-zero degrees. Climb to 1000 feet. Switch to Approach Control."

I turned the Sea King as directed, and prepared for the approach. Doing a CCA when you know that you are only a few miles off shore and that the weather is fine over the land, removes the worry of missed approaches and low fuel and the possibility of ditching before you run out of fuel. Miss the approach, try another, go ashore and wait for better weather. What could be easier?

At 1000 feet Victor Hotel was well above the fog bank, but when Approach turned the aircraft onto final approach course and started it down, things changed rapidly.

"Victor Hotel, you are on course, you are on glide path. Going slightly above glide path now, increase rate of descent. On glide path, come right to zero-one-two degrees. On course, on glide path. Approaching decision height, report ship in sight."

Decision height is just that, the altitude where you either have your landing spot—the ship's deck or the runway—and you decide to continue to the landing, or you execute a missed approach and take the aircraft around for another try. To go lower without the touchdown spot in sight is to risk flying into something, like the control tower or the ship's masts/superstructure.

---

*Fog is difficult to understand. Once, flying back from a ship off the same south coast as part of a flight of five aircraft, I came to understand fog better. Taking off, the ship was all clear, but once over land, we saw a thin layer of fog over the ground. It was so thin that looking down through it you could see every detail on the ground; houses, roads, farm fields, and up through it came radio towers and hilltops. When we called Yeovilton tower and were told the field was closed with zero visibility, we didn't believe it because we could see the ground so clearly from above.*

*In Britain, "closed" doesn't mean you can't land on the airfield, it just means you are on your own, so we decided to land without the tower's approval. I was number three in the flight, flying in a long, loose trail formation behind the first two Sea Kings. We rolled on final and one by one, I watched the first two disappear into the fog at 200 feet over the runway. Then it was my turn, and as soon as I entered the fog, visibility went from five plus miles to zero. Years before, I read about three Army CH-34s crashing one after the other when they hit ground fog at night in Germany. They could see the ground just fine from above but everything disappeared when they got down to 100 feet. At the time, I wondered how that could happen. Now I understood, understood completely.*

*I held the aircraft steady as I slowed down and touched down in the center of the runway with hardly a bump. I could hear the first two aircraft calling on the radio that they could not taxi off the runway because of no visibility at all. My crewman had jumped out to act as a ground guide but I could not see him beyond the rotor disk so I joined the other aircraft in shutting down right there on the runway. Tractors would tow us in when the visibility improved enough for the ground crews to find the taxiways.*

---

But now, I was over the sea and there was no runway, only the deck of a ship. At 125 feet, decision height, I looked up—nothing but gray fog, no ship in sight. Since I was now below the altitude of the ship's masts, I immediately applied power and began a rapid climb before I hit them.

"Approach Control, Victor Hotel, ship not in sight, executing missed approach," I called.

"Victor Hotel, Control, Would you like to try another CCA?"

"Control, Victor Hotel, negative. The fog is solid. I am now VMC (Visual Meteorological Conditions, i.e. clear of clouds/fog) above it again. Switching back to Center," the aircraft commander called. The aircrewman, trained as a navigator and communicator, had come up to the cockpit and at my signal, switched the radio frequencies back to Center so that I could concentrate on flying.

"Center, Victor Hotel, fog is solid, did not break out on CCA. I am going ashore to await your call when you are clear of the sea fog."

"Victor Hotel, Center, do not go ashore. We will attempt an ELVA (Emergency Low Visibility Approach)."

What do you do when you are far out to sea and you have done approach after approach in the fog and cannot see the deck? You are over the ship but it is invisible below you. What do you do when your fuel is running out and you don't have enough range left to make it to land? The last, the very last resort is an ELVA.

The difference between a CCA and an ELVA is that CCA uses aviation radar, much the same as is used at any good-sized airport. An ELVA, on the other hand, does not use aviation radar at all. Instead it uses the anti-aircraft radar that controls the ship's defensive weapons. The ship's defense system tracks you all the way down and since, when it is tracking you, it cannot track incoming threats, it is only used as a last resort. Too, a CCA is a smooth approach, with constant course corrections being supplied and altitude instructions given to keep you on a smooth glide path down.

In an ELVA, the ship holds a steady course directly into the wind. The anti-aircraft controllers just give you course directions and distance from the stern. Instead of smoothly descending at a constant rate as you slow your airspeed in a CCA, you start at 300 feet and 90 knots. Then, in steps as you get closer to the ship, you slow to 80 knots as you level off at 250 feet, then 70 knots at 200 feet, then 60 knots at 150 feet. In the final portion of the ELVA you are in a hover at 50 feet, directly off the stern. At that point you should be able to pick up the ship's wake visually and follow it to the flight deck. To help you along in finding the wake, the ship's deck crew throws floating fares overboard at certain intervals. You find the wake, follow the flares, and land aboard.

That's the theory anyway . . .

I had never done an ELVA , neither in a simulator, nor in a helicopter. Helo pilots all consider ELVAs one of those esoteric, arcane things that one quizzes copilots on, like back course ILS (Instrument Landing System) approaches and FM homing, not something that is actually done any more. No worries, though, since the weather above the fog is clear, the land is just a few miles away, and my aircraft has a couple hours worth of fuel left. I have plenty of time to try new things.

I turn the aircraft to follow the course directions provided and descend to 300 feet and 90 knots when directed. Shortly, I was once again in the fog and visibility was once again zero. The ship's wake is not visible, nor is a flare pot. I slow to 80 knots, then 70, then 60, as I descend in steps. Shortly I am in a near hover with barely any forward speed at 50 feet on the radar altimeter above the sea. I look up—only fog, gray and featureless. As I am about to call waving off, I see something move just below and in front of the aircraft's nose, and suddenly something bright orange flew down into the water. Continuing to hover slowly forward, I realize that what I saw was one of the deck crew actually throwing the flare pot into the water. Then the darker gray of the ship's stern is there, and then I hover aboard and follow the directions of the LSE's lit wands, vague through the fog.

Over the landing spot, I lower the collective and the deck crew runs under the rotor to chain the aircraft down. Victor Hotel and crew are safely aboard *Illustrious*.

My own deck crew, who had boarded the ship before she sailed, climb aboard as I shut the helicopter down.

"Sir, we are very surprised to see you," the Chief, the senior enlisted man, says.

Looking at the aircraft from side to side, I realize that I cannot see either ship's rail, meaning that visibility is less than 50 feet.

"You are not half as surprised as I am," I reply.

The mission was to get the helicopter aboard the ship and I have. The mission is complete. Luck and superstition?

## 30

# DAY AND NIGHT PASSENGERS
### GIBRALTAR ■ OCTOBER 1984

*As noted in an earlier chapter, the US Navy and Marine Corps are very fussy about how far out to sea you can fly single aircraft. If you are a section of two, you are not as limited, but they still get concerned if it is much more than 25 miles. The Royal Navy, on the other hand, has no such rules. They consider you competent enough to decide if it is too risky, after one of the five senior officers, the "Authorizers" in the squadron, sign off your flight plan. You present your plan to the Authorizer, tell him what the weather is in your mission area and that you are qualified to do the mission. Of course, if you are one of those five officers, you can sign off your own flight without reference to anyone else. As a flight commander, I was one of those five officers.*

### DAY

After a busy period onboard HMS *Illustrious,* the command decided that since they would be doing only ship drills for two days, my aircraft would not be needed, so I could take my maintainers and fly ashore to HMS *Rooke,* the Navy Base in Gibraltar, for some rest. "Liberty Call, now Liberty Call," is always welcome news to men deployed onboard ships.

After two days ashore and several non-flying adventures, we went back to work with a mission to fly to a British submarine 40 miles out in the Mediterranean and hoist a Royal Navy admiral and his aide onboard the helicopter for a ride back to Gibraltar (Gib). It was a calm day, sunny with light winds, easy. I had never done a lift off a submarine, nor had my copilot, but how hard could it be? After all, it's just holding a stable hover while the aircrewman pulls him up from the deck.

*We had flown this admiral once before. His VIP helicopter, a Lynx, had developed a fault and he needed to get from* Illustrious *to another ship that was about 20 miles away. We were available and were tasked with flying the admiral over to the other ship, never mind that our Commando Sea King was in no way a VIP aircraft. It was, of course, night, but for once, the weather was not bad. It should take about 45 minutes, tops, to complete this mission.*

*After the admiral was settled into his red troop seat, my aircrewman helped him put on a headset and adjusted the volume for him. On all Royal Navy aircraft, the ICS uses VOX (voice) instead of a transmit switch, so all anyone with a helmet or headset has to do if they want to speak over the ICS, is to start talking instead of having to push a switch. My aircrewman then said to the admiral, "Sir, I am very sorry but due to defense budget cuts the in-flight movie has been canceled. However, to make up for it the crew will play you a concert," whereupon he pulled a kazoo out of his flight suit pocket. At the same time, my copilot turned around in the left seat with a penny whistle in his hand. They both began to play for the admiral while I lifted the helicopter into a hover and took off into the night. The admiral did not say a word, but I'm told his eyes were very wide. Just under an hour later, we were back on the deck of the* Illustrious, *mission complete. No official comments were made on the concert.*

---

Now after the adventure with the night flight, we were to fly the same admiral again, as noted earlier, this time from a submarine back to Gib. We arrived over the sub on time to find a small group of people assembled on the sub's sail (the vertical portion of the sub that stands above its main deck)—the admiral, his aid, and several of the boat's company to assist in the transfer. The admiral would come up first, followed by the aid. As I came into a hover, my crewman prepared the hoist for the lift. He attached a "horse collar" to the hoist's hook and prepared to let it down. The idea is that the crewman lets out enough slack line so that the person being lifted is easily able to put it on without inadvertently being lifted up into the air. As he let the cable down, I tried to maintain a steady hover.

Trying to maintain a steady hover over a submarine's sail turned out to be a difficult task for a Commando Sea King. Typically, helicopters doing lifts off submarines would have an operational Doppler hover capability with radar that automatically allows the helicopter to maintain a constant hover position and altitude over water. Doppler measures the difference between radar points to provide a reference to the autopilot so that it can keep a constant position over the water, because a pilot cannot. Water looks like water and does not provide the visual clues a pilot needs to determine whether or not he is moving laterally or climbing or descending. While Commando Sea Kings do have the equipment installed, it is not maintained or tested since it is not part of the Commando's mission. The controls are "blanked out," that is, a plastic plate installed over them so that the pilot cannot activate the system. Since there is no Doppler, the pilot must see the submarine itself to get references he needs. If you are hovering above the sail there is very little submarine visible and minimal reference. Still, I can hover, so I'll just have to concentrate.

Another difficulty factor is that submarines, like all ships, roll in the waves. On a large ship, like a carrier, it is usually not a problem, but on a sub, the top of the sail moves back and forth quite a bit, even in calm seas. The problem for the man working the hoist is to time the start of raising the passenger just right, ideally when the sail is moving toward the helicopter so that the acceleration is not so great that it jerks the passenger off the sail instead of raising him smoothly.

That's the theory anyway . . .

Just as my crewman started the hoist up, the submarine's sail reversed direction and the admiral came off the deck so fast it nearly dislocated his shoulders. As my crewman swung him into the aircraft cabin, I could see he was not happy, not happy at all. The lift of his aid went without incident, no reversal this time, and in short order we were headed back to Gibraltar.

I had been briefed that the admiral was an old helo pilot and I could see him calm down as we headed back to Gibraltar at 500 feet. He knew exactly the difficulties of hoist off ships and did not hold a grudge at now being two inches taller than he had been before the sudden yank off the sail and into the air. His aid came up to the cockpit and asked if it would be alright if the admiral came into the cockpit and flew part of the way back. I replied of course it would be alright, since we routinely flew single pilot. The copilot climbed out of the seat and gave the admiral his flight helmet.

After the admiral was strapped into the copilot's seat, I introduced myself and gave him the flight controls. As an old instructor pilot, I kept my hands close to the controls but he settled right in and did a creditable job of flying. His frown was now a smile at being a pilot again instead of sitting behind a desk. In 15 minutes we were on final into Gibraltar's single runway. I offered to let him do a couple of touch and goes, but he declined and gave me back the controls for touchdown. After clearance from tower, we left the runway and began to taxi to our parking area.

At this point we must digress. When we came into Gib for our two days of liberty, the seven men in my ground crew had been working for a straight week onboard *Illustrious* without a chance to do their laundry and were completely out of clean clothes, both uniforms and underwear. As soon as they had the aircraft put to bed, the Chief inquired at the base laundry if it would be possible to get one-day service on washing their clothes. Informed it would, they all left their uniforms at the laundry, changed into civies, and proceeded with Liberty Call. The next day, their clothes were not back from the laundry, some problem with the washing machines. Day two and their uniforms were still not back; whether or not they had their uniforms, they had to go back to work and could not work in civilian clothes. The Chief, being a resourceful man, managed to arrange to borrow coveralls for them to work in, but alas, the coveralls were not of the right sizes, nor were they even vaguely the same color, with some half covered in paint of various colors. On several of the lads, the coveralls were far too short, stopping half way up their calves. Never mind, they would do until the proper uniforms were returned, tomorrow for sure.

Back to our flight with the admiral—the lads saw us land, and being in a good mood after a night of liberty in a port advertising 365 bars, they decided to give us a "proper" welcome. So, in their mismatched coveralls, they lined up, all eight of them, and as we taxied by, heading to our parking spot, they all gave a salute by putting their hands to their ears and waggling them at us while sticking out their tongues. About two seconds into this "salute" they began to realize that it was not the Royal Navy lieutenant copilot in the left seat, but someone much older. About one second after that they began the process of trying to sink into the payment.

The thought that went through my head was that the worst they could do to me was to send me home. The lads, well, I was pretty sure flogging was no longer allowed . . .

The admiral did a double take and to his everlasting credit, returned the "salute" in the same spirit by putting his hand to his nose and waggling it at the lads while sticking his tongue out back at them. Just before he climbed out of the seat, he clapped me on the shoulder and with a laugh told me what a pleasure it was to fly again and see that morale in the Fleet Air Arm remained as high as ever. Not a word did he say about being two inches taller after his inadvertent launch from the sub's sail.

When I looked over to where the lads had been lined up, there was not a soul to see.

## NIGHT

The mission was simple: depart Gibraltar at 2000 hours, well after dark, and deliver a single passenger, a Royal Navy captain, to a fleet auxiliary ship, a supply ship with a single helicopter landing spot on the stern. The interesting part of the mission was that the ship was over 100 miles out to sea in the Atlantic and had no navigation aids, such as a radio beacon, onboard to help us find her. To add a little difficulty factor, there was a solid overcast, meaning it would be a very dark night over the water, and visibility was only about a mile over the entire area between the ship's location and Gibraltar. On the odd chance that we could not find the ship, we were given diplomatic clearance to divert to either Portugal or Morocco, if we did not think we would have enough fuel to make it back to Gibraltar. Spain was out of the question because Spain and the UK, NATO Allies or not, were feuding over Gibraltar's status again, or more properly, feuding still. Since I was the AC, I decided on Morocco, with the hearty concurrence of my copilot and crewman. For added insurance, I had the aircraft fully fueled so that we could remain airborne for over five hours, if necessary, plenty of time to reach either alternative.

In the Royal Navy Commando Sea King squadrons, aircrewmen are not mechanics. If you are away and your helicopter needs oil, the pilot had better know where to put it. The aircrewmen are instead trained radio operators, photographers, loadmasters, and navigators. My aircrewman had done all the calculations on wind drift, magnetic variation, etc., and would be giving me constant course directions as were flew. We knew that if the ship was where it was supposed to be, our aircrewman would navigate us to it in short order. We also knew that if it wasn't, we would get a night in Tangier.

After we started up the aircraft, our passenger came onboard. Our aircrewman fitted him with a floatation vest and a helmet and we were set to go. I taxied the Sea King to Gibraltar's single runway for a takeoff to the east, and after tower clearance, we departed. As soon as we cleared the runway, Tower directed us to change radio frequencies to departure control. Departure directed me to turn right to a course that would take us out through the middle of the Strait, keeping us clear of Spanish and Moroccan airspace. As I cleared the Rock of Gibraltar, the lights on shore disappeared; it was another black night over the sea, nothing to look at except when we passed directly over a ship headed in or out of the Straits. We could see its lights below us for a few seconds as we passed overhead.

I had the altitude hold set to 500 feet so that we would stay out of the clouds somewhere above us, not that it made any difference. Looking forward, it was only black. The air was smooth and the stability system was working fine, so I just had my hands resting lightly on the controls as the aircraft flew itself through the night. My copilot had his penny whistle out again and was practicing some Scottish tune. My aircrewman had the red cabin lights on and his maps and charts spread out on the cabin deck. Every now and then he muttered things like, "I wonder where we are?" while pouring over the charts. This was strictly for our passenger's benefit, since my navigator knew exactly where we were, but he never missed a chance to mildly mind-mess senior officers. Every few minutes he would give me a minor course correction and an estimated time of arrival at our target ship.

The captain passenger unstrapped from his seat and came up to stand between the pilot's seats. He wasn't nervous, exactly, when we started the flight, but was less than fully comfortable. Now, seeing us so calm as we flew through the darkness, he relaxed too. He introduced himself and told us he was a submariner by trade, but had finished his command and now had nothing to look forward to but desks and paperwork. I laughed, knowing full well that if you are an RLO (Real-Live Officer, as opposed to a technician like a warrant officer) and stay in long enough, it happens to everyone, no matter what your job was, pilot, submariner, or commando.

The night seemed to clear a little. The overcast and blackness was still there but we were seeing ship's lights at greater distances. When my crewman told me we were 20 minutes out, I gave the ship a call and got a prompt reply. They were ready for us and would have favorable wind across the deck when we arrived. In another ten minutes, I could see a ship's light directly on the helicopter's nose. My crewman had called it exactly right and the ship was exactly where they said they would be.

I called the ship for landing. We were cleared for a starboard approach, coming in on the right side for a smooth, routine landing. Just before the captain disembarked, he came to the cockpit again to shake my hand. He said, "This may be routine to you, but it's amazing to me."

An hour later we were back on the ground in Gibraltar and I thought to myself, the captain was right that it was routine to us and that's what made it amazing. It was a perfect flight and yet I remember it. Cheated death again . . .

# 31

# FINAL FLIGHT WITH THE ROYAL NAVY
## CORNWALL, UNITED KINGDOM ■ JUNE 1985

---

*After two years as an exchange officer, I was ready to go home. The Royal Navy Commandos could not have made me feel more welcome, could not have given me more responsibility, more adventures—Norway, ships, Gibraltar, Scotland, Egypt, Cyprus— but I was ready to go home. As with most tours, as the end came near, I was assigned missions of less and less importance; in a way I went from being the male lead to being a supporting character actor, you might say.*

---

The last flight was to be an easy one, number three on a flight of three going from Yeovilton to "Coldnose," and then out into the Channel to work with a submarine on practice personnel hoists. As with the hoist of the admiral and his aide off Gibraltar, it would require some precision hovering because if you are in position to pick up a person, you sometimes cannot see much of the actual submarine. As noted earlier, water looks like water, making it very difficult to hold a steady position, but all in all it would not be too taxing on a fine day like this one. In fact, in the end it required nothing at all from my aircraft. The other two Sea Kings took care of all the work and I was released to go home early.

I refueled at Culdrose and headed back east across Cornwall's Bodmin Moor back to Somerset. It was a nice day, flying single ship at 500 feet above the ground, enjoying the view of Jamaica Inn country, Daphne du Maurier country, knowing full well that this quite probably would be the last time I'd see it this way. The next time, I thought, I won't have a multimillion British pound helicopter at my command: I'll be just driving a car like everyone else.

I am flying by myself today, no copilot in the cockpit and only my crewman in the back. No load, no worries, a nice way to end two years as an exchange officer from the US Marine Corps to the British Royal Navy.

Thirty minutes into the one-hour flight, my aircrewman calls calmly, "Fixed wing rolling in at 4 o'clock." His voice sounds a little too calm.

Since he did not say "jet" I automatically assume it's a Chipmunk, a small two-seat prop training aircraft, from one of the local air stations, out to have a little fun with the passing Sea King. Normally I would not play but it's my last flight and a beautiful day over the moor, so why not?

How you fight a fixed-wing when you are flying a helicopter depends mostly on what the fixed-wing does and what kind of fixed wing he is. If he is a high-speed fighter, like an F-4, you are in good shape because he cannot turn with you. If he comes down to helicopter altitudes, he is in every anti-air system in the world's range, so he must keep his speed up, which means that you can always out turn him. If he is an attack aircraft, like an A-4, he can turn but still not as rapidly as you can. But whatever he is, you must see him immediately so that you will know what he intends to do, how he is going to attack. In either case he cannot stay down with you too long because fighters rapidly burn up all their fuel at low altitudes.

Your first move is to fly directly toward him, gaining as much speed as you can. You put him right on your nose so that you increase the closure rate and thereby decrease the time he has to lock you up in his sights. While you are turning, you climb to 200 or 300 feet above the ground so that you have a little bit of maneuvering area below you, but not so much that he can get below you and skylight your aircraft. If you survive his first pass, you try to disappear. He cannot stay down low for long because as I said, he is burning a lot of fuel there and is still vulnerable to anti-aircraft fire.

If he is diving on you, wait until he is just about in gun range, and turn hard away from him. You must actually displace the aircraft over the ground, not just change heading. As you turn, watch his wings. When he turns to line you up in his sights, you turn hard the other direction and slip toward the ground. He may not be able to follow and will pass you by. As he starts his turn to come back, you hide behind a terrain feature, if you can find one, and you hope he gives it up and goes away. He probably won't though. A kill is a kill and five makes him an ace.

If he comes down to your altitude of 200 or 300 feet instead of diving on you, you immediately descend to 100 feet holding at as much speed as you can get out of the helicopter, and just before he gets into gun range, you pull up your nose and start a cyclic climb. He will be watching you and will pull his nose up to keep you locked up. When you see his nose start up, you immediately push yours back down. If he follows you and pushes his nose down too, he will fly into the ground before he realizes what just happened. I almost got an A-4 that way back at Yuma in the WTI course. I could see his wings wobble as he wanted to follow me but realized what I was doing just as he started to move his nose.

If you are being attacked by an armed helicopter and you are flying a transport helicopter, there is a 100 percent chance he will kill you within 90 seconds of getting in range. If you are flying an armed helicopter there is a 90 percent chance that you will both get off shots and will kill each other in about the same time frame. No helicopter can out turn another.

But this is not a helicopter attacking, it's a fixed wing. In all cases, you must always keep him in sight. Lose sight and die. So I turned my Sea King hard to starboard, adding power and adding rudder to get the nose around quicker. Looking up through the greenhouse I saw my "attacker."

Spitfire

It was a real Spitfire, painted in Battle of Britain colors, and could only have been a private aircraft. The pilot came down to see if this Royal Navy helicopter wanted to play for a few minutes.

I could not believe that I was looking at a Spitfire, already leveling his wings in a dive and closing in on my helicopter to within gun range. If this was real, I would quite probably be dead in a few moments. A literal chill went up my spine and I felt 40 years melt away. WWII had returned and now I was in it.

I went through the motions of fighting a fixed-wing, but we had not trained to engage World War II fighters. I had flown T-28's, a single engine low-wing aircraft like a Spitfire, though with nowhere near the performance of a Spitfire, and I knew how quickly that aircraft could turn. I found out immediately that even a helicopter couldn't turn with a Spitfire. We did three passes, two more after the first surprise one, and there is no doubt in my mind that he "killed" me on every pass. None of the "got you," "no, you didn't," "did too"—no, he had me on every pass. We both knew it. In my mind, I could see the six machine guns on his wings firing and see the tracers growing bigger and bigger as they hit my Sea King.

After the third pass, I rolled wings level at 500 feet and 110 knots. The Spitfire came alongside, slowing to match my speed like only a WWII fighter can. Modern fighters stall out at speeds higher than the max speed of a Sea King. The pilot held position at three o'clock while my crewman took pictures of him against the backdrop of the moor, and then with a waggle of his wings, he added power and climbed up to the right and was gone. Both the Spitfire pilot and I were smiling the entire time.

My crewman and I said nothing as we continued on back to Yeovilton—nothing to say. We had an experience that few people get to see now, had taken a small trip back in time, a warrior from Vietnam and a warrior from WWII greeting each other. For a few minutes, that river of time stopped and the 40 years were gone. Then they came back and we were alone in the sky over the brown moor.

Forty minutes later, I landed at Yeovilton and taxied back to the 846 Squadron ramp. I shut down Sea King VH bureau number ZA-293 after 2.7 hours of flight time. My exchange tour with the Junglies was over.

Cheated death one final time with the Royal Navy. Luck and superstition, that's all it is.

## THE WALL, 20 YEARS AFTER
### SEPTEMBER 1989

---

*I think we humans imagine we get over things, but then something always happens that shows us that we really do not. The best we can do is to suppress . . .*

---

On a warm, sunny, late-summer's day, I stopped off to see some old friends, friends I had not seen in 17 years. You see, I was learning to be a bureaucrat at a government "college"— the Defense Systems Management College (DSMC), at Ft. Belvoir just south of Washington, D.C. After 20 years of flying helicopters around the world for the Army, National Guard, the Royal Navy, and Marine Corps, I had to face the inevitable for career officers: a tour in an office, in an office building, in DC . . .

At our college they were worried about us. The course was very intense, with a lot of pressure on all the students, so they were worried about our physical health, as well as our mental health. They gave us blood tests to check our cholesterol levels and classes on how to relax while we learn about buying weapons of mass destruction, office supplies, and everything in between. Some of their students had had heart attacks while attending and one committed suicide before even graduating. I feel the pressure too. I don't know what it is, but somehow, using the weapons of war never bothered me as much as the act of buying them. Maybe the idea that you personally may have to pay the ultimate price for defending your country *right now* is more what I always imagined military life would be. Instead, I am to become another tiny cog in the bureaucracy in the endless government offices of the Washington metro area.

If I stay long enough, maybe I will be like the others in the office, praying that I will not die of a heart attack or stroke in the traffic and monotony of office life, instead of praying that I can get through one more dark night boat launch in an old, tired helicopter and my friends won't have to scrape up what is left of me from the wreckage and take it home to a closed coffin funeral.

But my friends, my old friends, I visited them again on that warm, sunny, late-summer's day. Our college class took a two-day trip to Capitol Hill for briefings by the Congressional Military Liaison Staffs. After the morning in-briefs we watched hearings in the conference rooms, the House and Senate in action, and talked to our own state representatives and senators if they were in town. On the second day I was bored with bored politicians reading scripts to an empty chamber and bored with bored witnesses reading scripts to a nearly empty committee table.

So, on the second day, I left at the first opportunity. I walked out of the Capitol Building with no plan in mind, except to enjoy the clear, warm late-summer's day. Because Labor Day had passed, most of the tourists were gone, except for retirees and foreigners, both groups posing self-consciously in front of the monuments. The rest of the people on the Mall, mainly men, seemed to be connected to the government: bureaucrats, staffers, contractors, lobbyists, mostly in the uniform of dark suit and tie. Some were military in uniform or running shorts. All were walking quickly.

But, there were women on the Mall, too, perhaps bureaucrats or contractors or staffers. Perhaps secretaries or students, still pretty in their lightweight summer clothes against the heat of the day. They seemed to be walking slower, enjoying the warm, sunny day.

The day itself seemed nearly perfect—less than 80 degrees, no clouds, no haze, and the buildings gleamed white. I had the strange thought that the whiteness of the buildings could mean either purity or sterility, as one of my college literature teachers explained how colors are used to invoke feelings, and wondered why I was even thinking such things. Colors and feelings had not crossed my mind in years. You must avoid feelings when you are flying, lest you be distracted.

As I walked down the hill toward the Smithsonian, I felt my tie begin to choke me and my seldom-used sport coat (blue, all Marine officers own a blue blazer, which is always worn with gray or tan trousers, always) becoming too hot, so I removed both. I stuffed the tie in the jacket pocket and slung the jacket over my shoulder. As I walked down the Mall, I stopped at the Aerospace Museum to touch the moon rock as I always do when passing by, for both luck and to remember the summer of '69 when my then wife and I watched the moon landing with friends in their trailer just outside Fort Rucker, Alabama. It was a few weeks before I got my wings as an Army helicopter pilot and a very significant time in my pre-war, pre-son, pre-college education life. We all cheered as we watched Armstrong step down from the ladder on the little black and white television.

The Washington monument stood straight against the sky in front of me, with the flags around its base snapping in the afternoon wind. As I walked toward it, I decided to keep on walking and visit my old friends. I knew roughly where I would find them, but my first and only visit had been several years ago, so now I would have to search a little before I found them.

On that trip, five or six years before, I took my 12-year-old son with me to visit them. I think he saw them, but only in the way I saw WWII monuments or even Civil War statues when I was his age—history, remote, not real and certainly not connected to his father in the 1970's or to him in the early 1980's. I showed him their names on the wall and although he did not know it, the place where mine would have been if the North Vietnamese gunner had fired a half second sooner.

I had forgotten where my friends were on the wall, so I had to ask one of the volunteers to look them up in his book for me. Their section is near the central V, deep down in the wall. There are six of my friends there. Other friends are scattered along the wall, but these six are together, one name after another. They died together when their CH-47C Chinook blew up, five or six thousand feet above Laos in the spring of 1971. Their names are low so I squatted to read them and to touch them, one by one on the black wall.

The first one was an old man, at least by 1971 Army helicopter pilot standards, of 35, a Navy veteran before he enlisted in the Army to fly. This was his second trip to the war. The first tour he had flown scouts, LOACHs, undoubtedly, some of the most dangerous helicopter missions in the war, and he survived those aircraft with many Air Medals, a Purple Heart, the Distinguished Flying Cross, and his life. But in 1970 he had a wife and three kids, so for his second tour, he chose what he thought would be a safer aircraft, a transport, not a hunter-killer. On his last flight he was the copilot, learning to be a cargo pilot and providing seasoning to a new, first tour AC.

His name, the AC's name that is, is there too. It was his first tour and maybe as a brand new aircraft commander (AC) he was a little less ready to lead combat missions as dangerous as the one that killed him, but that happens in war. The missions must be done and he was the AC, ready or not. At 25 he was still single and, as a Mormon, he kept to his faith's tenants of no drinking or smoking. This kept the rest of us from knowing him very well, since drinking and swearing and what might be considered ill behavior were usually involved in all the non-work activities back then.

This crew had a third pilot and his name is there, too. He is there because he did something stupid. He might have gotten his name there in his own right, had he lasted longer, but instead he is there with the crew of that Chinook, even though his name was not on the flight schedule that day.

---

*During Operation Lam Son 719, the invasion of Laos, so many helicopters were going down—107 destroyed and 600 damaged in six weeks—that orders from Division Headquarters directed that only aircrews on an assigned mission were to cross the border. Like I said, he wasn't supposed to fly that day. He was one of the few pilots who did not share his hootch with anyone, so he did not have a roommate to report him missing. For that matter, no one even knew he died or was missing from the company area until the day after the helicopter was shot down and he did not show up for a scheduled morning launch. We started looking for him and finally, one of the maintenance crew remembered seeing him board the downed aircraft, camera in hand, as it taxied out for that day's missions. He must have gone to take pictures, as pilots sometimes do. He probably wanted some shots of the Ho Chi Min trail. Hard to take them when you are flying and besides, you get better camera angles from the back than from the cockpit.*

---

I remember being 19, like he was when the Chinook blew up, and I remember knowing for a fact that death only happened to other people. He had no wife and was a "Newbie" so no one really knew him well or knew anything about his family. Do they still keep a picture of him on the wall or mantle, his new silver wings bright against the green of his dress uniform?

The flight engineer, the senior enlisted man on board, had shared many flights with me. He was a dark haired young man, good natured, always covered in grease, and apparently not afraid of anything. Well, he never admitted or showed signs of being afraid, anyway. I don't remember whether or not he was married. After 17 years, the details have dimmed considerably and the pictures he had taped to the armor inside his aircraft are vague now. What had not faded was the pride he took in his aircraft, something that made the pilots always glad to fly his Chinook.

The other two were also young, caught up in the war like the rest of us. The crew chief was blond and friendly, as he looked at the world through thick glasses. He was really looking forward to the day when he would be flight engineer of his own Chinook and could paint the pictures he wanted on the side of the aircraft up by the crew door on the starboard side. The door gunner wasn't a grunt that got tired of walking and volunteered to fly, like many of the door gunners were. He was a crew chief, too. He just volunteered to be door gunner when his aircraft was in for maintenance or not on the flight schedule. He too wanted his own Chinook, had one picked out in fact, but until then he enjoyed the view from over the M-60D's barrel as we flew along.

As I touched the third pilot's name, I couldn't help but say out loud, "You dumb-ass." The others died doing their jobs but this one died because he was 19 and invulnerable. Then I nearly cried.

You see, it was a beautiful, warm, late-summer day. The young girls in their summer dresses and shorts were walking on the Mall, many of them, the age that our wives and girlfriends were then and the age our daughters are now—my son's age now.

Women my age were at the Wall, too, but I tried not to look at them, afraid of what I might see. My wife might have been one of them, if the North Vietnamese gunner that hit me and took my Chinook out of the sky had pulled the trigger a half-second sooner.

My throat was dry and my eyes were blurry as I started to leave. As I turned from the Wall to go, I saw two of those lovely young girls standing behind me. Standing near together, they might have been sisters, tan with blond streaky hair. Both of them stared at me, looking half way between shock and pity, or maybe just in surprise that men really did get the way I was when they visited the Wall on a late-summer's day. Were they children of the wall, daughters of names on the polished black stone or only tourists, looking at dusty history? Maybe either or both, I don't know.

By the time I passed the Washington Monument on my way back up the hill, I was under control again. Pilots, aviators, especially Marine aviators, must always be under control—death before uncool.

When I visited the Wall that day, I was nearly 40, and learning to be a military bureaucrat in Washington. My friends on the wall are still in their late teens and twenties. They still live in my mind, just like they were in 1971.

The day they died, we packed all their things, took down their plaques from the wall of the Playtex Officer's Club, erased their names from the aircrew boards in the Club and in Operations, and then we went back to flying. The day after they died, a stranger entering the company area and walking around would never have known they had ever been there.

But their names are there on the Wall. For those of us still here, one by one, our flying days have ended, and our war is history, like Korea and WWII were to us back in 1971. Maybe someday I'll go visit my friends again, but not too soon. Not on a warm, sunny, late-summer's day when the young girls walk the Mall in their summer clothes.

## REEFING

*There comes a time when you cannot do it anymore. That is, you cannot do it at the level that is required to be fully successful as an aviator. Anything less than full concentration is simply death for you, and perhaps for your passengers, too. Perhaps the closest way to explain it is by asking the question, "when do you reef a sailboat's sails," i.e. make them smaller, reducing speed but keeping the boat from being over-powered, capsized or smashed by the wind? The wind is rising, what to do? Reef now or wait, thinking things will get better and the wind will drop? Answer—the first time reefing crosses your mind, do it, do it right then. If you wait until after that moment, it may be*

*too late to reef and the boat may go down under too much sail, the mast shat-*
*tered and the sails shredded. And when you start thinking of dead guys instead*
*of closing the door when you enter the mental room marked "flying," it is*
*time to reef.*

I thought about it again as I sat at my desk. Well, not really a desk, since only the senior officers and senior civil servants at Naval Air Systems Command (NAVAIR) have a real desk in a room with a door, but more of a shelf in a cubical. While I was going through my training to become a bureaucrat, another friend and his entire crew died in a helicopter crash. That was three years ago but I sat there in my cube and counted to myself all the men I knew who had died when their aircraft crashed. I started after Vietnam. Why count those who died in war when there are so many more out there to start with?

I quit counting at 43. That is not forty-three men killed in a single crash, but one here, two there, a crew of four there, over the seventeen years that had passed after I left Phu Bai. Five, when a Chinook loaded with 29 passengers flew into a mountain in Vietnam's I Corps. An OH-58 crashes somewhere in Germany and one of my former roommates from Vietnam dies in it. One when his Chinook comes apart after a single-point failure at Fort Carson. Three, when their Frog came apart in flight over the Joshua Tree National Monument. One, when his 46 rolled over on the deck of an LPH and sank into the Pacific taking him with it. One, when his T-28 left a smoking black hole in the Florida sand before he even finished flight school. Two, when their Cobra hit a power line in Greece at 150 knots. One, when his Cobra went into the Intercostal Waterway for no reason anyone could fathom. Another when his 53 did not return from a mission and they found the wreckage in too many pieces to determine why it went in. On and on and on. And each time, we would go to the chapel and sing the hymn about God watching over those who fly, but it seems He often doesn't. . . .

That one in October 1988 took two friends, one a crew chief—a good man, competent and a fine Marine—the other a close pilot friend from Med cruises past who I had taught tactics and all the hard things that make you a better combat pilot and flight instructor. Fun guy, but easy to make fun of in his middle-west, un-hip manner and everyone did, not that he seemed to mind.

I trained my friend to be a Weapons Tactics Instructor, a WTI, then the highest designation in Marine Corps helicopter aviation. He was a good student and learned well. Not to say that his training wasn't exciting, it always is when you push yourself and your aircraft as far as they can go. But, you can be a good student, have a good well-maintained aircraft, have the best training you can get and enjoy life in general, no matter how good a shape you keep yourself in, you still die.

---

*While flying on NVGs back on one of my Med cruises across northern Morocco one nice, moonlit night, we almost died, he and I and the crew chief in the back of our 46. It would have been one of those crashes where the aircrew flies directly into a mountain with no evasive action taken, one of those crashes like the Playtex Chinook in I Corps Vietnam back in 1971. An accident that sometimes leaves accident boards shaking their heads but is no mystery to those of us who fly NVG a lot. The weather—excellent; the visibility—excellent. All that would have remained would have been just a black spot after the fuel had burned off on a mountainside with aluminum fragments in it and small bits of DNA that they would put in a full sized coffin. The flag would be folded and the shots fired, but the aluminum box they buried would have been nearly empty.*

*I was the aircraft commander and the WTI. My friend was my student doing one of his final navigation flights before we moved into training tactics with the goggles. We planned a route out across the desert, total flight time, one hour from takeoff to landing. We would takeoff from the Moroccan airbase southeast of Tangiers where we conducting our exercise, fly a five-legged course out across the desert on NVG and return to the base. Simple. Because it was a navigation hop, and my friend was the student navigator, I would fly and he would navigate for the entire run.*

*Takeoff was normal, climb out was normal. What a fine night! The moon was high already and the night was clear—no haze—and it felt good to be in the air. The blue lights in the cockpit under the goggles showed all the instruments nicely and our course was as plain as if we were flying in daylight. On the way out we did a little mild buzzing of a hilltop where a friend was camped as part of the exercise, nothing serious, but a low pass to let him know we were thinking of him. And to rub it in that we were flying and he was not.*

*The third leg promised to be as uneventful as the first two. We were not flying low. In fact, we were about the same altitude as we would have been in the daytime, 500 feet or so above the ground. We made our turn from the second leg onto the third, and were tracking on course. In front of us, we could see quite clearly through the goggles a tall mountain, the one we had noted in our planning as 3,000 feet in height. We picked out a notch in the ridgeline on the top that we had marked on our map, and aimed just to the right of it as planned.*

*We were watching the ridge, green and sparkly through the lenses of the goggles. The air was smooth. Everything was normal. The altimeter began dropping rapidly from radar 500 feet toward zero.*

*Don't think of the color blue. Couldn't help yourself, could you? It's the same when things change in an experienced, focused pilot's cockpit. If you would be a pilot, you must, by definition, have excellent peripheral vision because you must see without looking directly at something. Over a short period of time, when you start flying, you learn to see movement. It gives you the ability to know something is changing without having to look directly at it. In the whole panel of 40 or more gauges in front of you, it just takes movement on only one and you instantly see it and your eyes go to it involuntarily. You cannot stop yourself from it, even if you tried.*

*And the altimeter moved . . . Down, hard down and fast.*

*We could see nothing in front of us, but the 200 feet low altitude warning light was on and then it was 125 feet and dropping and the cyclic stick was coming back in my right hand as the altimeter fell toward zero and impact with the ground. As the stick came back to my lap, the collective came up as I added all the power the aircraft had and at last the altimeter stopped falling. It bounced between 25 to 50 feet and then went "no-track," meaning we were higher than the 200 feet low altitude warning setting, as we cleared the ground below us. The low altitude warning light went off. A few seconds later, I lowered the power and the nose and we went back to cruise flight, the big ridge still sparkly in the moonlight in front of us.*

*We had come within 20 feet of flying into a ridge lower than the big one we were looking at. It was masked entirely in the shadow of the bigger ridge and we flew directly toward it without seeing it. Our fault. Had we planned properly, we would have known it was there and navigated accordingly. Our fault. My fault.*

*But we didn't die. No smoking hole in the hillside with bits of aluminum scattered about, no casualty assistance officers walking up to our houses with the news.*

*I trained my friend as best as I could and he was a good student. In time, I left the squadron to go to Washington to become a bureaucrat, and a few months later he went to the Weapons Tactics Instructor course at Yuma. He did well, too, from what I heard later. As a goodbye present, I gave him one of my dark green Norwegian Army turtleneck shirts left over from my Royal Navy days to wear against the Arizona desert night cold. Military bureaucrats don't need them, but Fleet Marine Corps pilots do.*

*The end of the WTI course is a graduation exercise that is very complicated and difficult, all planned and executed by the students. In it, every part of Marine and other forces aviation must come together. By accounts I heard later, he did his part well and at the end of the night he dropped his final load of troops and lifted off for the return flight to MCAS Yuma. WTI course complete, and after good work and hard flying, he was ready to go home to MCAS New River to train his squadron in all he learned. As he climbed out from that final landing zone in the Arizona desert, a Huey flew into the side of his CH-46E and both crews, eight men in all, died as their aircraft came apart and fell in flaming pieces to the desert. His fault? The Huey pilot's fault? My fault? The Marine Corps' fault? I wonder if he had on the Norwegian Army shirt I gave him when he died.*

---

In my mind they all stopped aging when they died. I may be 65 now, but they are all 28 or 32 or 20 still. They are not bald or fat and they are strong and confident when they laugh. Some drink too much, others not at all. They are married, they are single—either way it's forever in my mind. Those of us still here wonder what they know now that we don't. What's over there on the other side of life? Heaven? Hell? Anything? Nothing? Those of us here still cry, not necessarily for them—they knew the risk and took it anyway—but for what they missed; children growing up, baldness, spare tires, laughs over drinks about the good old days and because they now know something we do not.

In the end it comes down to being able to build separate rooms and when you enter one, you close the door on the last one behind you. The room you just left has house payments, sick kids, worries about promotion or relationships. The room you just entered, the one with "Flight" on the door, has only flying there—no ghosts, no fear, no regrets for those that died. But for me there came a time when I could not close the door any more. Those on the other side kept it open a little and the lock was sprung.

But in the years since I stopped military flying, they still die, the young men, some of them who are still my friends also die: a V-22 flown by a former student of mine goes into the Potomac off Quantico, another V-22 crashes in Morocco, a Chinook goes into the water in the Philippines, another Chinook, hit by RPG rounds, goes down in Afghanistan, a Huey crashes in California, a medical helicopter crashes in Arizona, a Shitter hits the ground in Afghanistan, a missile takes out a Blackhawk, a Huey and Cobra mid-air just north of Yuma, but I am not there to know them now, and I cannot go back. Not even if I wanted to. . . .

My final flight as a military aviator was on June 18, 1988 in CH-46E, bureau number 156436. According to my log book, I flew 30 minutes with lieutenant colonel, later Lieutenant General John Castellaw, call sign "Glad." I made one landing. I do not remember the flight, so it must have been perfect.

In 1992 I reefed. My missions were done. I am surprised to still be alive.

# GLOSSARY

| | |
|---|---|
| AC | Aircraft Commander (Army term) |
| ADF | Automatic Direction Finder |
| AFB | Air Force Base |
| AFTP | Authorized Flight Training Period |
| AGL | Above Ground Level, i.e altitude above the surface of the Earth |
| AH-1 | Bell Cobra or Sea Cobra, Army and Marine Corps Attack Helicopter |
| AHRS | Attitude Heading Reference System |
| AIM | Airman's Information Manual |
| AMTRAK | Amphibious Assault Vehicle used by the Marine Corps |
| APC | Armored Personnel Carrier |
| APU | Auxiliary Power Unit |
| ARVN | Army of the Republic of Vietnam |
| ASHB | Assault Support Helicopter Battalion |
| ASE | Automatic Stability Equipment |
| ATC | Air Traffic Control |
| AWS | Amphibious Warfare School |
| Blackhawk | Sikorsky-built US Army Utility Helicopter, UH-60 |
| BOQ | Bachelor Officer's Quarters |
| BRC | Base Recover Course |
| C&C | Command and Control |
| CCA | Carrier-Controlled Approach |
| CG | Commanding General |
| CH-46 | Boeing-built Sea Knight, Marine Corps Medium Lift Helicopter |
| CH-47 | Boeing Chinook Army Medium Lift Helicopter |
| CH-53 | Sikorsky-built SeaStallion Series Helicopter |
| Chalk | Army term for aircraft position in a multi-aircraft flight, i.e. the second aircraft is "Chalk 2," the third "Chalk 3," etc. |

Chinook   Boeing CH-47 Series Helicopter

CO   Commanding Officer

CQ   Carrier Qualification

CWO   Chief Warrant Officer, Grades 2–4

DA   Density Altitude

Dash 1, 2, etc.   Marine Corps term for aircraft position in a multi-aircraft flight, i.e. the second aircraft is "Dash 2," the third "Dash 3," etc.

DMZ   Demilitarized Zone

DSSN   Director of Safe, Standardization, and NATOPS

E&E   Escape and Evasion

ELVA   Emergency Low Visibility Approach

EMCON   Emissions Control

FAR   Federal Aviation Regulation

FBO   Fixed Base Operator

FFAR   Folding Fin Aerial Rockets

Fox Mike   FM radio

Frog   Boeing CH-46, used interchangeably with Sea Knight and Phrog

FSB   Fire Support Base also called Firebase

GCA   Ground-Controlled Approach

GED   General Educational Development— high school completion certificate

H&I   Harassment and Interdiction (a type of artillery mission)

HAC   Helicopter Aircraft Commander (Marine Corps term)

H2P   Helicopter Second Pilot (Marine Corps term)

MHH   Helicopter, Marine, Medium— designation of tactical CH-46 squadrons

HMT   Helicopter, Marine, Training— designation of initial training squadrons

Huey   Bell UH-1 Series helicopters

ICAO   International Civil Aviation Organization

ICS   Internal Communication System

IFR   Instrument Flight Rules

ILS   Instrument Landing System

| | |
|---|---|
| IP | Instructor Pilot |
| KIAS | Knots Indicated Airspeed |
| KIA | Killed in Action |
| IMC | Instrument Meteorological Conditions |
| LPH | Landing Platform Helicopter, a US Navy Helicopter Carrier |
| LPD | Landing Platform Dock, A class of US and British Navy Amphibious Ships |
| LSD | Landing Ship Dock, A class of US Amphibious Ships |
| LF6F | Landing Force, 6th Fleet |
| LOACH | Light Observation Helicopter Hughes-built OH-6 Cayuse Series Helicopters |
| LSE | Landing Signal Enlisted, a "Yellow Shirt" |
| LZ | Landing Zone |
| MCAS | Marine Corps Air Station |
| MEW | Marine Expeditionary Unit |
| MEW (SOC) | Marine Expeditionary Unit (Special Operations Capable) |
| MRE | Meal, Ready to Eat |
| NATOPS | Naval Air Training and Operating Procedures Standardization |
| NAVAIR | Naval Air Systems Command |
| NCO | Non-Commissioned Officer |
| NCOIC | Non-Commissioned Officer In Charge |
| NDB | Non-Directional Beacon, a homing radio that allows the pilot to fly to a navigation beacon or a commercial AM radio station |
| NEO | Nationals Evacuation Operation |
| NOE | Nap-of-the-Earth |
| NVA | North Vietnamese Army |
| NVG | Night Vision Goggles |
| OAT | Outside Air Temperature |
| OCS | Officer Candidate School |
| OD | Olive Drab |
| ODO | Operations Duty Officer |
| OH-6 | Hughes Cayuse Observation Helicopter, a LOACH |

| | |
|---|---|
| OH-13 | Bell Sioux Army Observation Helicopter |
| OH-23 | Hiller Raven Army Observation Helicopter |
| OH-58 | Bell Army Observation Helicopter |
| Ops O | Operations Officer |
| PA | Pressure Altitude |
| PAX | Passenger(s) |
| Phrog | CH-46, used interchangeably with Sea Knight and Frog |
| PMC | Portuguese Marine Corps |
| PSP | Pierced Steel Planking |
| PX | Post Exchange |
| PZ | Pickup Zone |
| R&R | Rest and Relaxation |
| RLO | Real Live Officer, i.e. a commissioned officer versus a warrant officer |
| RMI | Radio Magnetic Indicator |
| RN | Royal Navy |
| RON | Remain Over Night |
| RPG | Rocket Propelled Grenade |
| RPM | Revolutions per Minute |
| SAS | Stability Augmentation System, a semi-autopilot |
| SDO | Squadron Duty Officer |
| SEA | Southeast Asia |
| Sea King | British version of the Sikorsky H-3, The Mark IV Commando |
| Sea Knight | CH-46 |
| Sea Stallion | CH-53 |
| Shitter | CH-53 |
| Snake | AH-1 |
| SOCEX | Special Operations Capable Exercise |
| SOI | Signal Operating Instructions |
| SOP | Standard Operating Procedure |
| SWAT | Special Operations and Tactics |
| TACAN | Tactical Air Navigation System |
| TAD | Temporary Additional Duty |
| TDY | Temporary Duty |

| | |
|---|---|
| TERF | Terrain Flying |
| TH-13T | Bell instrument flight trainer version of the Army OH-13 |
| TOC | Tactical Operations Center |
| TRAP | Tactical Recovery of Aircraft and Personnel |
| U-6 | de Havilland Canada Beaver, Army Utility Airplane |
| U-8D | Military Version of Beechcraft Twin Bonanza |
| UH-1 | Bell Huey, Army and Marine Corps Utility Helicopter |
| UHF | Ultra High Frequency Radio, used for communications |
| VC | Viet Cong |
| V/STOL | Vertical/Short Take-Off and Landing |
| VFR | Visual Flight Rules |
| VH, VK, etc. | Royal Navy 846 Squadron Aircraft Identifiers, e.g. "Victor Hotel" |
| VIP | Very Important Person |
| VMC | Visual Metrological Conditions |
| VNE | Velocity Never Exceed |
| WO1 | Warrant Officer, Grade 1 |
| WOC | Warrant Officer Candidate |
| WTI | Weapons Tactics Instructor |
| XO | Executive Officer |

# ACKNOWLEDGMENTS

Many thanks to Doug Brooks, Al Venter, and Neall Ellis for helping me find the path to getting this book published.

A special thank you to my best friend, lover, wife, and editor, Mariellen, for encouraging me to write, being patient while I did, and then editing my work over and over again. Without her this would never have happened.